for Alex

Ribbon Culture

Ribbon Culture

Charity, Compassion, and Public Awareness

Sarah E.H. Moore
*Centre for Criminology and Sociology, Royal Holloway,
University of London, UK*

First published 2008
This paperback edition published 2010 by
PALGRAVE MACMILLAN

Palgrave Macmillan in the UK is an imprint of Macmillan Publishers Limited,
registered in England, company number 785998, of Houndmills, Basingstoke,
Hampshire RG21 6XS.

Palgrave Macmillan in the US is a division of St Martin's Press LLC,
175 Fifth Avenue, New York, NY 10010.

Palgrave Macmillan is the global academic imprint of the above companies
and has companies and representatives throughout the world.

Palgrave® and Macmillan® are registered trademarks in the United States,
the United Kingdom, Europe and other countries.

ISBN 978–0–230–54921–0   hardback
ISBN 978–0–230–24789–5   paperback

This book is printed on paper suitable for recycling and made from fully
managed and sustained forest sources. Logging, pulping and manufacturing
processes are expected to conform to the environmental regulations of the
country of origin.

A catalogue record for this book is available from the British Library.

A catalog record for this book is available from the Library of Congress.

10   9   8   7   6   5   4   3   2   1
19 18 17 16 15 14 13 12 11 10

Printed and bound in Great Britain by
CPI Antony Rowe, Chippenham and Eastbourne

Contents

Acknowledgements

I wish to thank a number of people who have provided useful criticism and advice during the writing of this book. Frank Furedi has not only offered many useful suggestions during the course of this project, but he has also supported me throughout. Mary Evans and Alisdair Spark have also provided stimulating advice and much encouragement. Fabienne Jung, Ralph MacKenzie, and Jacqueline Moore also deserve special mention for their help and support. Many of my students at the University of Kent and Rochester Independent College have sparked thought-provoking discussions over the years – without them I imagine I'd have become a reclusive writer. This book is based on doctoral work funded by the Economic and Social Research Council (ESRC), and I gratefully acknowledge their financial assistance.

Lastly, I would like to thank my whole family, and especially my husband, Alex Clayton, for their love and support.

Preface

Ribbon Culture is a book about the origin and meaning of 'awareness' ribbons, such as those worn for AIDS or breast cancer. A large part of the book is given over to discussing the relationship between charity 'flag days' of the early twentieth century, the US practice of tying yellow ribbons round trees, and the red- and pink-lapel ribbons. The book identifies a clear shift in terms of the meaning and use of charity tokens, of which 'awareness' ribbons are taken as the most recent example. During the early twentieth century, the charity pins worn on people's lapels – flags, as they were often referred to – symbolised one's belief in a collective cause and mainstream social values. The Remembrance or Memorial Day Poppy, the most famous and long-standing flag day campaign, remains a 'pro-social' symbol, in the sense that it embodies a sense of national pride and indebtedness to those who defended national sovereignty. The charity lapel ribbon, the first of which was launched in 1991, spoke of an altogether different mindset. Donning a red AIDS-awareness ribbon was, at least in the early 1990s, a gesture of defiance, an expression of annoyance with mainstream policies and attitudes concerning HIV and AIDS. Charity tokens, once a sign of decency and decorum, could have 'a message'; being charitable could be a bit daring, cool, even. More importantly, and somewhat confusingly, the charity token had become an emblem of individual, as opposed to collective, feeling.

My aim in writing the book was to argue that this trajectory in charity token-wearing is illustrative of a far more significant and entrenched socio-historical shift. Reading *Ribbon Culture* now, it strikes me that thinking about the nature of charitable giving allows us to make sense of this shift. Put simply, giving to charity *means* different things in different cultural and historical contexts. 'Charitableness' and 'compassion' should not be taken as self-evident attributes. When journalists and sociologists claim that people 'care more' today than in the past they are simply taking the fact that charitable donations are greater now than they were a decade ago as straightforward evidence of a rising tide of compassion. This is like taking the increase in the sale of valentine's cards as evidence that people are more romantic today. As Blumer argued in his classic article on variable-analysis, we need to ask what human action means in a given context to have any grasp of social phenomena like card-giving or charitableness. Understanding the meaning behind the latter is particularly important, because it can give us an insight into shared ideas about what it means to be 'fully' or 'properly' human in a given society. For example, social historians frequently explain the zeal for British philanthropy during the nineteenth century in terms of it allowing for the expression of religious values. Charitableness was next to godliness – and giving to charity was therefore a means of confirming that one was a decent Christian.

In many instances, displaying that one has given to charity involves 'saying' something about one's state of virtue, and that may involve being a 'proper' Christian, being politically conscious, or being especially empathetic. What, then, we might ask, does the awareness ribbon infer about the wearer? Before attempting an answer I should add the necessary qualifying statement that, of course, *Ribbon Culture* explores all sorts of motivations for wearing a ribbon. Nonetheless, there is, I argue in Chapter 5, a dominant 'type' of ribbon-wearer. In the main, to wear a ribbon is to indicate that one is a deeply self-aware character, has a full emotional repertoire, and is emotionally expressive – it does not, in contrast, mean that one has knowledge of an illness or campaign, that one is in touch with sufferers or other campaigners, or that one is a representative for a cause. Ribbon wearing, then, 'says' that one is an *emotional* being – someone for whom 'personal beliefs' (see Chapter 5), authenticity, and emotional 'realness' are aspects of an essential humanness.

What is particularly interesting about ribbon wearing is that it is a deeply self-affirming act that typically involves seeing emotional expressiveness as good *in and of itself*. 'To thine own self be true', as Polonius platitudinously advises Hamlet. Yet, as Lionel Trilling points out, in the context of the play, Polonius' injunction actually equates to the instruction to 'act in accordance with your real aims and desires, *lest you deceive others*'. He is, in other words, recommending sincerity as a moral virtue, as opposed to authenticity. Conversely, it would be easy to misread the practice of ribbon wearing as being directed towards something – as involving the cultivation of knowledge about AIDS, for example, or spreading information about breast cancer. In fact, for most of the ribbon wearers I interviewed, the point of donning a pink- or red-lapel ribbon is simply to show that 'I am in a state of self-awareness', as opposed to 'I am aware of a specific something'.

The prizing of self-expression and emotional ingenuousness is part of an important shift in how we conceive of the relationship between self and society. A number of sociologists and cultural commentators have argued that, since the mid-twentieth century in particular, we have become increasingly atomised as a society, unwilling to follow social norms, roles, and customs, unhappy with social authority and institutions, and interested in asserting our individuality. Figures like Frank Furedi, Ulrich Beck and Elisabeth Beck-Gernsheim, Richard Sennett, and Christopher Lasch have written about various aspects of this trend. *Ribbon Culture* also hopes to elucidate this shift, though it is perhaps more 'purely' sociological in its approach, emphasising the dialectical nature of the relationship between self and society – the impossibility and undesirability of achieving 'pure', unhindered self-expression, the contingency of such gestures on social conventions and norms, the perniciousness of the myth that the 'social' self is not the 'real' self. The other thing that *Ribbon Culture* stresses concerning the shifting ideas about the individual and society is the role of the 1960s counter-culture. I suggest that the UK and USA (and no doubt other countries besides) underwent a 'counter-cultural turn' during the mid-1970s whereby defiance of social conventions and annoyance at social institutions came to be seen as normal and self-evidently appropriate attitudes. As an entrenched socio-cultural current, the counter-cultural ethos involves a broad disapproval of the status quo, as well as a sense of vague annoyance with mainstream social authorities and institutions. Why is this a problem? *Ribbon Culture* suggests that the legacy of the counter-cultural turn is, to put it bluntly, a propensity for unreflexive nay-saying and an empty rhetoric of defiance. It is telling, for example, that more people sign petitions than vote in general elections in the UK, that almost anyone can wear a t-shirt emblazoned with the face of Che Guevara (irrespective of their political leanings), and that a charity token can become a symbol of an otherwise unacted-upon annoyance concerning the treatment of AIDS sufferers. If self-expression has become a virtue in and of itself, it is best, it seems, if it involves some sort of 'flight from', as opposed to 'flight to' (to borrow from Roszak), if it involves a vague disapproval of mainstream society – and 'awareness' ribbons are products of this culture.

For me, this is a central line of argument in *Ribbon Culture*. The book is also, perhaps more obviously, a critique of the 'culture of ostentatious compassion' (as Patrick West has it) that seems to have grown up in the UK and USA over the last few decades. Indeed, this is what most reviewers have taken to be the book's 'main point'. To show that one cares deeply has become a fashionable gesture; the most striking evidence for this is the fact that the ribbon, and then the empathy wristband, are seen by many (wearers included) as fashion items. It strikes me that this is even more apparent now than it was when I wrote the book. Wristbands, for example, have passed through their fashion cycle and become passe. The range of 'awareness' ribbons continues to grow, colours being re-used irrespective of their symbolic function in designating a specific cause or charity. On sitting down to write this preface I idly did a Google search for 'awareness ribbon'. The first page came up with a list of 'items to buy' that included a 'breast cancer awareness ribbon gold Swarovski crystal charm' and a 'sterling silver ovarian cancer awareness ribbon charm'. Showing compassion clearly remains a fashionable endeavour, and the problems with this – that a cause can come to be seen as faddish, that compassion itself becomes a fleeting, unsustained emotion, that certain problems and illnesses are glamourised – remain just as pertinent as when I wrote the book.

The backdrop to all this is, as I discuss in the book, the changing role and strategies of the third sector. During the 1980s the UK government instigated a 'contract culture' and encouraged charities and private coporations to bid for welfare service contracts. This laid the groundwork for the current 'mixed economy' of welfare, whereby welfare services are provided by private companies, charities, and state-funded organisations. It has always struck me as interesting that the left-wing British media frequently decry the state's meting out of welfare provision to the private sector, yet never offer similarly critical accounts of our increased dependence on charities to provide, amongst other things, prisoner rehabilitation, services for the blind, and certain emergency rescue services. There's not enough space here to discuss the various problems with this, except to say that the rationale for rolling out a welfare state in the UK was partly based upon the problems with charitable provision of basic welfare services and the belief that such services should be provided universally and by the state.

Charities' involvement in a 'contract culture', along with the increased numbers of marketing graduates going into the charity sector, the growing recognition within the sector that canny advertising increases revenue, and increased competitiveness between charities, has led to the commercialisation of charity. In other words, charities are increasingly required to act and think like private corporations to win government contracts and make money. Charities take on commercial sponsors that share 'market terrain' (and, in turn, a new 'cause-related marketing' has sprung up), adopt snazzy advertising campaigns, and create lines of merchandise. One only need look at the pink-ribbon awareness campaign to see that charity is now a thoroughly commercial enterprise.

I was partly motivated to write *Ribbon Culture* in order to show up the problems with this. Many people who have read the book, despite sharing its general thesis, have expressed the view that I'm unnecessarily critical of charities because, after all, the 'most important thing' is that charities make lots of money, irrespective of donors' motivations and the methods charities employ. I would like to end this Preface by responding to such comments. That people give to charities out of guilt, worry, peer pressure, the desire to be cool – this *does* matter, and the conversations I have had with ribbon wearers and wristband wearers have led me to believe that it matters greatly. As recent research has shown, charities need to encourage long-term commitment from their donors, and this involves building up a relationship that is based on something more than a catchy tag-line, slick advertising, or fleeting guilt. Needless to say, cultivating meaningful relationships with donors is of increasing importance given the current economic climate. To convince your donors that a cause has a certain caché, or that a charity token is the next 'must-have', might shake money from the rafters in the short term, but it does nothing to encourage donors to push for real political change or investigate the problem or illness – it also does nothing to stop donors dropping their donations when a cause goes 'out of fashion'.

Much more disturbing, though, is that charities might unnecessarily stir up fear concerning a problem or illness for the sake of raising money. Most of the young female pink-ribbon wearers interviewed for this project were scared (their word) of developing breast cancer sometime soon. Most of them wore their ribbons in complete ignorance of the fact that 80 per cent of women who develop breast cancer are post-menopausal and that breast cancer has a 76 per cent survival rate. The breast-cancer awareness campaign, of which they are, after all, contributors, has done little to allay their fears. After all, this is a charity-led campaign that involves countless beauty and clothing companies using the pink-ribbon motif on their products – it is invariably young women who are targeted with this merchandise, which is good for companies who are eager to raise their profile amongst this market segment, but not so good for young women who are bombarded with pink-ribbon merchandise, all of it feeding a nagging suspicion that 'it could be me'. Indeed, whilst writing *Ribbon Culture* I was phoned by a company trying to sell me health insurance and, as part of his pitch, the salesman deftly led me through a highly emotive speech that focussed on women's 'normal' fears about breast cancer (which, unquestioningly, I should share). Even my protestations that I was a healthy 25 year old woman did nothing to put him off his stride. Breast-cancer charities should be tempering, as opposed to contributing to, the culture of fear that surrounds this illness: indeed, that should be part of their mandate.

Finally, and most importantly, the indignant question that 'surely charities making money is a good thing?' presupposes that we should judge charities by the same standards as companies. Private corporations might be oriented to seek out profit by any means, but this should not be charities' primary rationale. *Ribbon Culture* argues that charities have a responsibility to provide accurate, helpful, and educational information about their respective causes. We should have no such expectation of a company. A drinks manufacturer markets it product with the sole purpose of making money; their adverts will, without scruple, encourage us to believe that their drink is 'the best' and is likely to transform our lives. If a breast-cancer charity were to explicitly or implicitly suggest comparable things about breast cancer – that we should see it as the most significant of illnesses, that it is the worst thing that can happen to a woman – we should see that charity as having failed in its remit. That certain charities get pretty near to suggesting these things should anger us greatly, and should spur us on to see beyond the 'ribbon culture' that has become so pervasive as to obscure the serious questions about the role of charities and the meaning of compassion.

Sarah Moore

1
Introduction

Ribbon culture

Princess Diana wore one, Bill Clinton wore one, and Kramer, a character in the hit sit-com *Seinfeld*, got beaten up for not wearing one. Since its emergence in 1991, the awareness ribbon has achieved the kind of cultural status usually reserved for religious symbols and big-brand icons. Drawn onto people's hands to protest the Madrid bombings, emblazoned across wine bottles, t-shirts, and mugs, tied to tree branches, and (of course) worn on people's lapels, the ribbon symbol is one of the most visible and well-recognised symbols in the world. Even eBay, the online marketplace, makes use of the looped ribbon motif to identify charity auctions. In the USA, the birthplace of the awareness ribbon, the range of causes for which people 'show awareness' is staggering: people can wear a ribbon to 'show awareness' of the Oklahoma bombing, male violence, censorship, bullying, epilepsy, diabetes, brain cancer, myalgic encephalomyelitis (M.E.), autism, racial abuse, childhood disability, and mouth cancer, to name just a few.[1] In many instances, the US-based ribbon campaigns have provided the blueprint for those launched in the UK, where 'showing awareness' gained popularity a little later than in the USA. With the exception of the red ribbon and pink ribbon campaigns (launched in the UK in 1992 and 1993 respectively), most of the British awareness campaigns were launched in the late 1990s (for example, the blue ribbon for M.E., the white ribbon to 'show awareness' of violence against women,[2] the jigsaw autism ribbon, and the blue-and-pink ribbon for infant and prenatal deaths).

1

Whilst the ribbon has obtained considerable cultural currency, its meaningfulness as a symbol is recurrently debated by media commentators, cultural critics, and activists. The ribbon has been described variously as the new religious cross (Fleury, 1992), the new peace symbol (Garfield, 1995), schmaltzy (Seidner, 1993), and a 'support symbol' (Heilbronn, 1994). Whilst some might attribute this confusion to the ribbon's capacity to speak to and for all (Heilbronn, 1994; Tuleja, 1994), or its necessary dynamism as a 'living tradition' (Parsons, 1991, p. 11), it seems likely that the ribbon in fact inhabits a much more complex place in our culture than many have previously acknowledged. Indeed, to understand ribbon wearing we must first address and unpack several points of analytic complexity. The ribbon is, for example, both a kitsch fashion accessory, as well as an emblem that expresses empathy; it is a symbol that represents awareness, yet requires no knowledge of a cause; it appears to signal concern for others, but in fact prioritises self-expression.

It was just such seeming ambiguities that originally sparked my interest in ribbon wearing. Over time, my thinking came to be focussed on one question: what does it mean to 'show awareness'? At first glance, it appears to be a relatively straightforward social practice. Much of the literature produced by awareness-campaign organisers suggests that 'showing awareness' is simply a means of demonstrating one's compassion for a particular group of sufferers. This is clearly true up to a certain point. However, the more one examines 'showing awareness', the more puzzling this social practice becomes. What does it accomplish? It is certainly debatable that it increases the visibility of suffering and encourages understanding of a particular disease or syndrome. Clearly 'showing awareness' raises the profile of a number of notable and worthy causes, otherwise charities would not produce and market awareness ribbons. But as a social practice, it extends beyond a simple case of charitable publicity. In some instances, for curious reasons, 'showing awareness' is perceived by wearers to be a very personal gesture, an activity that is discrete and private. Yet the use of the ribbon to symbolise a *personal* emotional response to suffering is surely at odds with its *universal* application as a symbol of compassion and awareness, regardless of the nature of the cause, or the specific characteristics of the ribbon wearer's feelings. Not only this, but the idea that 'showing awareness' is a private practice seems rather contradictory. The Pink Ribbon line of underwear, for example, launched by Estée Lauder, is sold on the premise that these pink-ribbon-motifed bras and knickers enable women to 'show awareness' of breast cancer. It is quite clear, however, that the extent to which one's underwear can 'show awareness' is limited to the frequency with which one shows one's undergarments to the man in the street!

Ribbons worn on people's outer garments – obviously the more common means of 'showing awareness' – tend to be similarly unrevealing. Bizarrely, certain colours stand for a range of causes. A blue ribbon can denote awareness of Internet censorship or of sufferers of M.E. or mouth cancer. A green ribbon might suggest awareness of tissue and organ donors, sufferers of ovarian cancer, or Tourette's syndrome. A purple ribbon can signal awareness of Alzheimer's sufferers, people with epilepsy, or the homeless.[3] In this context, the ribbon is more likely to induce confusion than awareness.

Equally baffling is that ribbon wearing requires very little commitment to a given cause. Indeed, wearing a ribbon does not mean that one is an active or staunch supporter of a particular charity (when I asked one ribbon wearer whether she saw herself as a supporter of the cause for which she wore a ribbon she replied, 'I wouldn't go that far'). At the funeral of victims of the Oklahoma bombing, Bill Clinton wore a ribbon of purple, yellow and black to 'show awareness' of the dead, the missing, and the children.[4] In so doing, he demonstrated how easy a gesture of awareness actually is, and how empty an expression of compassion can be.

The evident imprecision of the ribbon's meaning is connected to the vagueness of the term and practice of 'showing awareness'. Awareness consists of neither knowledge nor experience of a particular cause. It does not require any concerted action, nor any relationship with a sufferer. A central aim of this book is to develop a sociological conception of 'showing awareness' that might help us to gain a better understanding of this often-used, though ambiguous, term. It is sufficient to mention here, by way of introduction, that 'showing awareness' is primarily conceived of in this study as a means of *disclosing* the self. Bill Clinton's enthusiasm for ribbon wearing is surely deeply suggestive of his interest in appearing to be a genuine, emotionally mature human being, rather than engaging in serious contemplation of the suffering of each of the groups for which he wore a ribbon. It would seem that, in many instances, 'showing awareness' is more about the ribbon wearer than the sufferers of any given disease.

The affliction is tailor-made to suit the wearer. As the homepage for Pinmart, a US-based distributor of awareness ribbons, so tellingly declares, '[w]e are sure you'll find the right ribbon for you'.

Scholarly accounts of ribbon wearing

Considering the rich possibilities the phenomenon of ribbon wearing presents to sociology and other social science disciplines, it has received very little attention from academics. The yellow ribbon – the first to be widely used – is, by a large margin, the ribbon that features most regularly in the academic press. This ribbon was first used in the USA, during the Iranian hostage situation in 1979, and then later during the 1991 and 2003 conflicts in the Gulf. It is uncovering the yellow ribbon's status as an 'invented tradition' – a tradition that follows an historically contingent cultural dictum – that is often held to be the rightful analytic purpose of academic work on this subject matter. As such, most academic studies on yellow-ribbon tying aim to understand and elucidate the historical background out of which this social practice emerged (see, in particular, Heilbronn, 1994; Larsen, 1994). Whilst it is commonplace for such studies to trace the origins of this symbol, there are few in-depth discussions on *why* the yellow ribbon became so popular during the late 1970s (and again during the early 1990s). In his opening discussion on the invention of traditions, Eric Hobsbawm suggests that the practice of tracing the origin of traditions is useful, first and foremost because it enables us to understand a particular social and cultural context. Invented traditions are

> important symptoms and therefore indicators of problems which might not otherwise be recognized, and developments which are otherwise difficult to identify and date ... *The study of invented traditions cannot be separated from the wider study of the history of society, nor can it expect to advance much beyond the mere discovery of such practices unless it is integrated into a wider study.*
> (Hobsbawm, in Hobsbawm and Ranger [eds], 2001, p. 12. Italics added.)

Following on from this, I believe that it is ascertaining how the emergence of the yellow ribbon (and later ribbons) relates to and reflects wider socio-historical developments that is of real interest. To this end, I not only examine the origin of the yellow, red, and pink ribbon campaigns (see Chapter 4), but I also trace the project of 'showing awareness' back to the countercultural period of the 1960s (Chapter 6).

In contrast to the yellow ribbon, later ribbon campaigns are often passed off as extraneous, kitsch, or meaningless fads; the notion that they may provide leverage for cultural or sociological analysis is not granted much serious consideration within academia (see Garfield, 1995; King, 2006, for exceptions to this). This presupposition reveals a bewildering lack of awareness (or even observation). Ribbon wearing has become an increasingly visible aspect of our social reality, a form of mass participation in a society that is otherwise experiencing a decline in other forms of such activity (voting, involvement in civil society etc.). Moreover, the ribbon campaigns of the 1990s – most notably the red AIDS-awareness ribbon and the pink breast-cancer awareness ribbon – are themselves indicative of wider social and cultural developments. The ribbon campaigns tell us much about the manner in which we conceive of victimhood and illness in contemporary society, and point to the development of a particular identity, rooted in emotion and self-expression.

In addition to this, academic focus on the yellow ribbon has precluded a consideration of the development of ribbon-wearing practices. This study suggests that there is an evident trajectory of ribbon wearing, from the use of the yellow ribbons during the Iranian hostage situation, through to the use of awareness ribbons in the 1990s. Among other things, studying the trajectory of ribbon wearing reveals to us how the relationship between supporter and victim has developed and enables us to chart the emergence and development of the project of 'showing awareness'.

Overview of the book

In very broad terms, this book explores the sociological implications of awareness ribbons, such as those worn for AIDS or breast cancer. To this end, I examine the origin of ribbon campaigns, trace the project of 'showing awareness', explore the meanings that ribbon wearers attach to the symbol, and consider how awareness manifests itself (as a certain emotion or identity, for example). My analysis is based on data collected from 20 in-depth interviews, 70 questionnaires, and participant observation, as well as a wide range of secondary sources (see the Appendix for my methodology). The book includes discussions on, among other topics, the lived experience of risk, the nature of contemporary mourning practices, the sociology of compassion, the marketing discourses of charities, and the relationship between awareness and consumerism. These various points of discussion also work towards a more general assessment of contemporary society. In particular, my work shows up a two-way social trend in which a heightened interest in personal authenticity is coupled with a widespread distrust and repudiation of social forces (such as social institutions, state government, and social authorities).

Ribbon wearing is conceived of in this book as a social practice directed towards showing the self to be emotionally expressive and ingenuous. The ribbon is seen, first and foremost, as a symbol of self-awareness and empathy, one that suggests much about the meaning of compassion in today's society, the nature of self-identity, and our attitude towards illness. This conception of the ribbon partly arises out of the idea that compassion is afforded a particularly central place in today's culture. In this respect, the ribbon should be seen alongside the recent craze for empathy wristbands, the Red campaign launched by Bono, Live 8, the Make Poverty History campaign, companies' cause-related marketing, and charity telethons, to name but a few elements of the 'culture of compassion' that has grown up over the last 15 years.

What this book does *not* provide is a sustained account of ribbon campaigns as social movements, and it is necessary to justify this a little here. Firstly, it is worth pointing out that most ribbon campaigns have been launched by charities. Indeed, most of the ribbon wearers I interviewed for this project saw the ribbon as a charity symbol, and regularly compared it to stickers given away by charities and the Armistice Day Poppy. Moreover, and as I discuss in Chapter 4, whilst the red AIDS-awareness campaign and pink breast-cancer awareness campaign both have some connection to the gay-rights movement and Women's Health Movement respectively, these ribbon campaigns have been co-opted into the mainstream culture. Ribbon wearers do not, for the most part, belong to minority groups. In fact, the vast majority of ribbon wearers who took part in this research (and I have no reason to believe they are atypical) were young, white, middle-class women. Not only this, but the majority of ribbon wearers lack interest in any political objectives or organised social action (though the ribbon is widely taken to constitute an expression of annoyance at social authorities). There are, of course, exceptions to this lack of interest in activism. In Chapter 5, I explore the use of the ribbon as a resource in community-action campaigns, where ribbon wearing becomes a much more politically oriented practice.

Nonetheless, on the whole, ribbon wearers aren't activists, and the ways in which they express annoyance at social authorities are all the more fascinating as a result. Ribbon wearers might be concerned about a lack of funding, or problems of cultural visibility for certain groups, but they rarely engage in discussions about sources of inequality, or the state and voluntary sector's respective roles in welfare provision. Whilst sociologists and politicians have long bemoaned the rising tide of political apathy in both the UK and the USA, it is curious to find such political disengagement amongst those ostensibly interested in social issues. Oxfam's recent Make Poverty History campaign is another illuminating example of this. One of the more politically oriented campaigns, Make Poverty History, launched a white wristband in 2005 to coincide with the G8 summit in Edinburgh. Interestingly, the campaign's website reveals that whilst eight million people bought a white wristband in 2005, only eight hundred thousand people contributed to the online campaign. This is not only deeply suggestive of white-wristband wearers' lack of interest in organisational or political objectives, it might also be seen as evidence of their wish to be seen to support a cause, regardless of the finer details of the campaign. As I argue throughout this book, ribbon wearing, like wristband wearing, has more to do with self-presentation than political engagement.

Structure of the book

Chapter 2 seeks to provide a theoretical framework for ribbon wearing. Here I explore selected sociological accounts of symbolic behaviour (particularly the work of Erving Goffman), sociological conceptions of identity (especially those provided by Giddens and Beck and Beck-Gernsheim), and selected literature on charity-giving and compassion. Particularly important points of discussion in this chapter are risk-consciousness, the cultural meaning of compassion, and the implicit rules of self-presentation. This chapter also introduces the idea that ribbon wearing inheres in a particular identity. This identity – based on emotional literacy, self-awareness, and a sense of imminent illness – is particularly salient in late modern societies in which individuals are urged to be highly reflexive and compassionate. Indeed, emotional qualities have come to be seen as important facets of identity in contemporary society, and this chapter considers the rise of such 'feeling-based identities' (Furedi, 2004, p. 144).

The next two chapters are concerned with the historical background to ribbon-wearing practices. **Chapter 3** examines flag days of the first quarter of the 20th century, including the Armistice Day Poppy. **Chapter 4** looks at the emergence and development of the yellow, red and pink ribbon campaigns, the three most prominent campaigns in the USA and the UK. This chapter concludes with a consideration of the relationship between ribbon campaigns and earlier flag days and a discussion of the development of ribbon-wearing practices. This cultural–historical analysis is followed by a focussed discussion of ribbon wearers' motivations for wearing the ribbon in **Chapter 5**. This part of my work explores the use of the ribbon as a symbol of solidarity with homosexuals, as a resource in community-action campaigns, as a mourning symbol, and as a symbol of self-awareness.

Exploring the origins of the contemporary interest in 'showing awareness' is the subject of the following chapter. **Chapter 6** traces the contemporary project of 'showing awareness' back to the countercultural turn that took place during the 1960s in the UK and the USA. It is suggested that the countercultural ethos of the 1960s – premised on self-expression and an anti-establishment attitude – remains salient in today's society. A desire for self-awareness and distance from mainstream society are, for example, important features of the contemporary project of 'showing awareness'. This chapter includes a rigorous analysis of the 1960s counter-culture, based upon, among other things, political speeches, fashions of the period, films, novels, newspaper and magazine articles, and art criticism. This analysis is followed by a discussion of the pertinence of countercultural values to an understanding of contemporary society, and 'showing awareness' in particular.

Chapter 7 suggests that awareness often manifests itself as worry about a particular disease, particularly for female pink-ribbon wearers. It combines a critical assessment of the fund-raising techniques employed by the breast cancer awareness campaign with an analysis of young female pink-ribbon wearers' attitudes towards the illness. I also suggest that young women's fear of breast cancer may speak of a more general perception that our lives are fraught with inescapable dangers and hidden threats. Contributing to this social trend, the breast cancer awareness campaign frequently suggests that young women – the target group of its corporate sponsors, but by no means the group most affected by breast cancer – should be constantly aware that they are at significant risk of developing the illness. The chapter ends with a consideration of the campaign's promotion of a particular conception of femininity, one that represents women as sickly, body-conscious, beautiful, and buxom. The campaign thus stirs up, rather than allays, fears that breast cancer strips women of their femininity.

It is hardly surprising, given these women's worry about breast cancer, that they see charity as a fund from which they themselves will draw in the future. **Chapter 8** opens with the observation that many of the pink-ribbon wearers who took part in this research viewed their charitable donations as contributing to a fund that they would draw upon themselves at some point. This, I argue, is unsurprising considering their sense of worry about breast cancer. It also implies a certain attitude towards charity, one that sees personal investment and insurance, rather than state-provided welfare services, as the most efficient means of welfare provision. Though participants saw the charity sector, rather than the state, as the ideal provider of welfare, they were by no means acritical about charities. Indeed, research participants (both red- and pink-ribbon wearers) regularly compared charities to companies, often so as to highlight the unfavourable techniques employed by the former. The last part of this chapter examines compassion in contemporary society. Here I suggest that the discourse of compassion that accompanies the awareness ribbon, a rhetoric that has become so compelling as to make a refusal to accept its legitimacy tantamount to inhumanity, has transformed this emotion into a neat, marketable commodity.

2
Ribbon Wearing: Towards a Theoretical Framework

> All of us are fragments, not only of general man, but
> also of ourselves. We are outlines not only of the
> types 'man', 'good', 'bad', and the like, but also of the
> individuality and uniqueness of ourselves. Although
> this individuality cannot, in principle, be identified
> by any name, it surrounds our perceptible reality as
> if traced in ideal lines. It is supplemented by others'
> view of us, which results in something that we never
> are, purely and wholly.
>
> (Simmel, 1908, 1971, 'How is Society Possible?',
> pp. 10–11)

Simmel's above comments may well chime with the reader's experience of the self in late modern society. Perhaps most resonant is
Simmel's reference to our sense of our selves as 'outlines'. The use of
this word evokes the feeling that our identities are sketchy, incomplete. Neither the social self nor the private self enjoys a sense of full-
ness, 'wholeness', or 'pureness'. Simmel suggests that this
dissatisfying sketchiness is a necessary outcome of the incongruity
between the social 'me' and the private 'I'. At the same time,
Simmel's observation that our private selves are supplemented by
'others' view of us' implies (but does not concede) the inadequacy of
viewing the self as divided between its 'social' and 'private' aspects.
Simmel fails to follow through these implications to observe that the
perception of our selves as incomplete – as neither *fully visible* to others nor *fully distinct* – is in fact a false perception borne out of an

10

imagined or contrived dichotomy between the social self and the private self.

In a predominantly secular society, we rely upon others to affirm our existence, to see and acknowledge us. At the same time, there is a part of the self – the best part of the self, we are told – that is conceived of as imperceptible to others, as private and essential. It is an important facet of our social existence that we are seen and recognised by others; however, to allow one's self to be seen *fully* is tantamount to eschewing the essentiality or distinctness of the hidden, private 'I'. The dual fear of indistinctness and invisibility is, I believe, one of the most significant existential dilemmas for the late modern individual. As with other dilemmas of this nature, it is formatively shaped by how we live and how we view our selves (particularly in relation to others). Spurred on by consumerism, impelled by the discourse of therapeuticism, we are driven to seek out our essential, distinct selves in today's society. However, we are also bound by the underlying knowledge that to find the self we must turn towards others for affirmation. 'Pure' self-expression and self-realisation are in fact endless quests in search of unreachable goals. It is in this context that ribbon wearing – at first glance an entirely faddish, inconsequential activity – appears to me to be a highly significant and symptomatic aspect of contemporary social reality. What I intend to demonstrate in the course of this book is that ribbon wearing is in fact indicative of the manner in which we understand our selves and others in late modern society. If we feel ourselves to be sketchy and incomplete, then ribbon wearing is a particularly salient example of how we attempt to traverse the perceived gap between the private, essential self and the social, knowable self.

Indeed, ribbon wearing – like other forms of symbolic behaviour – involves making the self visible and readable, a process that is of great sociological interest. The tacit rules that direct self-presentation, the range of expressive equipment we have access to, the sense of belonging that shared symbols can engender – all these areas reflect a foundational concern in sociology with the relationship between self and society. Whilst such points of discussion, conceived of in the abstract, are sociologically interesting, we should recognise that rules of self-presentation, expressive equipment, and shared symbols – or any such aspects of social life – are historically contingent. Ribbon wearing, for example, is a form of symbolic behaviour that could only emerge under conditions of late modernity. Sociologists have identified a number of factors that characterise this period, including increased self-reflexivity, an interest in self-identity and emotional disclosure, a process of individualisation, the emergence of Lifestyle Politics, and a heightened risk consciousness. It is this social context that forms the backdrop to the contemporary practice of 'showing awareness', and this book returns again and again to such themes.

Before we attend to the historical origin of this social current, we need to consider the main dimensions of ribbon wearing as a social practice. Ribbon wearing is viewed in this book as a form of symbolic behaviour that enables the articulation of a particular identity (one that is based on emotional expressiveness). It is also, of course, a *charitable* practice, one that suggests much about the meaning of compassion in today's society. As such, this chapter provides an introduction to three central themes in the book: symbolic behaviour, identity, and compassion and charity. There are common threads that run through these areas of discussion: gender, the emotions, consumerism, and fashion are perhaps the most important of these. Whilst this chapter attempts to provide something like a theoretical framework for understanding 'showing awareness', it does not try to isolate one social theory as especially instructive. Indeed, the book makes use of an eclectic mix of scholarly work, including Simmel's writing on fashion, Marx's work on commodity fetishism, Goffman's theory of self-presentation, Beck and Beck-Gernsheim's work on individualisation, writings on the risk society, and Malinowski's ideas about the 'gift relationship'.

Symbolic behaviour

Symbolic behaviour in fact encompasses a range of social action, including the use of national and religious symbols, language and gestures, and the maintenance of personal appearance (use of clothes, hairstyles, and make-up, for example). The awareness ribbon might be seen as an expression of empathy, though it is also, and perhaps more obviously, an aspect of personal appearance. The discussion below draws upon examples of symbolic behaviour that might be considered to serve broadly similar purposes, such as badge wearing, observation of dress codes, and adherence to fashions.

Symbols represent the person, serving to make one's identity, emotions, and beliefs recognisable to others, often (though by no means always) in a way that seems to correspond very closely to personal sentiments. The notion that there is coalescence between social and personal meaning in symbolic behaviour, or even that a symbol might have a unitary, dominant meaning, is by no means accepted within the social sciences. According to Abner Cohen, one of the most prominent theorists in this field, symbols are 'normative forms that stand ambiguously for a multiplicity of meanings' (Cohen, 1977, p. 117). Similarly, it is the tension between social and personal meaning that interests Raymond Firth. The prime reason for studying symbolic behaviour, he writes, is to

> grapple as empirically as possible with the basic human problem of what I would call disjunction; a gap between the overt superficial statement of action and its underlying meaning. On the surface, a person is saying or doing something which our observations or inferences tell us should not be simply taken at face value; it stands for something else, of greater significance to him.
>
> (Firth, 1973, p. 26)

Certainly, symbols have significance beyond their general, shared meaning, and this is an important consideration for sociologists. However, we should be careful not to draw too strong a distinction between personal and social meaning. Even behaviour that seems deeply personal is dependent upon social codes of meaning, such as language.

Of course, some types of symbolic behaviour are more obviously group oriented than others, such as the styles developed by subcultures and other social groups at the margins of mainstream society. Such 'tie-signs' as Ruth Rubinstein refers to them, include gothic clothes and dreadlocks (Rubinstein, 1995, Chapter 15). These symbols often signify shared values for those within a particular social group, and thereby facilitate interaction between group members. More importantly, perhaps, they help delineate 'them' and 'us' relationships. A subculture's dress code often serves as a means of clearly marking out group members, concomitantly indicating their sense of belonging to a particular group and their disassociation from others. The Mods, for example, a working-class subculture that emerged in the early 1960s in the UK, adopted an ultra-neat

style that parodied mainstream culture and differentiated them from
the macho rockers:

> [t]he motor scooter, originally an ultra-respectable means of trans-
> port, was turned into a menacing symbol of group solidarity ...
> Union jacks were emblazoned on the backs of grubby parka anoraks
> or cut up and converted into smartly tailored jackets. More subtly,
> the conventional insignia of the business world the suit, collar and
> tie, short hair, etc. were stripped of their original connotations of
> efficiency, ambition, compliance with authority and transformed
> into 'empty' fetishes.
>
> (Hebdidge, 1979, pp. 104–5)

Such stylistic codes constitute tacit rules that underscore a sense of
commonality. As Najar puts it, '[o]ne can say that sharing the same
costume, the same critical attitude and types of clothes, creates a sen-
sory, non-verbal type of communication between the members of
social groups' (Najar, 1995, p. 404).[1]

Not only do symbols reiterate a sense of belonging, they also enable
self-expression. It is worth emphasising here that these two functions
of symbolic behaviour are neither mutually exclusive nor sequential:
a subculture's dress code may well solidify membership to the group *and*
articulate a group member's sense of self. Nonetheless, a number of
theorists wish to draw a distinction between symbols that are used to
affirm a sense of belonging to a group, and those that express specifically personal feelings or beliefs. In this way, Rubinstein differentiates
between 'tie-signs' and 'tie-symbols', emblems that are worn or used
temporarily to represent an individual's emotions or sense of self
(Rubinstein, 1995, p. 13). Examples of tie-symbols include CND badges,
'message' t-shirts, and the awareness ribbon (the latter, Rubinstein
comments, was 'the most visible tie-symbol in 1992–1993' [ibid.]).
Unlike tie-signs, Rubinstein argues, tie-symbols can express either pro-
social or anti-social sentiments (ibid., p. 206). In either case, these symbols represent a distinctly personal response to social issues.

Other theorists emphasise that even symbols that appear to have
been personally chosen to reflect the particular personality of the
individual are subject to social norms and cultural connotations.
Erving Goffman's work on self-presentation is particularly pertinent
to this conception of symbolic behaviour. Goffman argues that social

interaction is structured by a set of tacit rules that inform how we present ourselves to others. In social situations, Goffman suggests, we commonly present a 'personal front', a façade that is composed of a range of 'expressive equipment' (sex, rank, clothing, gestures, posture etc.) (Goffman, 1969, pp. 32–40). Such props are crucial, Goffman argues, for we are each performers (that is, a 'harried fabricator of impressions') hoping to adequately represent to others a character 'whose spirit, strength, and other sterling qualities the performance [is] designed to evoke' (ibid., p. 244). However, Goffman by no means wishes to suggest a separation between social actor and personal identity, though his metaphor of the stage might encourage such a view. Rather, he argues that a character (or, as it is sometimes seen, the self) emerges out of the performances that we give and is therefore itself a product of the rules that govern social life. The self, Goffman writes, is a 'dramatic effect arising diffusely from a scene that is presented' (ibid., p. 245).

For Goffman, the self is *dramatically realised*. 'All the world is not, of course, a stage', he famously commented, 'but the crucial ways in which it isn't aren't easy to specify' (Goffman, 1969, p. 78). In this way,

> the means for producing and maintaining selves do not reside inside the [person]; in fact these means are often bolted down in social establishments. There will be a back region with its tools for shaping the body, and a front region with its fixed props. There will be a team of persons whose activity on stage and in conjunction with available props will constitute the scene from which the performed character's self will emerge, and another team, the audience, whose interpretative activity will be necessary for this emergence. The self is a product of all these arrangements.
>
> (ibid., p. 245)

This is not to say that our actions are scripted, Goffman argues, but simply to point out that we draw upon a 'repertoire of actions' that are well rehearsed and known to have certain effects on certain audiences ('we all', Goffman writes, 'act better than we know how' [ibid., p. 80]). In this context, the idea that we personally choose symbols to express a sense of self is somewhat misleading. According to Goffman's logic, what is important about, say, the wearing of a Greenpeace badge, is not that the badge wearer wishes to express a personal belief in the need to protect the environment, but rather that he wishes to demon-strate to others that he believes as much and should be seen accord-ingly. In so doing, he draws upon the implicit rules of self-presentation that determine how we deliver our performances and how they are received by others.

Goffman urges us to acknowledge the existence of tacit social rules that govern our use of symbols in certain social situations. Affirmation is a powerful incentive that ensures compliance with such rules; cen-sure and disapproval are equally powerful disincentives that deter rad-ical departure from normative behaviour. 'If I do not conform to ordinary conventions, if in my mode of dress I pay no heed to what is customary in my country and in my social class', Durkheim writes, 'the laughter I provoke, the social distance at which I am kept, pro-duce, although in a more mitigated form, the same results as any real penalty' (Durkheim, 2002, p. 112). Of course, a symbolic code is rarely felt to constitute oppressive social rules. A man who attends a reunion with his old public school friends, for example, is likely to enjoy don-ning his old school tie to show his continued and deep sense of com-mitment to the group. He may well feel that the group's values are an extension of his own personal values, and that the group's identity is an expression, albeit an exaggerated one, of his own identity. Indeed, such symbolic behaviour is often deeply complex, shaping one's sense of self and relationships with others, and reflecting, amongst other things, one's status, cultural capital, and values.

Wearing an old school tie is, moreover, a practice closely bound up with gender identity, a dimension of symbolic behaviour that is par-ticularly relevant to ribbon wearing. A man wearing such a symbol to a reunion may well be reliving a spirit of competitiveness and pres-tige, and thereby affirming his sense of belonging to an 'old boy's network'. Such behaviour highlights a central difference between the symbolic codes of masculinity and femininity. As Craik puts it, '[w]hereas techniques of femininity are acquired and displayed through clothes, looks and gestures, codes of masculinity are inscribed through codes of action, especially through the codes of sport and competi-tion' (Craik, 1994, p. 13). Femininity is achieved through the careful maintenance of personal appearance, a technique that effectively transforms women into objects to be looked at; as John Berger famously put it, *'men act* and *women appear'* (Berger, 1977, p. 47). Certainly, the female ribbon wearers I spoke to were much more likely

than the male participants to see the awareness ribbon as an adornment (see Chapter 5). In this respect, the ribbon embodies certain
implicit gender norms and participates in the circulation of a particular conception of femininity, especially where it is given as a gift by
a mother to her daughter.

On other occasions, social rules governing the use of symbols are
explicit and strictly enforced. Berger and Luckmann point to the coer-
cion from various institutions (especially the church and the military)
to take part in various symbolic acts so as to confirm and legitimate
institutional values and procedures (Berger and Luckmann, 1966,
p. 88). Similarly, shop workers, nurses, the clergy, police officers, and
students are often required to wear uniforms, which might include
ties, overalls, shoes, and (in the case of cashiers) name-badges. Unlike
a subcultural dress code, a uniform is devised and enforced by social
institutions to reiterate an official code of conduct (Rubinstein, 1995,
p. 67). In other instances, symbolic behaviour is strictly imposed on a
particular group as a means of persecution. During the First World
War, for example, men who refused to enlist were made to wear white
feathers. These were meant to symbolise their weakness, and to emas-
culate them further, young women were recruited to hand out the
feathers (Gullace, 1997). We might also note the use of uniforms in
Nazi concentration camps, where each apparently aberrant group was
made to wear particular symbols on their clothing. In both cases, the
wearing of certain symbols is enforced by social authorities wishing to
mark out particular social groups as deviant.

Howard Becker, the prominent symbolic interactionist, emphasised
that certain behaviour (refusing to enlist during times of war, for
example) is labelled deviant because it contravenes a socially constructed moral code (Becker, 1973). According to this perspective,
meanings are socially produced, rather than inhering in actual objects,
people, or acts. For Becker, this by no means entails that meaning is
created and imposed by an anonymous, external social force. Rather,
he sees meaning as the product of a process of interpretation and
negotiation that takes place during social interaction (ibid., pp. 182–3).
Of course, on some occasions there is an unreflexive consensus about
meaning, though this is in itself a means whereby meanings are passed
on (Kaiser, 1985, pp. 187–8). Symbolic interactionism, perhaps more
than any other sociological perspective, has sought to demonstrate that
people take an active role in producing meaning, albeit as members

of groups. Blumer, who coined the term 'symbolic interactionism', was deeply critical of social theory that conceived of people as the carriers of social structures. 'Such sociological conceptions do not regard the social actions of individuals in human society as being constructed by them through a process of interpretation', Blumer argued. 'If a place is given to interpretation', he added, '[i]t is regarded as merely an expression of other factors (such as motives) which precede the act, and accordingly disappears in its own right' (Blumer, 2002, p. 73).

Though there is some merit to such an approach, it is important to acknowledge the impact of wider cultural and social factors upon this process of interpretation. This is not to suggest that human beings are the passive recipients of symbolic meanings, but simply to point out that their behaviour is *framed* by social processes and institutions. The rise of modernity, for example, is widely believed to have had a significant impact upon symbolic behaviour. A number of theorists have convincingly argued that symbolic meaning has become increasingly ambiguous in modern society as traditional sources of authority have declined and the process of individuation has become pervasive. Richard Sennett, for example, suggests that clothes, once seen 'as matters of contrivance, decoration, and convention' (Sennett, 1993, p. 65), now 'appear to have something to do with the character of the person wearing them' (ibid., p. 72). Though evident in the mid-eighteenth century with the emergence of 'house clothes', this attitude towards clothing has been particularly pronounced since the mid-nineteenth century, and particularly in urban areas (Sennett, 1993, pp. 64–72). Before this period, Lofland argues, city life involved 'an ordering of the urban populace in terms of appearance and spatial location such that those within the city could know a great deal about one another by simply looking' (Lofland, 1973, p. 22). By the late nineteenth century, however, symbols had come to have little relation to social status or ties, and because of this it became increasingly difficult to assign meaning to symbolic action. As a result, categorising people on the basis of their appearance became an unreliable means of identification.

The ineffectiveness of this process of categorisation is ever more evident in our heterogeneous, late modern societies. Certainly, it is sometimes difficult to pin down precisely what the ribbon signifies about its wearer. The yellow ribbon, for example, has not only been used to support troops fighting in the Gulf, but also to spread awareness of teen suicide, to support the nanny Louise Woodward, and to protest teens' restricted iInternet access.[2] Moreover, the ribbon motif frequently appears alongside other symbols. Yellow ribbons, for example, are often tied to pictures of those who died in the September 11 attacks in New York and are frequently pinned to houses in the USA alongside national flags (Santino, 1992, pp. 27–8). Similarly, it is possible to buy a red AIDS-awareness ribbon with the image of an angel, religious cross, rainbow, dove, the pope, a star, or a jewel in the centre. Such adjuncts to the ribbon design mean that the symbol can be used to infer a wide range of meanings.

Berger et al. (1979) explain the widening field of symbolic meaning in terms of the emergence of multiple sources of authority in modern society. They argue that fathoming an order to, or a relation between, symbols is increasingly difficult in a society in which there are few shared symbolic meanings, such as those provided by religion. Similarly, Mary Douglas claims that '[o]ne of the gravest problems of [modern society] is the lack of commitment to common symbols' (Douglas, 1996, p. 1). Douglas argues that social controls, such as religion, have come to seem pernicious, a development reflected in symbolic renderings of the body ('the most readily available image of a system') that represent it as a burden, overly constraining and inferior to spiritual essence (ibid., p. xxxviii). As a result, 'symbolic life [is] detached more and more from the task of relating an individual to his society and more and more freed for expressing his unique private concerns' (ibid., p. 171). The primary – at least the most obvious – purpose of symbolic behaviour in late modern societies is to facilitate the articulation of personal, rather than social, meaning. Certainly, the awareness ribbon seems to be directed more towards articulating personal sentiments of awareness and compassion than any shared meaning.

Looked at differently, the apparent individualisation of symbolic meaning in late modern societies masks a creeping uniformity. Symbols in contemporary society may rarely represent an unchanging or collective worldview, but they often connote decidedly standardised meanings, mainly, I would suggest, because they are frequently transformed into commodities. As I discuss in Chapter 4, the various personal meanings attached to the awareness ribbon are overshadowed by the idea that ribbon wearing is aimed at 'showing awareness', a broad, catch-all meaning that, just like an advertisement's tag line, is easily transposed from one ribbon campaign to the next.

The standardisation of the ribbon's meaning may well strike us as particularly odd considering that the symbol is widely seen to embody deeply personal sentiments of awareness and compassion. The same ambiguity might be noted about many other products in contemporary society. Levi jeans, for example, are widely seen to suggest a cool attitude, one that seems to be intimately bound up with the distinctive individuality of the wearer. Indeed, as Rubinstein points out, Levi Strauss has recognised and capitalised on 'the benefits of turning clothes into tie symbols', that is, into expressions of self-identity (Rubinstein, 1995, p. 206). However, the advertising for such clothes delineates a particularly narrow type of individuality: adverts show us that young male Levi-jean wearers are quick-thinking, confident, and comfortable anywhere, whilst young female Levi-jean wearers are thin, aloof, and savvy. Such advertising 'sells' individuality. Modern consumerism, as Colin Campbell noted, is premised upon a 'philosophy of self-expression and self-realization' (Campbell, 1987, p. 201). This 'spirit' of consumerism is, Campbell argues, essentially 'romantic in inspiration', as it is based upon a hedonistic impulse, a desire for novelty, and an unquenchable search for self-realisation (ibid.). Yet, this romantic ethic is *rearticulated* in contemporary advertising in such a way as to transform ideas about self-identity into glib patter promoting 'realness', authenticity, and 'being yourself'. The important thing to note here is that clothes (and other commodities) are often believed to reflect a sense of individuality *in keeping with*, rather than regardless of, this rather prescriptive conception of self-identity.

What is particularly novel here is the emphasis placed on clothes as a mark of pure individuality. Yet fashion, as Simmel noted some one hundred years ago, is peculiar in the sense that it enables both conformity *and* differentiation. 'Fashion' he commented, 'is the imitation of a given example'. 'At the same time', he wrote, 'it satisfies in no less degree the need of differentiation, the tendency towards dissimilarity' (Simmel, 1904, 1971, 'Fashion', p. 296). As such, 'the individual derives the satisfaction of knowing that [a fashion] adopted by him ... still represents something special and striking, while at the same time he feels inwardly supported by a set of persons who are striving for the same thing' (ibid., p. 304). Simmel seeks to show us that the dual desire for sameness and difference is in fact a profound aspect of social reality, one that is evident elsewhere if we look hard enough. 'The whole history of society', he declares at the start of his essay on fashion, 'is reflected in the striking conflicts, the compromises, slowly won and quickly lost, between socialistic adaptation to society and individual departure from its demands' (ibid., p. 294). The only problem with such a neat formulation is that it suggests too clear-cut a distinction between society and the individual, and implies that both exist in a 'pure' form.

Identity

Identity is a rather bewildering sociological concept, not least because it is associated with an incredible range of behaviour and human faculties. Yet identity, as Dennis Wrong notes, 'is the most widely used concept these days in the social sciences' (Wrong, 2000, p. 10). Indeed, contemporary sociology is dominated by discussions about identity, from resistant identities to reflexive self-identity. With all the talk of identity it is easy to forget that this concept is a relatively recent addition to the sociologist's lexicon, and one that did not, as Bauman points out, feature in the work of the classical sociologists (Bauman, 2004, p. 16). It was only in the 1950s that the term came to be widely used in the social sciences to refer to a person's biography or individual life history. Even during this nascent period in the study of identity, defining the concept proved to be difficult, as Eric Erikson, one of the most influential researchers in this field, comments,

> Identity and identity crisis have in popular and scientific usage become terms which alternately circumscribe something so large and so seemingly self-evident that to demand a definition would almost seem petty, while at other times they designate something made so narrow for purposes of measurement that the over-all meaning is lost, and it could just as well be called something else.
> (Erikson, 1968, p. 15)

A social psychologist, Erikson put forward a conception of identity that took into account both the individual's capacity for self-reflection and the impact of family and peer groups on self-development. Identity, Erikson suggested, is an ongoing 'process of simultaneous reflection and observation' whereby an individual assesses himself in comparison to others (ibid., pp. 22–3). It is, Erikson comments, a mainly unconscious process of 'increasing differentiation' (ibid.) resulting (save for identity crises) in a 'subjective sense of invigorating sameness and continuity' (ibid., p. 19). Wrong sums up Erikson's conception of identity as 'an individual's not necessarily fully conscious sense of self, reflecting the continuity of her/his life history and the synthesis of various past identifications with others, especially in the family' (Wrong, 2000, p. 11).

Whilst Erikson's definition seems straightforward enough, we might reasonably ask how we might go about studying identity. After all, identity, for Erikson at least, is an intangible, unquantifiable aspect of human experience. We can't ask people directly what their identities consist of, as Richard Sennett, then a student of Erikson, found during his first research project:

> 'My what, young man?' an elderly Boston matron replied when I asked her to describe her identity, point-blank over tea in the Somerset Club ... An identity involves a life-narrative rather than a fixed image of self, I kindly explained to her ... and a recognition that others' lives intrude into one's sense of self. Equally kindly, she wasn't having any of it: 'We go our separate ways, dear'.
>
> (Sennett, 2001, p. 175)

Indeed, this conception of identity raises a number of questions. How, for example, can an individual express his life history *in its totality*? And to what extent can a person describe her identity in concrete terms (that is, through language)? How valid is a narrative account of identity? (Do we really experience identity as a story with a start, middle, and end?) As Bourdieu points out, '[t]o produce a life history or to consider life as a history, that is, as a coherent narrative of a significant and directed sequence of events, is perhaps to conform to a rhetorical illusion' (Bourdieu in Du Gay et al. [eds], 2000, p. 298). Of course, many of us conform to this rhetorical illusion, but we should realise that in doing so we reshape past events, shave off seemingly superfluous details, and elaborate upon others. A life story becomes a plot, the desire for coherence *transforming* each episode into an integral part of a meaningful narrative structure. If we elicit any response from people when we ask them what their identity consists of, it is likely to be a retrospective interpretation of past events shaped by an idealised self-image in the here and now.

For these reasons I did not ask research participants to provide a potted life history. Instead I asked them to explain why they supported the charities they wore ribbons for, what had first prompted them to wear a ribbon (and, if applicable, why they continued to do so), whether the ribbon symbolised particular values, how they viewed other ribbon wearers, and their relationship to sufferers. Some interviewees did volunteer something like a life narrative − they spoke of seminal events that had helped create an interest in a certain cause and described ribbon wearing as a logical extension of previous behaviour or attitudes. Others discussed their sense of compassion in terms of their relationships to others, and most notably their family members (several young women, for example, spoke about their mothers' charitable behaviour and how it had influenced their actions). A significant number of interviewees, however, were unable, or unwilling, to conceive of their ribbon wearing in terms of such an explanatory framework. One young woman, for example, told me a series of disjointed stories about people dying suddenly (some were urban myths, some she had heard from friends or her mother, a nurse). She was clearly preoccupied by such stories, to the extent that her account was decidedly incoherent. What was particularly interesting was her presumption that I shared her particular outlook and concerns, her belief, in other words, that the deeper meaning of what she was saying was self-evident. In fact, I was flummoxed by her responses, and finally asked her why she was so concerned with death, since, I added, everyone has to die at some point. 'But people don't have to die *young*', she replied caustically. Such a comment, so illuminating of certain elements of this young woman's identity (her sense of compassion for sufferers of illness, her relationship to her family, her various superstitions, for example), would not have been possible if the interviewee had been asked or encouraged to relay her experiences in a narrative structure.

Moreover, Erikson's approach only takes into account the more personal, biographical aspects of identity. Our identities are surely also shaped by wider, social conditions, such as economic position, social norms, and cultural background. Similarly, it is not simply our interactions with peers and family members that shape our identity, but also our place within large-scale, 'imagined' social groups, such as a nation or an ethnic minority. For a number of social scientists, a person's 'social identity' is rather different from his 'personal identity' (Jenkins, 1996). The former involves a process of association with 'we' groups and disassociation from 'them' groups; the latter involves a process of identification and differentiation *within* a 'we' group (Deschamps and Devos, 1998, pp. 4–8). Such a conceptualisation might be neat, but it also creates the illusion that the individual has two separate identities. Certainly, it encourages the belief that sociologists should restrict their investigations to the consideration of 'social identity', and leave the exploration of 'personal identity' to those with a better grasp of individual subjectivity, such as psychologists or philosophers.

In contrast, some sociologists emphasise that even the apparently personal aspects of identity are contingent upon socially constructed norms and conventions, a view that is supported in this book. In her work on gender identity, Judith Butler claims that becoming a recognisable person requires the adoption of familiar, social modes of representation, such as language. This, she suggests, is a point often neglected by philosophers who write 'on the assumption that whatever social context the person is 'in' remains somehow externally related to the definitional structure of personhood, be that consciousness, the capacity for language, or moral deliberation' (Butler, 1990, p. 16). For Butler, 'the person' is not intrinsic or naturally emerging, but rather a socially constructed category achieved by adhering to certain frames of meaning and patterns of behaviour. Gender, for example, is not a matter of 'being', rather it is a matter of 'doing' (ibid., p. 18).

Butler suggests that the 'performance' of gender regulates identity, desire and sexuality so that the neat binaries of 'masculine' and 'feminine' 'are understood as expressive attributes of male and female' (ibid., p. 17). In this account, gender is the corollary of a hegemonic discourse that prioritises heterosexuality and masculine subjectivity (ibid., pp. 5–10). However, she argues that gender 'ought not to be construed as a stable identity or locus of agency from which various acts follow ... rather, gender is an identity tenuously constituted in time, instituted in an exterior space *through a stylized repetition of acts*' (ibid., p. 179. Italics added.). For Butler, it is the gaps in gender performance – the points at which we are not required to repeat gendered acts – that offer up the possibility for resistance.

Butler's analysis, illuminating as it is about the mechanisms of social regulation, wrongly conceives of gender as something that is ultimately separable from the person who performs it (indeed, the very notion of performance implies as much). Yet the person who 'performs' gender is surely *already* gendered, a point that Butler herself alludes to in her suggestion that the person is constituted by socially produced meanings and patterns of behaviour.[3] This inconsistency in Butler's work raises an important question: how can we reconcile the idea that a social identity, such as gender, is at once *external* to the self and located *within* the self?

One answer might be found in Carolyn Steedman's (1997) autobiographical account of her experiences growing up in a working-class family in the 1950s. In one seminal episode, Steedman (then aged four) and her father are caught picking bluebells in a privately owned forest (ibid., pp. 49–51). The forest keeper shouts and jeers at her father, causing 'a dramatic eruption' (ibid., p. 50). Steedman recalls being struck by her father's vulnerability and the tenuousness of his status as an authority figure. 'All the charity I possess lies in that moment' (ibid.) she tells us, a remarkable admission considering her antipathy towards her father, a man who 'dictated each day's existence' (ibid., p. 19). It is her father's very person – not simply an antiseptic 'stylised act' he is repeating – that appears to be at stake in this encounter, no doubt a 'gap' in performance that Butler would see as offering up the possibility for subversion. For Steedman, regardless of her antagonism towards her father and the social system he represents, this experience provokes a deep, visceral feeling of discomfort and pity, a sense of 'dislocation', as she puts it (ibid., p. 51). Steedman's account highlights that even repressive social identities can be integral to our sense of self and our relationships with others. Her work is directed towards a consideration of the interrelationship between lived experience and socio-historical developments:

> [f]ixing my father ... in time and politics can help show the creation of gender in particular households and in particular familial situations at the same time as it demonstrates the position of men and the social reality represented by them in particular households. We need historical accounts of such relationships, not just a longing that they might be different. Above all, perhaps, *we need a sense of people's complexity of relationship to the historical situations they inherit.*
>
> (Ibid., p. 19. Italics added.)

I adopt a similar approach to the study of ribbon wearing. This social practice reflects a cultural-historical development in which a discourse of compassion has come to constitute a moral vocabulary. Such a discourse is difficult to resist, particularly as exhibiting compassion is widely associated with authenticity; we are embedded, in other words, in a culture of compassion, in which showing that one cares deeply affirms one's very sense of self. Indeed, I would suggest that compassion is not only a prized character trait, but has come to constitute a central aspect of identity in contemporary society. Such an identity requires, amongst other things, the idea that one's actions and beliefs stem from a particularly intense sense of compassion, self-identification as a caring person, and recognition from others that this is the basis of one's identity ('my family call me the caring one!' one interviewee told me happily). This identity is seemingly based on individuated experiences and feelings. Such an identity is therefore markedly different to those that sociologists usually turn their attention to – those based on class, gender, ethnicity, and nationality – and this is where Erikson's conception of identity *is* relevant to our discussion.

Erikson's notion that identity constitutes personal biography reflects a certain socio-historical context in which identity becomes the task of the individual (Bauman, 2004, p. 18). In this respect, and as Dennis Wrong argues, identity is the consequence of a historical shift that took place some one hundred years before the term became a sociological buzzword. For Wrong, the notion that we each have a particular life history

> reflects the freedom and mobility available under conditions of modernity, confronting individuals with a wide array of choices and holding them responsible for those that are made ... Identity is inescapably a result of the rise of individualism as a value-set distinctive of modernity.
>
> (Wrong, 2000, p. 11)

Thus a process of individuation was set in place during modernity, though it would be some one hundred years before it reached far enough to facilitate the creation of personal biographies. Indeed, we should not forget that the rise of modernity during the nineteenth century ushered in the seemingly inexorable social identities of class, gender, and nationality.

Today, however, we forge our identities through 'multiple histories, media and archives that are subject to revision, mobilization, and recombination' (Outhwaite and Ray, 2005, p. 195). We make use of such sources of identity not only because they seem to offer up an incredible range of possibilities for personal development, but also because sources of more solid, lasting identities are no longer accessible. As Beck and Beck-Gernsheim comment, in our late modern societies, 'historical models for the conduct of life' have become obsolete (Beck and Beck-Gernsheim, 2002, p. 26). In this context, identity in late modern societies might be seen in terms of a lack of substance, coherence, and permanence. For Bauman, it is precisely these deficiencies that made identity such a prominent area of study during the second half of the twentieth century. 'You tend to notice things and put them into the focus of your scrutiny and contemplation', he notes, 'when they vanish, go bust, start to behave oddly or otherwise let you down' (Bauman, 2004, p. 17). Left with no 'ready-made identities or categories that we can unproblematically slip into' (Rutherford, 1990, p. 24), our attention is focussed on the difficult task of developing our own personal biography, for ourselves, by ourselves.

For Beck and Beck-Gernsheim, developing this type of identity has become an imperative in late modern societies. In fact, the notion that each person should run his or her own life has come to shape most of our actions, a development these authors refer to as individualisation. This process, they argue, has become a defining feature of education, family relations, welfare benefits, and the job market: in all of these areas, individuals are required to prioritise their personal objectives and see themselves as autonomous of social relations. Individualisation has, in short, become institutionalised; looking at one's life in terms of individual aims, costs and gains is unavoidable. Identity is subject to this same process. Biographies, Beck and Beck-Gernsheim note, are now hatched together by individuals who must take sole responsibility for the outcome of their decisions. 'Opportunities, dangers, biographical uncertainties that were earlier predefined within the family association, the village community, or by recourse to the rules of social estates or classes', they note, 'must now be perceived, interpreted, decided and processed by individuals themselves' (Beck and Beck-Gernsheim, 2002, p. 4).

As a result, the individual is required to plan his own life, scrutinise his motivations and decisions, and reflect, on a more or less constant basis, on what might be the most efficacious course of action. 'At each moment', Giddens writes, 'the individual is asked to conduct a self-interrogation in terms of what is happening. Beginning as a series of conscious questions, the individual becomes accustomed to asking, how can I use this moment to change?' (Giddens, 1991, p. 76). In this context, reflexivity is not simply a method of assessing a situation, it is a practice integral to the creation of identity. The self becomes 'a reflexive project' in which even the body becomes a site for continual assessment and improvement (ibid., p. 77; see also Shilling, 1993, p. 5). A 'self-identity', as Giddens refers to it, is reflexively understood by the individual, who is thereby able to integrate otherwise disparate elements of his/her life history into a coherent narrative (Giddens, 1991, p. 215). In this context, we might see ribbon wearing as a practice aimed at fostering reflexive self-identity. Certainly, it is commonly directed towards showing a sense of awareness about a particular illness or cause. More generally speaking, ribbon wearing seems to reflect the freedom available to individuals in late modern societies to create their own identities.

In fact, as we see in Chapter 5, the practice of 'showing awareness' often involves decidedly uniform, habitual behaviour, even though it seems to be self-directed and deliberate. As Colin Campbell insightfully points out, we should recognise that 'there is a distinction between performing a deliberately chosen act in an habitual manner and habitually deciding to do something but performing it in a self-conscious and deliberate fashion' (Campbell, 1996, p. 162). 'It is important to remember', he adds, 'that every single deliberate, reflexive, freely chosen, rationally calculated, and willed action contains the potential to become the first step in the construction of an unconsidered and automatic, habitual routine of conduct' (ibid., p. 163).

Certainly, whilst 'showing awareness' might require a level of reflexivity in the first instance, it often manifests itself as, amongst other things, a nagging sense of worry that subsumes itself into everyday practices and routines. Where it eventuates in such routines, the type of reflexivity described by Giddens is in fact decidedly disenabling. More akin to compulsive self-scrutiny than rational evaluation, this brand of reflexivity may well speak of and reiterate a deep sense of uncertainty and incompleteness. 'Anxiety', Kellner writes, 'becomes a constituent experience for the modern self. For one is never certain that one has made the right choice' (Kellner, 1996, p. 142). Even seemingly straightforward or mundane tasks become cause for concern in a society in which nothing is certain or self-evident. We are, for example, told that loved ones might do us more harm than good; we attend health and safety meetings about the risks posed by otherwise harmless, everyday objects; we are made aware of the harm we might unintentionally do ourselves, by our lifestyles, by falling in love, even.

For Ulrich Beck, our increased consciousness of risk is related to a process of 'reflexive modernization', whereby we have become concerned with the problems incurred by technological development, such as ecological and nuclear disasters (Beck, 1992, p. 21). 'Risks, as opposed to older dangers', Beck writes, 'are consequences which relate to the threatening force of modernization and to its globalization of doubt' (ibid.). Side-effects, malfunctions, and by-products become central concerns for those living in technologically advanced societies. Knowledge about risks becomes a central means of defence, though it is also 'open to social definition and construction' (ibid., p. 23). In this way, risk reports can be 'changed, magnified, dramatized or minimized' (ibid.).

Similarly, Furedi argues that '[t]he media play an important role in the shaping of perceptions of risks' (Furedi, 1997, p. 52). Indeed, and as we see in Chapter 8, pink-ribbon wearers' concern about breast cancer is shaped by the ways in which the illness is represented in the breast cancer awareness campaign. 'Since most people gain their information through the media rather than through direct experience', Furedi points out, 'their perception is moulded by the way information is communicated' (ibid.). However, Furedi is critical of Beck's suggestion that the process of modernisation has created particularly harmful risks. Instead, he argues that the contemporary concern with risk is symptomatic of a widespread aversion to change in today's society and the weakening of social institutions that might have previously provided a basic sense of security (ibid., p. 67). According to Furedi, then, a sense of uncertainty is a response to a particular social context, rather than a response to the actual scale or nature of risk in contemporary society.

We will pick up this line of discussion again in Chapter 7, where we examine ribbon wearers' sense of worry about the illnesses for which they wear a ribbon. At this juncture, however, the idea that we are particularly susceptible to a risk consciousness in contemporary society is pertinent because it is deeply suggestive of a certain approach to the task of self-identity. Such a widespread lack of certainty is not only likely to prompt feelings of worry or anxiety, it is also likely to produce a desire to find something that will provide a sense of conviction, especially for the purposes of forging and asserting an identity. In this context, the emotional aspects of the self are relatively reliable features of personal identity. As Deborah Lupton notes, '[i]n a world which is experienced as uncertain and changing being able to cling to the notion of an "emotional self" that is at least partly stable provides some degree of certainty about the self' (Lupton, 1998, p. 168). At the same time, an emotional self is ostensibly flexible and self-referential, and therefore satisfies, in no less degree, the desire for an identity that is unconstrained by any really concrete or externally imposed model of behaviour. As Christopher Nolan comments, we are regularly confronted with the idea that '[t]he true or real person is the one who begins with the self, as opposed to social institutions outside the self, and "honestly" and "authentically" emotes his or her inner tides outward' (Nolan, 1998, p. 7). As a result, and as Furedi puts it, 'the question of identity is increasingly associated with feeling' (Furedi, 2004, p. 143).

It is unsurprising, therefore, that the expression of emotional sentiments has gained a certain cultural currency, a development embodied by the emergence of what Furedi refers to as a 'therapy culture' (Furedi, 2004). Taking a rather different stance to Lupton, Furedi sees the emergence of an 'emotional self' as an extension of the process of individuation:

> [t]he significance attributed to the feelings of the self reinforces and intensifies the historic tendency towards individualisation. The feelings of the self are private, personal matters that differentiate and distance people from each other. The emotionalisation of the self heightens the sense of individuation by shifting the focus inward.
>
> (Ibid., p. 144)

An integral aspect of this process of individualisation is the decline of external sources of authority. In other words, it is a process borne out of necessity as much as a desire for an authentic self. Lacking shared symbols and belief systems, 'one is left with one's feelings', as Nolan puts it (Nolan, 1998, p. 5).

This is not to suggest that our identities are developed autonomously of social norms and cultural currents and reflect 'pure' emotional experiences. After all, and as Gerth and Mills point out, 'in order for inner feelings to become emotions, these feelings must be linked with socially recognizable gestures and the person must become aware of them as related to the self' (Gerth and Mills, 1965, p. 20). Indeed, there are 'fashions in the vocabularies of emotion' (ibid., p. 56) that shape the ways in which we discuss, represent, and understand emotional experiences. In her research into emotional experiences, Lupton found that being emotional was frequently equated with displays of compassion (Lupton, 1998, pp. 44–5). Such an understanding of the emotional self is unsurprising given the pervasiveness of a discourse of compassion in contemporary society. 'The language of caring has permeated so deeply', West argues, 'that even political conservatives have appropriated it'. 'We grew accustomed in the 1990s to Bill Clinton and Tony Blair promising to "reach out" to us, to "feel" and "care" for us', he comments, adding that now '[e]ven Republicans in the US and the Tories in the UK ... talk of compassionate conservatism' (West, 2004, p. 68). Such a rhetoric of compassion has been judged by some to constitute a cynical attempt to curry favour with the electorate. Indeed, for Stjepan Mestrovic we are living in a *postemotional* world, saturated by vacuous cultural representations of emotion; 'postemotionalism refers to the use of *dead*, abstracted emotions by the culture industry in a neo-Orwellian, mechanical, and petrified manner' (Mestrovic, 1997, p. 26). It is 'a displaced, viscerated compassion' (ibid.) that greets us when we turn on our television sets, read our newspapers, or listen to our politicians, Mestrovic argues. Exploring the implications of the standardisation and abstraction of emotional responses is a central point of concern in this book. Before we consider such arguments more fully, it is necessary to examine the nature of charity in contemporary society and the cultural meaning of compassion.

Charity and compassion

The lapel ribbon is often taken to be a symbol of compassion for a particular group of sufferers. We should note, for the sake of conceptual clarity, that there is a distinction between manifesting a compassionate act and exhibiting one's compassion. In reality, of course, the two are intimately connected. Ribbon wearing, for example, requires a charitable donation, and therefore establishes a relationship – however tenuous – between donor and sufferer, but is also directed towards showing the wearer to be a compassionate person. As a method of self-presentation, showing compassion is intriguing behaviour (to whom is the display of compassion directed? What kind of discourse accompanies such a display? What are the assumed meanings and connotations of showing empathy?). The motivation behind an act of compassion is no less complex. After all, such behaviour can be much more than (or, indeed, much less than) a demonstration of concern for others. This is not to suggest that compassionate acts are not motivated by a desire to attend to others' suffering. It is simply to point out that an act of compassion might be informed by other concerns too, such as the wish to alleviate guilt, the belief that one's kindness will be repaid in some way ('what comes around goes around'), or simply the notion that doing something compassionate is what one *ought* to do.

Understanding what motivates people to show compassion is further complicated by the fact that expressions of compassion may well be intangible and spontaneous. Social scientists, especially psychologists, have therefore often focussed on official (and measurable) acts of compassion and, in particular, charity giving. Such academics have isolated a wide range of 'donor motives', from countering negative emotions of guilt, to conforming to group norms (see Clary et al., 1998). As Farsides notes, most of these motivations inhere in either an altruistic or an egoistic drive, though the former is often seen to exist in only a partial form:

> [a] person with an altruistic motive is motivated to bring about other-benefits. If that goal is achieved, the person will experience satisfaction, and it is the anticipation of such satisfaction that motivates the behaviour. The latter fact compels some thinkers to say that such partially altruistic acts are 'ultimately' egoistic ... The main contrast drawn here is between such motives and *wholly* egoistic ones, for which other-welfare is only ever – at best – *contingently* required for satisfaction. A person with wholly egoistic goals is truly motivated only to bring about self-benefit. Even if this requires that another must be helped to make such self-benefit possible in the circumstances, other-benefit will only ever be properly understood as instrumental to self-benefit.
>
> (Farsides, 2005, 22n)

Charities, Farsides goes on to point out, satisfy donors' egoistic or altruistic inclinations by fostering 'exchange' or 'communal' relationships, respectively (ibid., pp. 4–5). Charities wishing to develop the former type of relationship treat their donors as self-seeking consumers, whilst those that seek to foster 'communal' relationships see their donors as likeminded supporters.

Certainly, many of the interviewees who took part in my research made use of such language: a number spoke of wishing to support a cause, whilst others clearly had a more egoistic attitude towards charity giving (see Chapter 8). Nonetheless, the notion that charitable behaviour is varyingly altruistic or egoistic (or a mixture of the two) seems rather reductive. Of course, Richard Titmuss comments, donors' behaviour is never *purely* altruistic. It 'could not be, for ... no donor type can be depicted in terms of complete, disinterested, spontaneous altruism. There must be some sense of obligation, approval, and interest; some feeling of inclusion in society; some awareness of need and the purposes of the gift' (Titmuss, 1997, p. 306). What standard typologies of charitable behaviour usually fail to explore is the relationship between donors and their social and cultural environments, and the resulting ambiguities in terms of motivation and meaning. Giving to charity is not always done for straightforward reasons and, like other social behaviour, it is often shaped in complex ways by our relationships to others, our awareness of social norms, and our surroundings (whether, for example, we are approached by a charity collector at work, at home, or on the street).

The point I wish to emphasise here is that analyses of charitableness should not be limited to 'weighing up' donors' motives, but should attempt to provide nuanced accounts of this behaviour. In-depth accounts of charitable behaviour are crucial if sociologists are to gain a deeper understanding of this aspect of social life. Indeed, in some instances, compassion does not simply involve one's relation to others, but it also constitutes an integral aspect of one's identity. Assertions that 'Yes, I'm the kind of person who cares', as an American *Save the Children* advert puts it (Moeller, 1999, p. 53), are clearly more directed towards self-identification than a recognition of others' suffering.

In more subtle ways, too, acts of compassion might be shaped by the wish to affirm a sense of personal identity. During the mid-nineteenth century, a period during which charitable provision for the poor far exceeded that provided by the state in the UK (Whelan, 1996, p. 15), charitable acts affirmed a sense of religious virtue (Fraser, 1984, p. 127). This is not to suggest that British philanthropists of this period were not motivated by a genuine concern with improving working and living conditions in the newly industrialised urban centres. It is simply to emphasise that expressions of compassion are informed by prevailing ideas about the place and meaning of compassion in any given social context.

Similarly interested in the cultural meaning of compassion, Barker-Benfield suggests that the rise of British philanthropic organisations during the nineteenth century was related to the emergence of sentimental fiction and, more generally speaking, a 'cult of sensibility', during the mid-eighteenth century (Barker-Benfield, 1992, p. 294). It was middle-class women who dominated the reading and writing of this literature, as the domestic sphere became the primary site for consumption of cultural products such as novels (ibid., p. 395). Moreover, femininity came to be closely associated with emotional responsiveness during this period, an attribute that was deemed to make women particularly suited to the reading and writing of sentimental literature (Jones, 1990, p. 11). As Jones comments, middle-class women were believed to possess a 'special capacity for sympathy and feeling', which was thought to manifest itself as an especially caring disposition (Jones, 1990, p. 11). As a result, the 'flood of reform organizations' that emerged in the nineteenth century were 'rooted in a middle-class, female constituency' (Barker-Benfield, 1992, p. 294). Of course, we are more accustomed to think of Victorian charity as the preserve of middle-class, male philanthropists. Certainly, figures such as Lord Shaftsbury and Dr Barnardo were highly influential in organising provision for the poor. This type of philanthropy is markedly different, however, to the benevolence associated with upper-middle-class women. Whilst the former was often seen in terms of the high-minded, rational pursuit of social progress, the latter was regularly seen as a morally virtuous pastime.

The relationship between Miss Brooke and the boring religious scholar Casaubon in George Eliot's novel *Middlemarch* (originally written in 1871) is a pertinent illustration of these gender differences. Eager to develop a more rational approach to (amongst other things) her house building project for the rural poor, Miss Brooke receives lessons from her new husband, in academic disciplines usually reserved for men:

> [t]hose provinces of masculine knowledge seemed to her a standing-ground from which all truth could be seen more truly. As it was, she constantly doubted her own conclusions, because she felt her own ignorance: how could she be confident that one-roomed cottages were not for the glory of God, when men who knew the classics appeared to conciliate indifference to the cottages with zeal for the glory?
>
> (Eliot, 2003, p. 64)

Exasperated by Casaubon's indifference towards her benevolent pursuits, Miss Brooke is plagued by an underlying concern that, as a woman, her vision is clouded by an irrepressible sense of compassion and an inclination for selflessness:

> [a]ll her eagerness for acquirement lay within that full current of sympathetic motive in which her ideas and impulses were habitually swept along. She did not want to deck herself with knowledge – to wear it loose from the nerves and blood that fed her action; and if she had written a book she must have done it as Saint Theresa did, under the command of an authority that constrained her conscience.
>
> (Ibid., p. 86)

Miss Brooke *feels* compassion, it drives through her veins and tingles her nerve endings, forcefully 'sweeping' her along in a wave of emotion. In today's society, such emotional experiences may not be accompanied with quite the same sense of female inadequacy, but they are certainly still associated with femininity (see Thoits, 1989, pp. 321–2; Hochschild, 1983). Many of the ribbon wearers I interviewed, for example, described compassion as a deeply feminine trait. Not only this, but they believed that women were far more likely to give to charity, an assumption that is borne out by statistical data (Farsides and Hibbert, 2005).

It is not simply gender norms that shape charitable behaviour in today's society. We should also note that social agencies (charities, state and local government, and the media) often provide models or outlets for expressions of compassion. For example, government policies often furnish individuals with the means of expressing their 'moral potentialities' (Titmuss, 1997, p. 306). Similarly, the cultural representation of compassion – the moral vocabulary through which acts of compassion are discussed and the ways in which empathy and victimhood are portrayed – is likely to shape charitable behaviour. Following a broadly similar line of argument, a number of commentators have suggested that the media's reporting of tragic events can have an important impact on charity giving. During the 1990s, Susan Moeller argues, charity campaigns and the media's coverage of crises inspired a nonchalant attitude towards suffering in the USA, which in turn caused a decrease in charitable donations (Moeller, 1999). She suggests that the media were particularly at fault in creating this 'compassion fatigue': '[h]ow they typically cover crises helps us to feel overstimulated and bored all at once' (ibid., p. 9). Moeller argues that the media's over-reporting and sensationalisation of tragedies causes the public's compassion to be stretched to its limit (ibid., pp. 17–53).

For a number of theorists, however, our sense of compassion in today's society is distinguished more by its presence than its absence. Certainly, data for the UK shows that charitable donations have increased in recent years, prompting authors of a recent survey on charitable donations to suggest that we are entering a 'new era of increased altruism'.[4] There has been a similar increase in charitable donations in the USA (donations from individuals increased by 1.4 per cent in 2004),[5] though it is less marked in a country in which charity is viewed as a core value (indeed, US citizens make more charitable donations than the citizens of any other country [Brooks, 2006]).

Taking a rather broader view of charitable trends, a number of theorists have suggested that the interest in charity today should be seen in the context of large-scale socio-historical shifts, and in particular the emergence of modernity some 150 years ago. Natan Sznaider, for example, argues that the rise of modernity ushered in an especially 'compassionate temperament'. Sznaider suggests that civic equality, a central principle of modern, democratic societies, has helped engender a sense of shared humanity and, in turn, a recognition of others' suffering (Sznaider, 2001, pp. 61–2). In addition to this, he argues, the workings of the capitalist market, though more often associated with impersonal, instrumental rationality, have in fact provided the basis for a compassionate sensibility. 'By defining a universal field of others with whom contracts and exchanges can be made', Sznaider writes, 'market perspectives extend the sphere of moral concern as well, however unintentionally' (Ibid., p. 9).

Putting forward a broadly similar line of argument, Iain Wilkinson argues that 'conditions of modernity involve us in both a heightened sensitivity towards pain and a developed imagination for the suffering of others' (Wilkinson, 2005, p. 163). Drawing on the work of Durkheim, Wilkinson suggests that modernity engendered a 'shared social experience of individualisation' (Ibid., p. 129):

> [u]nder these circumstances the idea of humanity itself, such as that declared in the works of Enlightenment philosophy, is likely to acquire 'sacred' value in so far as it accords with a common experience of seeking social recognition of one's moral significance and worth as a distinct individual.
>
> (Ibid.)

This historical development affords the possibility for a heightened awareness of others' suffering, Wilkinson argues, though he acknowledges that we should also be alert to the ways in which such a sensibility is manipulated for political ends or ideological purposes (ibid., p. 135). Indeed, whilst we might be more aware of others' suffering in contemporary society, a language of compassion is regularly employed by politicians to suggest their genuine concern for certain groups and their overall authenticity (Nolan, 1998; West, 2004).

We should also note the ways in which charities and their corporate sponsors draw upon a discourse of compassion. Indeed, the increase in charitable donations since the mid-1990s – which Wilkinson sees as evidence of a rise in public compassion – reflects, in part at least, charities' adeptness at marketing compassion. As Taylor points out,

> as a result of the market-based culture of the 1980s and 1990s, larger charities in particular [have become] increasingly entrepreneurial in response to funding pressures, adopting more aggressive approaches to the fund-raising marketplace and developing trading arms to generate earned income, whether from government contracts or from the sales of goods or services.
>
> (Taylor, 2001, pp. 133–4)

Though the New Labour government that came to power in 1997 attempted to counter the 'contract culture' that had developed within the charity sector, many large charities seem to have retained an entrepreneurial outlook.

Indeed, in many senses the charity sector is in much the same state today as it was some twenty years ago. Blair's government, like the New Right administration that preceded it, has continued the transference of welfare services into the private and charity sectors. Joint private, public and charitable provision of welfare services – the 'mixed economy' of welfare – is the program promoted by Blair as a compromise between a full-fledged welfare state and privately owned welfare services. The assumption underpinning this approach is that the state can not (and should not) be the sole provider of social welfare, a belief that is strikingly reminiscent of the political Right's criticism of welfare dependency (Gladstone, 1999, p. 1). Indeed, there seems to be widespread consensus across the political spectrum that the welfare state is no longer tenable or even desirable. In his discussion of the decline of the welfare state system across Northern Europe, Mauricio Rojas comments that,

> [w]hat we are witnessing is fundamentally a conflict between, on the one hand, collectivist, standardised and nation-centred social forms and ideas and, on the other, increasingly individualised, diversified and transnational ways of living and thinking. In other words, it is not only the concrete organisation of the welfare state but also its moral and ideological foundations which are becoming less and less compatible with an age of growing individual liberty.
> (Rojas, 2001, p. 108)

In this context, the dismantling of the welfare state is indicative of a particular attitude, one that sees consumer choice as the only legitimate basis for welfare provision, and funding for welfare as increasingly the responsibility of individuals and charities.

In such a social context, it is unsurprising that charities often present themselves as consumer-conscious organisations eager to 'sell' their causes in ever-new and exciting ways. As the National Council for Voluntary Organisations puts it, 'over time ... the voluntary sector is becoming more like the private sector'.[6] It is widely accepted, by the public and academics alike, that charities need to become more like companies if they are to be successful. Yet the top 500 charities already spend an average of between thirteen and fourteen percent of their total expenditure on fundraising, management and administration.[7] Certain charities devote larger sums to fundraising, including Cancer Research UK and Breast Cancer Care, the two most prominent distributors and promoters of the pink breast cancer awareness ribbon in the UK. The latter devotes 18.75 per cent of its total expenditure to fundraising, whilst Breast Cancer Care, the charity that launched the pink ribbon in the UK, devotes 18.19 per cent.[8]

Whilst slick marketing might increase a charity's income, it also promotes a commercial spirit that, *by its very nature*, prioritises raising money above all other aims. The means whereby such a goal is achieved are rarely given great consideration. The charity telethon is a pertinent example of this. Such events have gained considerable public support since their emergence in the early 1980s (Tester, 2001, p. 117). Indeed, some seventy percent of the British public have donated money to Comic Relief, the biannual telethon to raise money for poor and needy children around the world (Wilkinson, 2005, p. 144). Whilst the telethon format might help raise substantial money it also, and crucially, transforms charity into a Friday night television spectacle. As Keith Tester argues, the 'dominant message of Live Aid', the first and quintessential charity spectacle, was that,

> remedying the problems of the world (that is to say, moral action oriented towards the suffering and misery of distant others), need not be dull and boring. It can be fun and exciting. Live Aid turned morality into a leisure time entertainment, a transformation that has been pushed ahead, in Britain at least, by both *ComicRelief* and *Children in Need*.
>
> (Tester, 2001, p. 117)

Compassion has not simply become a rather easy sentiment, Patrick West argues, it has become deeply fashionable. 'To today's collective "carers", the fate of the homeless starving Africans or dead celebrities is not actually of principal importance', West writes; 'what really drives their behaviour is the need to be seen to care' (West, 2004, p. 5). The awareness ribbon, West adds, is 'one of the most visible symptoms of the culture of ostentatious caring' (West, 2004, p. 23). Similarly, Furedi suggests that ribbon wearing is essentially an overt display of empathy

(Furedi, 2004, p. 55). Like other public displays of grievance, ribbon wearing is, Furedi argues, a deeply personal gesture of emotional solidarity, in a society in which genuine political engagement is lacking. For Furedi, as with West, the 'politics of emotion' is symptomatic of a general lack of social cohesion. 'In a highly fragmented and individualised world', Furedi writes, 'individual grievances can be temporarily shared through a common expression of emotion' (ibid., p. 54).

Whilst West and Furedi argue that displays of compassion speak of a lack of social cohesion, I would emphasise the commercialisation of compassion in contemporary society as an important factor in the increased appeal of ribbon wearing and other such charitable acts. 'Cause-related marketing' (CRM) has been a central marketing technique employed by companies since the early 1980s in the UK, and even earlier in the USA (Pringle and Thompson, 2001, p. 3). According to Pringle and Thompson, whose book provides tips for companies interested in launching a cause-related marketing campaign, CRM is a 'marketing tool which links a company or brand to a relevant social cause or issue, for mutual benefit' (ibid.). It might involve sponsorship of a charity or voluntary organisation, or a direct contribution to a particular cause (ibid.). The aim of this marketing technique is to promote a positive perception of a brand amongst consumers and this, in turn, is instrumental in increasing sales. From American Express's 'Charge Against Hunger' campaign, to Tesco's 'Computers for Schools' campaign, the range of companies that use CRM is vast and growing, especially in the USA, where charity is already big business (the sector's total revenue is over one trillion dollars).[9]

The interest in this type of marketing is unsurprising, given the many corporate success stories. For example, the cosmetic company Avon was able to successfully 're-brand' and raise awareness of their products amongst younger, fashion-conscious consumers by supporting breast cancer charities (ibid., p. 37). Avon launched their 'Breast Cancer Awareness Crusade' in the UK in 1992, and a year later in the USA, and quickly became one of the largest distributors of pink ribbons in both countries (ibid., p. 33). This campaign incorporates a remarkable range of events, advertising, and services: Avon has distributed over sixty million educational brochures, 'transmitted over 900 million impressions through print and broadcast media', and launched a marathon to raise money for breast cancer charities (ibid., pp. 35–6). The pervasiveness of Avon's campaign – aptly referred to by the company as a 'Crusade' – has secured them an enviable reputation as a company that cares.

The Breast Cancer Awareness Crusade has, of course, also increased revenue for the company. Sue Adkins, in *Cause Related Marketing: Who Cares Wins*, suggests that Avon is a prime example of a company that has made good use of this marketing tool. 'As a result of Avon UK's sponsorship of Fashion Targets Breast Cancer', she notes, 'it received an estimated £200,000 of complimentary advertising in print publications, and an estimated £300,000 of complimentary advertising through 1000 London Underground poster and 3000 bus shelter posters' (Adkins, 2005, p. 201). Not only this, but '[o]ver 1196 calls were made to the telephone hotline [providing information about breast cancer] and many callers expressed an interest in purchasing from Avon' (ibid.). How snugly do the roles of information provider and moneymaker fit together? Surely a company's interest in increasing sales will take precedence over issues of public health and education. A prime example is the way in which Avon, along with other companies that support the Breast Cancer Awareness Campaign, has helped convince young women – their target audience – that they should be worried about developing breast cancer, even though 80 per cent of sufferers are post-menopausal women. More generally speaking, CRM effectively transforms compassion and awareness into advertising buzz-words, and, as Samantha King puts it, 'packages generosity as a lifestyle choice through which individuals can attain self-actualization and self-realization' (King, 2006, p. 2).

Conclusion

This chapter has introduced the three central themes in this book: symbolic behaviour, identity, and charity and compassion. Though each of these aspects of social life are often deemed to be deeply personal, we have explored the ways in which they are shaped by social norms, codes of meaning, and rules of interaction. The symbols we use (from the language we speak to the clothes we wear), the identities we take on, and our expressions of compassion are all shaped by social forces, though this is by no means to suggest that they exist outside our control. From gender norms to rules of self-presentation, social forces inhere in our very beings. In order to capture this complex aspect of our existence, this book constantly moves between the particular (the meanings people attach to the ribbon, the lived experience of risk, the feelings embodied in the ribbon) and the general (the socio-cultural milieu shaping meaning, the structural origins of a 'risk society', the implicit rules that govern emotional expression).

Whilst this requires attention to the subtle nuances of ribbon wearers' accounts, it also necessitates an understanding of broad socio-historical shifts. This chapter has attempted to give a sense of the ways in which symbolic behaviour, identity, and charity and compassion might be subject to such developments. We found, for example, that symbolic meaning has come to seem increasingly differentiated, as collective beliefs and identities have declined. Under conditions of modernity, individuals have become more able and inclined to use symbols for the purpose of self-expression. Whilst such arguments reveal much about the way in which we conceive of symbolic behaviour in today's society, they fail to acknowledge that other social processes (such as commodification) have lead to the standardisation of symbolic meaning.

The emergence of self-identity is subject to a similar historical trajectory: modernity provided the basis for the reflexive, purposive project of the self in contemporary society. The recent emergence of 'feelings-based identities' is the obvious extension of this historical development, as such identities are suitably flexible and self-referential, yet provide an element of self-certainty. In this context, exhibiting emotions is not just a matter of fleeting and spontaneous self-expression, but a conscious display of identity. This has surely been aided by the culture of compassion that has grown up over the last two decades, a development underscored by the commercialisation of charity and the transformation of compassion into an advertising buzz-word.

3

Flags and Poppies: Charity Tokens of the Early Twentieth Century

The next two chapters explore the historical background to the awareness ribbon campaigns of the 1990s. Before we look at the specific origins of the yellow, red, and pink ribbons, we must consider possible historical precedents to these charity symbols. To this end, this chapter examines flag days and the Armistice Day poppy.

Flag days

Flag days are charity campaigns in which lapel pins (initially flags, but later, badges, flowers, and stickers) are given out in return for a donation. These tokens are an important fundraising tool for charities: poppies continue to be sold and worn to remember war veterans, many charities' street collectors give away stickers, and the Marie Curie Daffodil Day has become increasingly popular.[1] Whilst these tokens are widely worn today in the UK, it was at the point of their emergence, at the start of the First World War, that flag days were particularly prominent. It seems that flag days were peculiarly British events, though they were adopted by allied countries during the war. Mass-produced and worn on the lapel, early flag day tokens were, in a certain respect, the precursors to the awareness ribbon campaigns in today's society. Before we can consider this proposition more deeply, though, we need to examine the origins and objectives of early flag days.

In a publication for *The Voluntary Action History Society*, Fowler suggests that flag days may have been based on earlier fundraising events in the UK, known as Hospital Saturdays. These events date back to 1870, and continued to be a source of funding for charities until the mid-twentieth century (Cherry, 2000, p. 461; Gregory, 1994, p. 96). They consisted of 'house to house and street collections' for local voluntary hospitals (Cherry, 2000, p. 471) in which tokens were sometimes given out in return for donations (Fowler, *The Voluntary Action History Society*). The cost of running hospitals rose significantly from the mid-nineteenth century onwards, and Hospital Saturdays were a response to the need for extra funds (Cherry, 1997, p. 306). These events were not only meant as fundraising exercises – in fact they contributed very little to the income of voluntary hospitals – but also served to encourage the working class to subsidise the services they used, a goal that was in keeping with the Victorian ethos of self-help (Cherry, 2000, p. 471; Gregory, 1994, p. 96).

According to Fowler, the first official flag day occurred a month after the declaration of war, on 5 September 1914, and was organised by the Bristol branch of the Red Cross and the Glasgow branch of the Soldiers' and Sailors' Families Association (Fowler, a publication for *The Voluntary Action History Society*).[2] 'The first flag days seem to have been held for the 162,000 Belgian refugees who were flooding into Britain as the Germans moved through Belgium', Fowler notes. 'The arrival of these refugees offered the first real chance for ordinary men and women who were not able to enlist to become involved in the war effort' (ibid.). Subsequent flag days were aimed at helping war victims in France, Russia and Serbia:[3] 'By 1916, each ally had its own day on the national anniversary – for example, the French had theirs on Bastille Day – and the monies collected were shared between the appropriate organisations' (ibid.). These flag days helped to create support for the allied forces. 'The [flag day] movement has ... the object of stimulating appreciation of the work done by our Eastern Allies', *The Times* reported in an article about the Russian Flag Day, in 1915 (*The Times*, 11 May 1915, p. 5). The day included educational lessons about Russia and patriotic songs performed at the London Opera House. The appreciation was mutual: Russia, *The Times* reported, was holding an English Flag Day on the same day (ibid.).

There are several explanations for the emergence and popularity of flag days during the First World War. Fowler suggests that the success of these events lay in their appeal for all sections of society, not just the traditionally philanthropic upper and upper-middle classes

(Fowler, a publication for *The Voluntary Action History Society*). We might also reasonably surmise that an important motivation behind wearing a flag day token during this period was to assert a sense of national solidarity.

The desire to be involved in the war effort is reflected in reports in *The Times* about flag day events. Articles praised the tireless flag-day vendors and the generous donors and proudly recorded the amount of money raised by the public for the injured troops. Wearing a flag enabled those at home to respond to developments in the war; it provided flag wearers with a means of showing concern for embattled allies and appreciation for their successes. 'Russian Flag Day in London came at the right time to ensure a hearty response from the public', *The Times* remarked on the second annual flag day for Russia. 'The sweep of the Russian Armies through Bukovina and the interest of the people in the general offensive efforts on all the Allied fronts gave a support to the appeal of the flag-sellers which readily loosened purse-strings' (5 July 1916, p. 5). Newspaper reports also enabled allies to express their gratitude for British support and extol the virtues of British courage. 'Your help is most welcome, the need being great', Jonescu, the president of Romania commented in an article in *The Times* after the launch of a Romanian Flag Day. 'The Romanian people, proud to fight for the cause of liberty and civilization on the side of the nation that was first to proclaim the doctrine of the sovereign rights of small nations, see in the noble [flag day] movement a new proof of the unalterable friendship between the great British nations and the Latins of the East' (26 October 1916, p. 9).

Flag days were not only directed towards helping allies. A Lord Kitchener Flag Day, introduced in 1916, celebrated this 'national hero' (*The Times*, 29 July 1916, p. 5). An Ivory Cross Flag Day was launched in 1918 to raise money for dental aid for discharged servicemen (*The Times*, 14 March 1918, p. 15), and a Children's Society Flag Day provided money to safeguard the care of soldiers' and sailors' children (*The Times*, 8 June 1920, p. 18). 'Our Day' was launched in 1915 as a special flag day to raise money for British troops, and was particularly popular. 'Before the morning was very far advanced', *The Times* commented, 'the whole population appeared to be wearing the red Maltese Cross on a white background' (22 October 1915, p. 6). Nelson's Column became the unofficial 'symbol of the day', and passers by threw coins at the plinth as a means of demonstrating both their support for the troops and their belief in British fortitude.

In this context, it is interesting to note the ways in which the buying and selling of flag day tokens reiterated conventional gender norms. Flag day vendors were predominantly young, upper-middle-class women and men seemed to be particularly enthusiastic about buying and wearing flag day tokens. Newspaper articles in *The Times* applauded the 'bands of ladies' selling flags[4] and noted that upper-middle-class men working in London were particularly generous in donating money.[5] We might reasonably surmise that flag day appeals provided a means for men 'at home' to consolidate their identity as protectors of the nation, and to align themselves with the men taking a more active role in fighting the war. The young female vendors, on the other hand, might have been seen as the repositories of national hope and virtue, as symbolic, in other words, of what needed to be protected. Such ideas about masculinity and femininity were also reflected in the practice of giving white feathers to men who were perceived to be shirking their war-time duties (Gullace, 1997). As with the flag days launched during the war, the giving out of white feathers – an act that young women were asked to perform – reiterated the naturalness and legitimacy of gender norms, the idea, that is, that men should protect and that women should be protected. In their reproduction of such gender norms, both flag day events and the giving out of white feathers helped bolster a sense of pride in the national culture and a desire to maintain the status quo.

The poppy

Whilst flag days reiterated a sense of national unity and stability during the First World War, the Armistice Day poppy helped give expression to the tide of national mourning thereafter. The Poppy was launched at a time when enthusiasm for flag days was beginning to ebb; *The Times* reported an initial unwillingness to promote what was seen as another flag day event, but stressed the British Legion's view that 'Poppy Day will be a much more important function than the ordinary flag day' (*The Times*, 19 October 1921, p. 3). Indeed, the Poppy Appeal became immensely popular, raising increasingly large amounts of money over the next four-year period (*The Times*,

23 February 1925, p. 9). By the mid-1920s, 'the wearing of poppies on Armistice Day had become a habit that was almost universal' (Gregory, 1994, p. 102).

The poppy was in fact first launched in the USA, in 1918, and is worn in this country for Memorial Day (an annual day of remembrance at the end of May for those who have died fighting for the country). Since 1868, strewing flowers on the graves of those who died at war had been an official Memorial Day (or, as it was then known, Decoration Day) ritual, and this practice may have helped raise interest in poppy wearing, when it emerged in 1918 (*Washington Post*, 25 May 1975, DC1). The poppy was the creation of Moina Michael, who worked as the social secretary at the YMCA's Overseas Headquarters. Michael was inspired by a poem written by the soldier John McCrae, 'In Flanders Field' (Michael, 1941). In the poem a dead soldier addresses the reader directly and conjures up an image of red poppies growing between marked graves on a battlefield. The image is both horrifying and peaceful: the wave of red poppies, stubbornly grown up between crosses, evokes the blood-soaked battlefield at the same time as providing a sense of renewal. Indeed, for Michael the poem expressed a sense of optimism about the possibility for renewal, as much as it prompted consideration of those who had lost their lives in the service of the country (ibid.).

Poppy wearing was a well-established practice in the USA by the time the token was launched by the British Legion in 1921 (Connelly, 2002, p. 147). In the UK, the Poppy took its place alongside a series of temporary memorials created after the First World War to mark Armistice Day. As the historian David Cannadine notes, a number of the temporary commemorative displays, including the Cenotaph, were made permanent due to popular demand for war memorials: 'the Armistice Day ritual, far from being a piece of consensual ceremonial, cynically imposed on a divided and war-weary nation by a cabinet afraid of unrest and revolution, was more a requiem demanded of the politicians by the public' (Cannadine, 1981, p. 219).

In its original usage in the UK, the poppy was meant as both a charity token and as a commemorative symbol; it provided a fund for war veterans and enabled remembrance of those who had died during the war (Connelly, 2002, pp. 147–8). An essentially conservative institution, the British Legion promoted the idea that buying a poppy enabled one to repay a debt of gratitude to the dead by helping to support those who had survived the war, an idea that had been at the heart of Moina Michael's original conception of the symbol (Gregory, 1994, p. 105). Gregory points out that increased state welfare provision for ex-servicemen and the emergence of ex-servicemen's organisations after the First World War helped to create a widespread sense of support for war veterans that did not exist prior to this period (Gregory, 1994, pp. 93–9).

However, it seems that the poppy was predominantly a com-memorative symbol, rather than a charity token, in the years directly after the First World War in the UK. In this way, Cannadine suggests that the emblem served as a crucial means of formulating some collective understanding of death. During the First World War death had become a central, irrepressible concern: 'those six mil-lion who had served at the front had seen more death in their rela-tively brief spell of armed service than they might reasonably have expected to encounter in a lifetime' (ibid., p. 217) and, on the home front, 'scarcely a family in Britain ... had not suffered the loss of a father, a brother, a cousin or an uncle' (ibid., p. 211). Cannadine argues that

> [u]nder these circumstances, where traditional ceremony and tradi-tional religion seemed inadequate in the face of so much death and bereavement, alternative attempts were made to render such losses bearable in the years after the war. Two responses in particular merit attention: the one official, public and ceremonial; the other private, spontaneous and individualistic. The first was the construction throughout the country of war memorials, and the gradual evolu-tion of the ritual of Armistice Day. The second was the massive pro-liferation of interest in spiritualism.
>
> (Ibid., p. 219)

Cannadine's analysis is illuminating. However, he draws an overly rigid distinction between private and public means of understanding death during this period. After all, the public ceremonies that emerged at this time in the UK aimed to *reflect* the public's sponta-neous outpouring of grief. The press release from the Palace, in 1919,

urged that Armistice Day commemorative practices should be naturally emerging, rather than official and forced:

> [t]he Government feel that carrying out the King's wishes [for the
> ceremony] must be left to the sympathetic good will of the com-
> munity. No general instructions can ensure the success of a cere-
> mony which can only be truly impressive if it is universal and
> spontaneous.
>
> (in King, 1998, p. 24)

Indeed, the Armistice Day rituals often showed up the possibility of
creating a public ritual infused with personal meaning. 'What do we
commemorate during these hours?', an editorial in *The Times* pon-
dered after the second Armistice Day, in 1922:

> [n]ot, one may venture to think, physical victory, all-important as
> such victory was to the continuance of our race upon the earth;
> not even the cessation of the most intense and exhausting of wars;
> not even the vindication of justice against the violating hand of
> iniquity, essential as it is that that principal should be vindicated
> in their dealings with one another. None of these, primarily, but
> the lives of our brothers and sons who sacrificed themselves for
> our sakes and for the sake of all they held, and we hold, dear.
>
> (11 November 1922, p. 11)

The act of remembering lost loved ones − 'brothers and sons' − is
made into a public display of communal mourning, with a shared
belief in the rightfulness and worth of the 'British way of life' also
shaping proceedings. We might understand the Remembrance Day
poppy in a similar way, that is, as a symbol that enables both the
expression of personal loss and participation in a collective mourning ritual. In this context, wearing a poppy, like other Armistice Day
rituals, constituted an expression of personal loss as well as a statement of belonging.

Unsurprisingly, the Armistice Day rituals (including poppy
wearing) did not continue to function in this way for more than ten
years. As Alex King points out, '[b]y the late 1920s there was some
sense of change in the public mood. Armistice Day was becoming

more formal, less emotionally charged ... *The Times* found it
"a slightly more reasoned, slightly less emotional reverence" in 1926'
(King, 1998, p. 22). Around the same time some began to question
what they saw as the overly militaristic content of Armistice Day rituals, a development that was perhaps a result of the emergence and
popularity of an anti-war movement in the late 1920s (Connelly,
2002, p. 169). Although none of this halted poppy sales, it did bring
about a fall in the number of tokens sold and signalled the emergence of a rather ambivalent attitude towards war memorialisation
(ibid., p. 171). An anti-war sentiment also characterises the contemporary society, though the poppy is currently experiencing increased
popularity.[6] Interestingly, in contrast to the 1920s, the legitimacy
and aims of war memorialisation are not widely debated in today's
society; instead, it is generally accepted that we should memorialise
those who lost their lives, regardless of the political bases or the
impact of war.

Although it has experienced various shifts in its usage and meaning, the poppy has retained some residual meaning. Ultimately, the
poppy continues to symbolise national sentiment and solidarity in
today's society; media reports describe members of the Royal British
Legion as 'the Best of British', or suggest that the recent upsurge in
poppy wearing constitutes a 'new patriotism' and wonder whether
'we're made of quite the same stuff' as those who fought for the
country during the First World War.[7] 'It's something that I do believe
in', one of my interviewees told me, 'a lot of men died. And when
the Queen goes and lays the poppy wreath – I mean, we don't watch
that every year – but we do watch that, you know'. As with other
interviewees, she explained the poppy in terms of its capacity to symbolise *unity*, a practice that not only brings the nation together in a
collective display of commemoration, but also her family, to watch
the television broadcasts.

4
Ribbon Histories

Though we know that the ribbon originated from the USA, it is difficult to establish precisely *when* it came into existence. Whilst some point to the yellow-ribbon campaign that emerged in 1979 after 52 US citizens were taken captive in Iran,[1] there is evidence that there was a green ribbon worn to show concern about the Atlanta Child Murders around the same time (Engle, 2000; Sturken, 1997, p. 106). What is clear, however, is that by 1991 the ribbon's time had come. The reaction *en masse* to the invitation to 'tie a yellow ribbon' for troops fighting in the Gulf during this period meant that the yellow ribbon became a widely recognised symbol in the USA. As Larsen notes, '[f]ew symbols ... have been so quickly embraced by so many segments of society' (Larson, 1992, p. 11). Several months later, the red AIDS-awareness ribbon was launched, a symbol that was to transform a US practice into a global phenomenon. Indeed, the success of the red ribbon prompted numerous groups and charities to launch ribbon campaigns, the most prominent of which has been the pink breast-cancer awareness ribbon.

This chapter explores the origin and development of the yellow-, red-, and pink-ribbon campaigns. Not only are these ribbons the most well known and widely worn, but each of them marks out an interesting stage in the development of ribbon-wearing practices as a whole. The analysis that follows draws upon folklorists' accounts, academic studies, cultural criticism, media articles, and charity literature.

The yellow ribbon: tradition and sentiment

The first major yellow-ribbon campaign emerged in the USA in December 1979, and lasted until January 1981 (Parsons, 1991, p. 11; Cosgrove, 2001). During this time, people tied yellow ribbons around trees and wore yellow ribbon pins to show support for the 52 US embassy workers held captives in Iran (Parsons, 1991, p. 11). The campaign was organised principally by Penelope Laingen, the wife of one of the hostages. Inspired in part by the lyrics of a popular song released some six years earlier, Laingen had originally tied a yellow ribbon round a tree in her garden as a personal gesture of support for her husband. Her actions were soon reported in the media, along with her recommendations that others should follow her example. 'It just came to me', she told the audience of a CBS broadcast on 28 January 1980, 'to give people something to do, rather than throw dog food at Iranians. I said, "Why don't they tie a yellow ribbon round an old oak tree?" That's how it started' (Laingen, in Parsons, 1981). In March 1980, Laingen met with the spouses of other hostages and formed the Family Liaison Action Group (FLAG), an organisation that transformed the informal, spontaneous practice of yellow-ribbon tying into a more organised yellow-ribbon campaign (Parsons, 1991, p. 11).

A decade later, in 1991, the yellow ribbon gained nationwide popularity once more, this time as a symbol of support for troops fighting in the Gulf. 'Yellow ribbons appeared by the thousands across the United States', note Yocom and Pershing, 'around mailboxes and in town squares, on traffic signs, church doors, police cars, and pinned to people's clothing as boutonnieres' (Yocom and Pershing, 1996, p. 41). The prominence of the yellow ribbon during this period precipitated great interest in the symbol's history, and in particular its origin (see, for example, Heilbronn, 1994, pp. 154–6; Tuleja, 1992, pp. 24–6). This fascination was reflected in the American Folklife Center's 'hit parade of yellow ribbon reference enquiries', in which 'the question "Is the custom of displaying yellow ribbons for an absent loved-one a genuine American tradition?"' was 'number one' (Parsons, 1991, p. 9). Fuelling the interest in the origin of the yellow ribbon, media and cultural commentators regularly drew attention to the various historical uses of the symbol. In a study of media-reports about the yellow ribbon during this period, Heilbronn notes that '[s]everal sources felt the need to classify what appeared to be a highly distinctive and situation-specific behavior as only one example of a universal human behavior' (Heilbronn, 1994, p. 154). For example, the use of the yellow ribbon during the Iranian hostage situation and the 1973 folk song '*Tie a Yellow Ribbon Round the ole Oak Tree*' were seen as evidence that the yellow ribbon was in fact a recurring symbol in the US culture.[2] So strong was the desire to claim a central place for the yellow ribbon in the US culture, that several accounts of the ribbon's history suggested that yellow ribbons were worn by wives and girlfriends of cavalrymen during the American civil war. 'People will say "Is this a Civil War tradition?"', Parsons, the late folklorist and librarian at the USA's Folklife Reading Room, writes, 'as if an association with that central experience in American history would certify its authenticity' (Parsons, 1991, p. 9).

Such attempts to locate the origin of the yellow ribbon in the American Civil War, are deeply suggestive of the yellow ribbon's status as a symbol of national identity. Certainly, the symbol has been associated with a number of seminal military conflicts in US history (not only the American Civil War and the two conflicts in the Gulf, but also, though erroneously, the Vietnam war).[3] In this respect, the yellow ribbon is associated with ideas about national heritage and character, as well as a belief in the need to maintain the 'hard fought for' status quo. It is in this context that a number of writers have argued that the use of the yellow ribbon during the 1991 conflict in the Gulf helped to underscore traditional gender norms (Yocom and Pershing, 1996; Marks, 1991). These authors suggest that the yellow ribbon symbolises a particular relationship between men and women, one in which men are involved (willingly or otherwise) in a political struggle against foreign aggressors and women wait at home for the return of their brave loved ones (Yocom and Pershing, 1996, pp. 60–1). The widespread assumption that yellow-ribbon tying was a time-honoured national tradition surely helped underscore the idea that such gender roles were themselves natural and timeless.

In actuality, the yellow-ribbon motif – like gender norms – is neither naturally emerging nor eternal. Yellow-ribbon tying is in fact a relatively recent phenomenon. The folklorist Gerald Parsons points out that the popular John Ford film, *She Wore a Yellow Ribbon* (1949), 'remains the only demonstrable connection between the yellow ribbon and the Civil War' (Parsons, 1991, p. 10).[4] We might also note that Penelope Laingen, who tied a yellow ribbon around a tree whilst her husband was a hostage in Iran, was not acting on the basis of any grand historical imperative, but was mainly inspired by the hit song *'Tie A Yellow Ribbon Round the ole Oak Tree'* (Parsons, 1981). The song, first released in 1973 by Tony Orlando and Dawn, hit the number one slot in the national charts within months and sold three millions copies in the first three weeks of its release in the USA (Parsons, 1991, p. 10). The song tells the story of an ex-convict's journey home. He has written to ask his sweetheart to 'tie a yellow ribbon' round the old oak tree in her garden if she wants him back. He returns to find the tree covered in yellow ribbons. Interestingly, the lyrics of the song were inspired by a series of popular stories circulating during this period about a man returning from prison who asks his lover to tie a yellow (or in some stories white) *handkerchief* to a branch of an oak tree in her garden if she still wants to continue their relationship (ibid.; see also Parsons, 1981). The decision to change the central symbol from a yellow handkerchief to a yellow ribbon in the song was, as Parsons puts it, 'conditioned by requirements of versification', rather than due to the supposed historical pertinence of the symbol (ibid.).

The point to be emphasised here is that the development of yellow-ribbon tying as a social practice has a rather different origin to that asserted by those convinced of a Civil War connection. Like other 'invented traditions', yellow-ribbon tying is interpreted as a timeless practice in order to fulfil a certain desire for a coherent narrative of the nation's origin and development. Such a desire might become particularly strong when the nation enters conflicts, when, in other words, it becomes necessary to legitimate attacks on countries that seem to threaten the nation's time-honoured beliefs and way of life. A number of commentators, however, have emphasised the importance of seeing the yellow ribbon as a dynamic symbol that inferred different meanings for different people during the first conflict in the Gulf. Whilst 'yellow ribbons were, by and large, expressions of resolve', writes Tad Tuleja, 'homogeneity puts too simple a cast on a complex picture'. He adds, 'it ... ignores the sensibilities of millions of Americans − including many ribbon wearers themselves − who read the "patriotic" symbol as anything but totalising' (Tuleja, 1992, p. 24). Indeed, as an article in the *New York Times* highlighted, the symbol was 'flaunted with equal fervour by supporters and opponents of war, and by opponents of war who nonetheless support[ed] soldiers themselves' (3 February 1991, F3). The flexibility of the ribbon clearly helped to make the symbol immensely popular. It also, and rather more problematically, transformed it into a rather innocuous symbol of support. Indeed, in discussions about the symbols used during the conflict, the yellow ribbon was frequently set apart from more obviously political emblems, as is illustrated by the following story:

> [a] hospital worker in Louisville, Kentucky made headlines when supervisors asked him to remove a button from his uniform that read 'U.S. out of the Middle East, No War for profits' because it 'violated wearing political affiliations or slogans on uniforms'. At the same time, other employees wearing yellow ribbons were allowed to keep them on because ribbons did not have a specific political meaning.
>
> (Larsen, 1992, p. 17)

Similarly, the author Russell Banks explained in an opinion piece for the *New York Times* that he was 'cheered' by the yellow ribbons 'hanging throughout America', but had been 'made nervous by the proliferating American flags' which he believed symbolised an 'Us versus Them mentality' (*New York Times*, 26 February 1991, F26). Such responses in part reflected a wish to avoid the accusatory debates that had characterised the public response to the Vietnam war (Tuleja, 1992; Santino, 1992, p. 21; Heilbronn, 1994).

The desire for a neutral symbol of support also reflected a widespread notion that the proper function of the ribbon was to invoke emotional, rather than political, sentiments. Indeed, by the end of the conflict the ribbon had come to be widely seen as a repository of personal emotions of compassion, support and, in some cases, worry (Larsen, 1992, p. 11). What is particularly interesting about this use of the ribbon is that many of those who displayed the symbol had no specific relationship with any of the troops fighting in the conflict. Indeed, a survey carried out by Heilbronn found that many of those who had erected yellow-ribbon displays outside their homes did not have any personal connections to troops (Heilbronn, 1994, p. 171):

> [i]t was clearly unlikely, given the number of displays within the community, that all households would have a family member or

friend of the family in the Gulf. I asked for reasons for the display, expecting that respondents would cite a specific temporal event (seizure of hostages, dispatch of reservists, initiation of bombardment, or the actual ground assault) as the reason for their display. While approximately a third did provide an emotional connection to one or more persons in the Gulf, a surprising number named not a specific date or event, but provided an emotional or affective response to the crisis or war.

(Ibid.)

Heilbronn's findings highlight not just the widespread use of the yellow ribbon as a symbol of emotional sentiments, but also suggest a lack of interest in the political details of the conflict.

For many, the depoliticisation of the yellow ribbon – the most widely used symbol of the conflict – simply led to political issues being buried. Yocom and Pershing, for example, argue that the ribbon encouraged an unthinking nationalism that precluded serious, political debate (Yocom and Pershing, 1996, p. 52). Pointing to the Government's co-optation of the yellow ribbon, these authors suggest that the incorporation of the seemingly neutral symbol, along with the 'upbeat "support our troops" rhetoric', into public celebrations, 'simultaneously obfuscat[ed] public understanding of the accuracy and efficiency of the military technology used against Iraq' (ibid., p. 52).

Indeed, it is interesting to note that, unlike the Vietnam War, there was considerable and widespread public support for the 1991 conflict in the Gulf, which McLeod et al. put down to a comparable lack of 'formalized opposition' to the war (McLeod et al., 1994, p. 20). We might add here that the public debates surrounding the Vietnam war (taking place through, for example, protest groups, the underground press, rallies and talks) provided some possibility for moral positions to be more fully worked through. This is in sharp contrast to the fuzziness of debates surrounding the conflict in the Gulf, and in particular the 'support the troops' rhetoric used alongside the yellow ribbon.

Also cynical about the yellow ribbon's neutrality, Kenon Breazeale is highly critical of the commercialisation of the yellow ribbon campaign (Breazeale, 1992; see also Larsen, 1992; Yocom and Pershing, 1996, pp. 50–1). Breazeale points out that the conflict in the Gulf was accompanied by an incredible range of merchandise, such as 'jewellery, hand towels, mugs, placemats, Christmas tree ornaments' and, of course, the yellow ribbon (Breazeale, 1992, p. 32). These products, he argues, helped transform the conflict into a 'consumable spectacle' (ibid., p. 35). 'Until recently, the model by which modern governments encouraged their civilian populations to relate to military conflict was that of sacrifice', Breazeale notes (ibid., p. 31). 'The material culture produced for ODS [Operation Desert Storm]', he writes, 'reflects a transformed ideology that eliminates any message of necessary sacrifice and replaces it with a means of supporting war that seamlessly anneals patriotism to consumption' (ibid.). For Breazeale, buying a 'Gulf war product' was tantamount to 'buying into' the conflict, the latter requiring just as little deliberation as the former.

For Yocom and Pershing, the marketing of yellow ribbons lead inexorably to 'the attenuation of their power as symbols' (Yocom and Pershing, 1996, p. 77). We might reasonably add here that the ribbon's use as an expression of emotional sentiments helped weaken its capacity to articulate group meaning in any depth or detail. Instead, the yellow ribbon came to infer a very general, 'catch-all' meaning – support for the troops[5] – in an attempt to navigate the gap between public symbol and personal sentiment. A departure from the original meaning of the yellow ribbon as it was used by Penelope Laignen, the idea that the symbol represented a generalised statement of support may well have been shaped by the growing tenuousness of the relationship between the ribbon user and 'the troops'. As the ribbon wearer's relationship to sufferers became increasingly depersonalised and distant, the feelings expressed through ribbons were ever more diluted and non-specific. A personalised expression of love quickly became a general indication of support; a manifestation of genuine empathy became a vague and sterile display of awareness that was less directed towards an identifiable object.

The red AIDS-awareness ribbon: from AIDS activism to fashion accessory

The yellow ribbon caught the attention of a group eager to create their own symbol of support.[6] 'My neighbors in upstate New York had a daughter in the Gulf War', Frank Moore, a member of the group that created the red AIDS-awareness ribbon, explained to a reporter for the *New York Times*. '[T]hey tied a yellow ribbon around a tree in their yard. It wasn't a political thing, just a gesture of support for their child. I took that idea and suggested we turn it into something you could wear' (30 November 1997, 3C). This is how the red ribbon emerged, and with it the familiar looped-ribbon motif, the penchant for wearing the ribbon on the lapel, and the idea of 'showing awareness'.

The red ribbon was the brainchild of a group of seasoned AIDS activists, Visual AIDS.[7] Based in New York City, the group had already created the annual protest events, 'A Day With(out) Art' and 'Night Without Lights' (VisualAIDS.com). They launched the red ribbon in June 1991 at a Broadway award show, the Tony awards, though Jeremy Irons was the only notable celebrity who wore the symbol at the event (ibid.). Following the Tony awards, Visual AIDS teamed up with the charities Equity Fights AIDS and Broadway Cares to develop a more structured ribbon campaign (Garfield, 1995, p. 256). 'The Ribbon Project' was the result, a grass-roots philanthropic campaign aimed at promoting awareness of people with AIDS and HIV and raising money for research and services. The group did not copyright the red-ribbon design, hoping that as many people as possible would get involved in making and wearing red ribbons ('from kindergarden up', as a subsequent director of Visual AIDS put it [ibid.]).

Made up of mainly arts and media professionals, Visual AIDS certainly knew the power of a good symbol. Indeed, the group's involvement in the creative industries was an important factor in the development of the red ribbon and its message of awareness and compassion. 'Designs like the red ribbon brought theory and message down to a simple pop art moment', Aaron Betsky wrote approvingly in an article for the *New York Times* (30 November 1997, 3C). 'Most of the activist artists and designers were members of the first generation to come of age after Post-Modernism made it acceptable to beg, steal, and borrow any part of the culture, to make what the artist could call a work of art − or of politics or design' (ibid.). Borrowing and customising the already-popular ribbon motif, Visual AIDS blurred the lines between art, politics, and design to create a symbol with 'all the power of a good advertising gimmick and all the immediacy of a cry in the streets' (ibid.).

In this respect, the red ribbon was a descendent of AIDS activism of the 1980s, much of which sought to merge art and protest. The

'Art Against AIDS' project, for example, was launched in the mid-1980s (Crimp, 1991, pp. 5–6). The AIDS memorial quilt, started in San Francisco in 1987, provided a similarly creative means of memorialisation and protest (Sturken, 1997, p. 186). Two years later, the 'protest graphics' of Act UP, a radical group of gay activists, showed up the potential of art to drum home a message (Smith and Gruenfeld, 2002; Crimp, 1991, p. 12).

AIDS activists of the 1980s had united quickly in response to the AIDS crisis, and developed interesting means of engaging the public and rallying support. Adept campaigners, early AIDS activists generally took their cue from the gay-liberation movement that had emerged in the previous decade. Their 'gay lib precursor[s]' (Patton, 1998, p. x) had developed subcultural groups that furnished AIDS activists with an important source of support and identity (Frankenberg, 1989, p. 25). Of course, during the early 1980s it was widely believed that it was mainly homosexual men (and injecting drug users) who contracted HIV, and so AIDS was deemed to be a health problem that required the mobilisation of gay activists. Protesters widely believed that the conservative Reagan administration had failed to respond promptly to the AIDS crisis because of a bigoted attitude towards homosexuals (Patton, 1998, p. 16; Weeks, 1993; Pollak, 1992, p. 19).

During the mid-1980s, however, the US government and the public alike started to respond to the AIDS crisis (Patton, 1990, pp. 18–19). At the same time, Cindy Patton argues, many AIDS activist groups began to move away from their 'liberationist roots' and instead turned their attention towards developing an 'AIDS service industry' with the help of government agencies (ibid., p. 19). Central to this shift was a growing awareness that heterosexuals could contract HIV, a development that resulted in what Patton refers to as the 'degaying' of AIDS (ibid., p. 20; Adkins, 2001, p. 190). A similar shift was evident in the UK a few years later. There was, Simon Garfield argues, 'a slight sea change' during the late 1980s in the UK, 'with the epidemic shedding at least some of its stigmatism' (Garfield, 1995, p. 240; see also Berridge, 1992, p. 42).

By the early 1990s, representations of AIDS sufferers and discussions about the syndrome had entered the mainstream culture. In 1991 Benetton, the hip clothing retailer, broadcast a television advert in the USA and the UK that showed a man dying from AIDS

(Sturken, 1997, pp. 171–2). Though the advert caused controversy, it also reflected a growing sense of concern about the AIDS epidemic. The immense popularity of *Philadelphia* (dir. Demme, 1993), the Oscar-winning Hollywood film about a gay man with AIDS and his legal battle for compensation for unfair dismissal from his job, reflected the increased public sympathy for those suffering from the syndrome. Acknowledging the shift in attitude, numerous celebrities started to proclaim their support for AIDS charities. The gay British pop singer, Elton John, for example, suddenly became actively involved in promoting AIDS awareness: 'he sold his record collection for the THT [Terence Higgins Trust] (£181, 000), he modelled for the trust merchandising catalogue, he sang about AIDS and he set up his own foundation to distribute his record royalties' (Garfield, 1995, p. 242).

Though it might seem like something of a detour in our discussion of the red ribbon, this brief consideration of AIDS activism and the gradual acceptance of AIDS as a public health problem highlights something very important about the socio-cultural context out of which the symbol emerged. To put it simply, the red AIDS-awareness ribbon was launched at a point when the government, the media, and large sections of the public (including many celebrities) had accepted that AIDS was an important health problem that needed attention. As Marita Sturken points out, in the USA, awareness of AIDS and HIV was already widespread by the time the red ribbon was launched (Sturken, 1997, p. 173). In this context, it is difficult to see the red ribbon as anything other than a rather inoffensive emblem of awareness, rather than the radical protest symbol it was sometimes described as during the early 1990s. Even Barbara Bush, the wife of the then Republican president, risked little by wearing a red ribbon at the 1992 Republican National Convention (*Los Angeles Times*, 24 March 1993, F6).[8] Within a year of the ribbon's launch, the US Postal Service had created a red-ribbon stamp, further evidence that the symbol had been assimilated into mainstream culture (Yocom and Pershing, 1996, 74n). Indeed, the red ribbon had swiftly become, as an article in *Brandweek* put it, 'a universal icon' (30 November 1992, p. 14). The symbol had not only gained immense popularity in the USA, its country of origin, but had also been launched in most European countries. By the mid-1990s red-ribbon campaigns had been launched in numerous countries, including Senegal, Bangladesh, Sri Lanka, India, Cambodia and China.[9]

With the emergence of international campaigns came a perhaps inevitable competition for control over the red ribbon design. Red Ribbon International (RRI), a London-based charity, was one such group that threatened the original vision of The Ribbon Project.[10] Emerging in early 1992 to launch the red ribbon in the UK at a Freddie Mercury tribute concert, RRI aimed to control red ribbon distribution across Europe. By the end of the year, the charity had started to sell ribbons and safety pins for a profit. Visual AIDS were dismayed at these developments, and feared that RRI would transform the ribbon project into a commercial enterprise. In June 1993, RRI created further alarm by attempting to gain copyright for the red ribbon design as well as the phrases 'Red Ribbon' and 'AIDS Awareness'. Having previously worked in design and communications, the director of RRI aimed to transform the red ribbon motif into a slick emblem that would improve the fundraising capabilities of AIDS charities. 'It's no good if you actually do something that looks weak and badly designed', he commented. 'What I'm trying to get across to the NAT [National AIDS Trust] is to show how the corporate side can work for AIDS charities; you've got to take things out of the book of corporate imagery and make it work for you' (in Garfield, 1995, p. 260). At the heart of such a perspective is the idea that the red ribbon is a brand icon, 'compet[ing] in the same arena as Pepsi and Nike' (*New York Times*, 30 November 1997, p. 3C). For those convinced that the ribbon has a place alongside commercial brands, the red ribbon must fulfil the criteria of other brand icons, and remain 'non-threatening ... user-friendly ... [and] non-aggressive', as a later director of RRI put it (*The Independent*, 11 June 1995, p. 5).

AIDS awareness had certainly acquired a cachet usually reserved for big brands. Launched at a Broadway award show, worn by scores of celebrities, the red ribbon had, since its emergence, been associated with glitz and glamour. Indeed, for many, the red ribbon is, and always has been, a fashion accessory. Used by fashion designers, worn by models in fashion photographs, the red ribbon's status as *the* fashion accessory of the period was confirmed when it won a special award from the Council of Fashion Designers of America in 1993.[11] Visual AIDS, the Council commented, had created an 'eloquent statement of love and promise'; never, they claimed, had 'an accessory been so pure and meant so much' (Garfield, 1995, p. 257).

Realising the potential of incorporating the red ribbon motif into a range of 'accessories', opportunistic companies swiftly capitalised on the appeal of the symbol. A mere two years after the red ribbon's launch, 'AIDS Inc', as Paul Rudnick refered to it in an article in *Time Magazine*, was turning a significant profit (30 December 1996, p. 16):

> [y]ou can now buy ribbons encrusted with diamonds for $445 ... the Robinson-May department store advertises a diamante version in magazine advertisements, with only a portion of the proceeds going to fund Aids research. The Neiman Marcus chain has a project called 50 Against One, for which Paloma Picasso, Donna Karan and others have designed ribbon-related merchandise, including hats, belts and chocolates. A shop called Don't Panic on Santa Monica Boulevard, Los Angeles, has begun selling the red ribbon inside a glass ornament. It's called Miracles Happen.
>
> (*The Independent*, 30 March 1993, p. 20)

Seen more as a product than a protest, the ribbon quickly lost the capacity to articulate or engender any meaningful statement of belief. As Marita Sturken comments, 'over time ... the [red] ribbons came to signify *everything*' (Sturken, 1998, p. 173. Italics added). Anything the consumer wanted, at least. We see the extension of this in the recent Red campaign, launched by the pop singer Bono, in early 2006. The campaign involves companies, including Gap, American Express, Converse, and Motorola selling specially branded Red products and donating a proportion of their profits to the Global Fund to fight AIDS. Though it appears to be a philanthropic endeavour, the Red campaign is in fact an entirely commercial enterprise. 'Philanthropy is like hippy music, holding hands', Bono commented in an interview for the BBC. 'Red is more like punk, hip hop, this should feel like hard commerce'.[12] It's difficult to fault the logic behind the campaign: AIDS awareness has become deeply fashionable, the red ribbon has been transformed into a commodity like any other − the way was clear for AIDS awareness to be fully subsumed into consumerist practices. What is sacrificed in the process is genuine engagement with the issues concerning HIV and AIDS and any spontaneous, organic feeling of compassion.

Indeed, for many of those who are committed to AIDS activism, such initiatives as the Red campaign trivialise the syndrome. Such criticisms have also been levelled against the red ribbon; in fact, within two years of its launch, the red ribbon had come under serious attack from a number of activists and media commentators. Wearing the ribbon, it was argued, was 'something tokenistic, an empty gesture', or as an article in the *Los Angeles Times* put it, 'a hollow, politically correct statement' (*The Independent*, 30 March 1993, p. 7; *Los Angeles Times*, 24 March 1993, p. F1). By the mid-1990s, many joined Peter Tatchell, the British gay-rights activist, in arguing that wearing a red ribbon was 'too easy' a gesture to constitute real activism (Peter Tatchell in Garfield, 1995, p. 256).

Other commentators were critical of the AIDS awareness campaign's antiseptic portrayal of AIDS. David Seidner, for example, launched a particularly stinging attack on the red ribbon, in a 1993 edition of the *New Yorker*: 'Never in history', he wrote, 'has so much schmaltz been generated around an illness' (*New Yorker*, 28 March 1993, p. 31). Arguing along similar lines, Daniel Harris has claimed that the ribbon helped transform AIDS into a thoroughly kitsch illness (Harris, 1997). For both Seidner and Harris, the red ribbon campaign helped aesthetisise AIDS and thereby effectively obscured the pain and suffering caused by the illness.

Regardless of the critical backlash against the red ribbon campaign, the symbol experienced immense popularity throughout the early and mid-1990s in both the USA and the UK. In an article written in a British newspaper in 1997, Pleydell-Bouvier estimated that more red ribbons had been distributed in the UK than any other colour: whilst roughly 6 million AIDS-awareness ribbons were sent out every year during the early and mid-1990s period, Pleydell-Bourvier estimated, only 500,000 ribbons of all other colours combined were distributed annually (*The Independent*, 1 December 1997, p. 14). By the late 1990s, however, another ribbon had supplanted the red ribbon as the must-wear symbol of awareness.

The pink breast-cancer awareness ribbon: marketing breast cancer

The red AIDS awareness ribbon was bound to experience an ebb in its popularity. When showing compassion becomes a fashion statement, it invariably becomes subject to trends, and the search for novelty more generally. 'Blue is in; red is out', ran the photo caption for an article on ribbon wearing in *The US News and World Report*. 'What was Denzel Washington's purple ribbon about? And why did Geena Davis wear red and pink ribbons?', *Newsweek* asked, eager to reveal the newest trends in ribbon wearing (28 June 1993, p. 61). By 1997, the red ribbon had passed through its fashion cycle: as an article in the *New Yorker* put it, the 'red ribbon became a fashion accessory, then a must-wear statement of political correctness, then a cliché' (28 November 1997, B10).

At the same time, the pink breast-cancer awareness ribbon was quickly becoming the next 'must-wear' charity symbol. Launched in late 1992 in the USA and a year later in the UK, the pink ribbon helped transform the breast cancer awareness campaign into a highly visible movement. A National Breast Awareness Campaign had in fact been in existence in the USA since 1989 (Vineburgh, 2004, p. 137), though it was some six years later, and thanks to the pink ribbon, that breast cancer awareness became entrenched in the social consciousness. By that time the breast cancer awareness campaign incorporated a number of charities (in particular, Breast Cancer Care and Cancer Research UK in the UK, and the Susan G. Komen Foundation in the USA) and had attracted a large number of corporate sponsors.

Considering the symbolic importance of breasts in our culture − as the source of childhood nourishment and as the object of sexual fantasy − the popularity of the pink ribbon is perhaps unsurprising. What *is* curious, however, is that the pink-ribbon campaign emerged after death rates for breast cancer had began to decline in the USA and the UK. From the 1960s to the 1980s there had been a worrying increase in breast cancer deaths in post-menopausal women in many developed countries. By the early 1990s, substantial improvements in the treatment of the illness had contributed to a decline in the breast cancer death rate in the USA and the UK.[13] Not only this, but various government-funded health initiatives had been put in place in both countries during the late 1980s and early 1990s to help tackle breast cancer, including national screening programmes.[14] In this respect, the pink-ribbon campaign emerged at a point when breast cancer had already made it onto the political agenda.

If the pink-ribbon campaign emerged rather late to have an impact on government policy, this may well be due to the fact that it was launched by the philanthropic arm of a company, rather than by a feminist organisation or pressure group. Although pink ribbons were first distributed by the Susan J. Komen Cancer Foundation at its 'Race for the Cure', it was really when the pink-ribbon motif made it onto the cover of the glossy women's magazine *Self*, in October 1992 that the symbol became really prominent. The symbol had been the creation of Alexandra Penney, the then editor of *Self* magazine, though Evelyn Lauder, a vice president of the cosmetics firm Estée Lauder, was also highly influential in the development of the ribbon (see an interview with Lauder in the Lexington Herald Leader, 22 October 2005, online version). Lauder, a breast cancer survivor who was in the process of setting up a charitable trust to fund research into breast cancer, had been invited to edit *Self* magazine for the annual National Breast Cancer Awareness Month.[15] Lauder saw a fund-raising opportunity in the pink ribbon and the symbol was soon being sold at cosmetics counters across the USA, to raise money for breast cancer charities. Lauder's motivation for distributing the pink ribbon lay not simply in a general philanthropic impulse, but also in her annoyance at the relative lack of public and media interest in women's health, and breast cancer specifically. AIDS, she reasoned, killed far fewer people in the USA, and yet it received far greater publicity due to the popularity of the red-ribbon campaign (ibid.). Just as the red ribbon had served as a symbol of solidarity for those in the gay community, she reasoned, the pink ribbon would help bring women together to tackle breast cancer.[16] Indeed, for some, the pink-ribbon campaign has provided 'a compassionate, supportive community' for women, based on 'emotional and charitable support' (Vineburgh, 2004, p. 137).

Such language is strikingly reminiscent of that used by the Women's Health Movement, a feminist group that became especially prominent during the 1980s in the USA (Bass and Howes, 1992, p. 3). Indeed, as Barbara Ehrenreich comments, such feminist organisations 'helped to make the spreading breast cancer sisterhood possible' (*The Times*, 8 December 2001, Features). At the heart of the Women's Health Movement was a desire to wrest control of women's bodies and health from male medical professionals; women, it was argued, should seek to understand their bodies by themselves, for themselves (Zimmerman, 1987). Committed to creating a supportive environment in which women could cultivate an understanding of their health and bodies, the movement was founded on an ethos of self-help (hence the publication of several influential health manuals for women, including *The New Woman's Survival Catalog* [Grimstad and Rennie, 1973] and *Our Bodies, Ourselves* [Phillips and Rakusen, 1988]).

During the 1980s, a number of feminist campaigned for better treatment of breast cancer (notably the American journalist Rose Kushner). However, it was really in the early 1990s, and with the creation of the National Breast Cancer Coalition, in 1991, that breast cancer became a central point of protest for feminists in the USA (Myhre, 1999, p. 29). It was around this time that Charlotte Haley begun a grass-roots campaign to make women aware of the lack of government-funding for breast cancer. Haley made and distributed peach-coloured ribbons with a card that read, '[t]he National Cancer Institute annual budget is $1.8 billion, only 5 per cent goes for cancer prevention. Help us to wake up our legislators and America by wearing this ribbon' (in King, 2006, p. xxiv). This alternative origin story to the breast cancer ribbon is detailed in an article by Susan Fernandez, a member of the feminist organisation Breast Cancer Action. According to Fernandez, Haley's efforts soon came to the attention of Alexandra Penney and Evelyn Lauder, who had not yet launched their own breast cancer awareness ribbon. Their response was to contact Haley and ask her to join forces. Haley refused their offer, on the basis that she did not want her campaign to become too commercial. *Self* magazine consulted their lawyers, who recommended that they chose a ribbon colour other than peach to launch their own campaign: this is how the pink ribbon was born.

This is also the story of how the breast cancer awareness campaign came to be co-opted by powerful charities and their corporate sponsors. Supported by a glossy women's magazine and a major cosmetics firm, the pink-ribbon campaign was clearly commercially viable. Today, the list of corporate sponsors of the campaign includes much of the beauty industry (Revlon, Avon, Lancome, Clarins), numerous clothing companies (Gossard, Pretty Polly, Ralph Lauren, Betty Barclay, Jane Norman, Next), several food companies (McDonalds, Canderel, Haägen-Dazs), and even car manufacturers (Ford, Volvo).[17] Of course, there is not always an easy or obvious relationship between these companies and breast cancer awareness (as was amply demonstrated by Volvo's magazine adverts in which dual air bags were used to evoke female breasts). In a similarly bizarre magazine advert for a Pretty Polly bra, a provocative image of a woman wearing a padded bra was accompanied by the tongue-in-cheek tag line 'we've always been interested in raising awareness' (*Pink Ribbon*, October 2002). This reuse of the pink-ribbon-campaign slogan gives an extra meaning to the idea of raising awareness, one that is aimed primarily at promoting a product rather than improving women's chances of detecting breast cancer. The pink ribbon itself is subject to such commercial reinventions: from iridescent pink ribbons to pink pins encrusted with Swarovski jewels, the pink-ribbon motif has taken on a range of forms to suit the demands of companies interested in showing their support for a popular cause.

From tweezers to tissues, t-shirts to teddy bears, the range of breast cancer awareness merchandise on the market is enough to convince any consumer that the pink-ribbon campaign is a thoroughly commercial enterprise. The risk, of course, is that the products will fail to communicate anything meaningful about breast cancer. When I asked one of the young female interviewees who wore a pink-ribbon t-shirt what made her choose to wear the garment on certain days, I was seeking to understand whether there were certain situations, relationships, and experiences that prompted her to show her awareness of breast cancer. Her keen reply took me by surprise: 'I think "it's got pink in it, what goes with pink?" Actually I wear it with this skirt quite a lot ... '. 'I quite liked the look of it' another interviewee told me when I asked why she had bought a gold-plated breast cancer awareness ribbon. For a significant number of interviewees, the pink ribbon is a straightforward fashion accessory, something to wear with particular clothes and on matching coats.

The marketing strategies used to spread awareness of breast cancer have not gone unnoticed by feminists. Breast Cancer Action, a group of feminists based in San Francisco, have been particularly critical of the campaign and have exposed many of its corporate sponsors and charity advocates as having vested interests. The 'Think Before you Pink' website urges women to recognise that the pink-ribbon campaign evinces a decidedly narrow conception of breast cancer and its treatment. In terms of more scholarly work, critical accounts of the pink-ribbon campaign are rare; where the pink-ribbon campaign is dealt with, it is generally taken as a positive example of a new social movement. Samantha King's book, *Pink Ribbons Inc.* (2006), is one of the few exceptions to this (see also Desiderio, 2004). King explores the ways in which the breast cancer movement (the pink-ribbon campaign as well as the cancer-survivor movement) has been co-opted by companies. In the process, King argues, breast cancer has been transformed into an individual problem, rather than a social problem that requires collective action. Not only this, but the unflinchingly up-beat tone of the movement, with its emphasis on self-awareness and positive thinking, effectively conceals the actual experience of suffering.

Though such a representation of the illness might help sell products, for sufferers of breast cancer the pink ribbon campaign's 'tyranny of cheerfulness' is surely anything but cheering (King, 2006, Chapter 5). On a message board provided by Breast Cancer Care, sufferers of the illness discuss everything from what they're allowed to eat whilst having chemotherapy to Lorraine Kelly. One thread is from a woman expressing a niggling annoyance at the pink-ribbon campaign and, in particular, ASDA's marketing slogan, 'tickled pink'. The influx of replies soon makes this one of the larger thread on the message board, and the mixture of views gives us a real insight into how sufferers of breast cancer feel about the breast cancer awareness campaign. Whilst a significant number of posts argue for the importance of corporate funding and the harmlessness of pink-ribbon marketing, other sufferers express serious anger at the pink-ribbon campaign. Women dressed in sexy underwear and pink wigs in Marks and Spencer to 'raise awareness', overpriced breast cancer awareness products, annoyance at NHS Direct's website that has a link entitled 'pink and proud' for breast cancer sufferers − the women's anger is directed towards a culture that has transformed an illness into a schmaltzy, fluffy, cutesy bit of fun. The pink-ribbon campaign, as many posts acknowledge, is what is driving this cultural representation.

Such critical voices, however, are not widely heard. Whilst the mainstream media was quick to judge the red ribbon clichéd and tokenistic, the pink ribbon seems to be beyond reproach. Indeed, the ribbon's appeal as a fashion accessory and its use as a symbol of awareness are often deemed to sit comfortably with one another. The various glossy women's magazines created to raise money for breast cancer charities are testament to this: articles on 'living with breast cancer' and 'how I coped with breast cancer' are published alongside fashion shoots and advertisements for breast cancer awareness products. In this respect, the pink-ribbon campaign has gone much further than the red-ribbon campaign in acceding to a commercial orientation.

That the pink-ribbon campaign has been so smoothly co-opted by companies and the mainstream culture is perhaps unsurprising once the roots of breast cancer activism are examined more closely. Unlike AIDS activism of the 1980s, which was often oppositional in tone, breast cancer activism, from its inception in the early 1990s, sought a more conciliatory style of protest. This is not to suggest that the breast cancer movement was entirely uninfluenced by AIDS activism, which, after all, provided a blueprint for later disease activism, especially in pushing for a shift in identity-labels for sufferers (King, 2006, pp. 105–9; Myhre, 1999, p. 29). However, in other respects, the breast cancer movement adopted entirely different protest strategies to AIDS activists. Instead of direct action and angry protests, the breast cancer movement 'consciously worked to produce a normalized identity for the movement' (King, 2006, p. 109). 'Their aim', King adds, 'was to woo politicians, leaders in the world of biomedical research, and, in the case of some groups, corporate sponsors' (ibid.). AIDS activists threw fake blood at protests. Breast cancer campaigners signed-up corporate sponsors.

In this respect, the breast cancer movement was markedly different to the Women's Health Movement of the 1980s. Whilst the former may have fostered feelings of togetherness amongst women, it certainly does not inspire any political worldview. In fact, the movement has depended upon the public's acceptance of breast cancer as a politically neutral issue. As Cindy Pearson, the director of the USA's National Women's Health Network comments, 'breast cancer provides a way of doing something for women, without being feminist' (in Ehrenreich, *The Times*, 8 December, 2001, Features). Breast cancer activists' conscientious attempts to distance themselves from strident political debate may have helped raise money and influence federal spending, but it also paved the way for the depoliticisation of breast cancer as an issue. In this respect, it is unsurprising that 'doing something for women', as it was conceived of in the breast cancer movement, was so easily turned into celebrating femininity in the pink-ribbon campaign.

Indeed, one of the more surprising aspects of the pink-ribbon campaign is the extent to which it promotes a deeply conventional conception of femininity. After all, the ribbon is a girly pink colour. Less obviously, perhaps, fund-raising events tend to involve particularly feminine activities, such as interior design, cake decorating, various types of exercise, and female-only pyjama parties. Breast cancer charities sell bags, lipsticks, chocolates, clothing, earrings, teddy bears, and a whole host of other consumer products meant to appeal specifically to women. In such products, femininity, consumerism, charitable sentiments, and breast cancer awareness coalesce – and it is this strange but powerful alliance that has provided the impetus for the pink ribbon campaign.

Conclusion

If we consider ribbon campaigns alongside the early flag days discussed in Chapter 3, we can discern an important shift in the use and meaning of charity tokens. Whereas the yellow ribbon, like the earlier flag days, reiterates a sense of national solidarity and pride (however vague this might be for some ribbon users), the red and pink awareness ribbons suggest a faintly oppositional stance towards mainstream society. Growing out of the gay-liberation movement and the feminist movement respectively, the red and pink ribbons more closely resemble the 'anti-social' rather than the 'pro-social' tie-symbols discussed by Rubinstein (Rubinstein, 1995, p. 206). Furthermore, we should acknowledge that the awareness ribbon is an altogether different fund-raising tool to the former flag-day tokens. Charities in contemporary society have adopted slick marketing campaigns that do little more than raise the profile of their causes (and products). Certainly, whilst most of my interviewees knew very little about the particular illness for which they showed awareness, a number of them mentioned charities' marketing campaigns.

In this context, it is perhaps unsurprising that the awareness ribbon has become a much-recognised symbol with the kudos normally associated with big brands such as Nike or Coca-Cola. We see the extension of this commercial orientation in the recent craze for empathy wristbands. In an interview with *The Observer*, Michelle Milford, a spokesperson for the Lance Armstrong Foundation, acknowledged that the Foundation's yellow wristband, 'is a fashion statement, but we will happily take that because it is raising so much money for our cause'. 'It is great', she added, 'that the summer's hottest accessory is also raising money for cancer' (*The Observer* 8 August 2004, p. 9). In this respect the wristband, even more than the awareness ribbon, has taken on the qualities of a faddish fashion item. Indeed, the wristband is often sold in shops *as* an accessory, rather than a charity token, the most dramatic sign that compassion has become a commodity like any other. This is simply a logical extension of the commercial impulse driving the ribbon campaigns of the 1990s. Sponsored by companies, widely seen as a fashion accessory, the ribbon campaigns helped carve out a market in showing empathy. In this context, it was perhaps unsurprising that so many of my interviewees saw the ribbon as a disposable fashion accessory: eight out of my 20 interviewees commented that their decision to wear the ribbon was connected to whether or not the emblem matched the coat they wore.

It is reasonable to suggest from this that the awareness ribbon is in fact a different type of charity token to flag day tokens worn during the 1910s and 1920s, just as, in more general terms, charity has changed significantly since this time. Alongside this shift, we should also note that *being charitable* has also taken on a particular meaning in contemporary society; wearing a ribbon to show empathy for AIDS or breast cancer sufferers has decidedly different connotations to those associated with token wearing during the First World War.

Whilst a comparison between flag days and ribbon campaigns yields interesting insights into the development of charitable behaviour during the twentieth century, we should also attend to the similarities and differences between the yellow-, red-, and pink-ribbon campaigns of the 1990s. Taken together, these three campaigns show up an interesting trajectory in ribbon-wearing practices. If we trace the short history of contemporary ribbon-wearing practices, it is evident that there has been a gradual movement away from the ribbon's original symbolic meaning. This development is marked by a number of significant changes in how the ribbon motif is created, used, and understood. The significance of the ribbon's material properties, for instance, is no longer considered to be an important aspect of the ribbon's symbolism. Whilst the earlier yellow-ribbon campaigns involved local community action, the ribbon wearer today is much more likely to have bought her token pre-made from a store. Whilst the early yellow ribbons were often hand-made, there is a current craze for enamel or metal pins shaped like ribbons (Santino, 1992, p. 23).

As Heilbronn notes, 'the ribbon has developed a standardized format, a loop approximately six inches in length, worn with the tails of the loop downward. It has achieved such consistency that some now argue it no longer has its semiotic significance, and is merely a decorative sign of liberal sentiments' (Heilbronn, 1994, 175n3).

The most significant shift in terms of the ribbon's symbolism, however, is the move away from *tying* the ribbon (as around 'the ole oak tree') to *wearing* the ribbon. This rupture in ribbon-wearing practices takes place during the late stages of the yellow-ribbon campaign launched during the first conflict in the Gulf. From herein, the ribbon is more commonly worn than tied, signalling a gradual movement away from using the ribbon in a personal gesture that is ostensibly directed towards recognising, remembering, or celebrating a specific loved one. In place of this, the ribbon swiftly became an object of consumption and a means of exhibiting the wearer's emotions. A major contention of my work is that the shifting site in which the symbolic meaning of the ribbon is created – from the tying of the ribbon to the wearing of the ribbon – has, in turn, been coterminous with a shift in focus away from the sufferer and instead towards the ribbon wearer. The emergence of the idea that the ribbon serves as a symbol of the wearer's awareness is perhaps the most obvious indication of this development.

5
Symbolic Uses of the Ribbon

In this chapter we turn our attention to the particular meanings that ribbon wearers attach to the ribbon. The following discussion focusses on the four most common uses of the awareness ribbon: the ribbon's use as a symbol of solidarity with homosexuals, the ribbon as a tool in community-action campaigns, the ribbon as a mourning symbol, and the ribbon as emblematic of the wearer's self-awareness. The last of these categories receives the most attention here, as, according to my research, this is the most commonly cited reason for wearing a ribbon. The typology is based on data gathered from 20 in-depth interviews with British ribbon wearers, 70 questionnaires (some self-completion, some face-to-face), and participant observation carried out at Manchester Pride and Pink Aerobics, an event organised for breast cancer awareness month. The majority of ribbon wearers who took part in this research were white, middle-class British women in their early 20s (see Appendix, for notes on my methodology).

I should point out here that the uses of the ribbon outlined below are based on my research findings; in other words, it is not a typology that was constructed prior to research. In this respect, I believe that this chapter provides a highly valid summary of the central motivations for ribbon wearing in contemporary British society. It should also be noted that none of these categories are mutually exclusive; several of my research subjects fit into more than one of these groups.

The ribbon as a symbol of solidarity with homosexuals

Launched by a group of gay activists, distributed for the first time in the UK at a Freddie Mercury tribute concert, and used by numerous gay-rights organisations, the red AIDS-awareness ribbon has, since its emergence, been associated with homosexuality. I was interested to find out whether the red ribbon is still widely worn by those within the 'gay community', and therefore decided to attend Manchester Pride in late August 2004, an event that drew roughly two hundred and fifty thousand people.[1] Manchester Pride is a festival that celebrates gay, lesbian, bisexual, and transgender life and was started in the early 1990s to raise money for those suffering from HIV and AIDS.[2] On this basis, I thought it reasonably likely that I would find people wearing the red ribbon at this event.

However, my immediate impression was that there were in fact very few people wearing the red ribbon at Manchester Pride. Indeed, in the six hours I spent at the event, I only spotted and interviewed four red-ribbon wearers. The first person I interviewed, a 26-year-old man, was working on a stall for the Socialist Party Lesbian, Gay, Bisexual and Transgender Group, a group seeking to fight homophobia and, according to their leaflet, 'develop a mass movement for democratic socialist change'. This man, who worked in local government, wore his red ribbon during the annual AIDS-awareness week and at gay-activist events with the aim of 'showing and spreading awareness of the cause'. For this particular individual, red-ribbon wearing constituted a means of indicating his solidarity with what he perceived to be an embattled, minority group. He saw the red ribbon as a symbol of political activism, a 'call to arms', and, in keeping with this, he considered red-ribbon wearers to be 'politically minded' individuals. He seemed to view his sexuality as a site of political struggle, and was rather annoyed at the idea that the red ribbon might be worn as a means of 'advertising' sexual orientation for its own sake. He laughed at my question as to whether he'd become involved in the socialist party or gay activism first, because, as far as he was concerned, both his political and sexual orientation had developed organically and together.

The next two ribbon wearers I interviewed were running a stall selling the red ribbon, and were staunch AIDS activists. These two men wore the ribbon as a means of signalling their long-term support for gay men affected by AIDS and HIV. They both suggested that they wore the ribbon to indicate their sexual orientation, though, as with the young man mentioned above, they seemed to conceive of their self-identification as a means of supporting the 'gay community'. In this instance, red-ribbon wearing is meant to provoke either interest and compassion (from those outside of the 'gay community') or a sense of familiarity and comfort (from those within this group).

This is in stark contrast to the last person I interviewed at the Manchester Pride, a 21-year-old woman. This young student was wearing both a rainbow pin (a symbol for gay rights) and a red ribbon, though she admitted that she in fact wore both intermittently, 'depending on the jacket' she was wearing. Seemingly uninterested in the political struggle for gay rights, or the treatment of those with AIDS or HIV, for this woman, a key reason for wearing the red ribbon was 'to indicate [her] sexual orientation'. Unlike the other red-ribbon wearers mentioned above, this young woman did not see the ribbon as a symbol of her solidarity with other homosexuals; she expressed no sense of group affiliation, and was clearly uninterested in issues pertaining to gay rights. Interestingly, she associated red-ribbon wearing with, amongst other things, self-assuredness. She told me that she wore her red ribbon to 'show that she was aware', to demonstrate a sense of self-belief and confidence about her sexuality. Overall, this young woman's motivation for wearing the red ribbon is probably more akin to the use of the ribbon as a symbol of awareness (see below), than the use of the ribbon as a symbol of solidarity with homosexuals. Her reasons for wearing the ribbon certainly bore little resemblance to those of the other red-ribbon wearers I spoke to at Manchester Pride.

One of the main drawbacks to this set of interviews was that they were carried out in public, and there was, therefore, no possibility of building up much of a rapport with the interviewees and asking them more probing questions. It was fortunate, therefore, that one of the ribbon wearers who volunteered to take part in an in-depth interview could provide further insights into this particular use of the ribbon. This woman, a 27-year-old teacher, had worn the red ribbon for roughly six months when she was 20, with the aim of establishing her solidarity with the 'gay community':

> I guess I wore it because I wanted to make a statement about supporting homosexuals ... and for me it was more about homosexuality than AIDS at the time.

Interestingly, for this interviewee, wearing the red ribbon seemed to have been part of a rather tentative process of 'coming out':

> I wasn't out then, so maybe it was a subconscious thing ... I think it was an indirect statement and I wouldn't have wanted to discuss it. And I guess it was also because it was round that time that I seriously began to think about what was wrong with me ... Maybe it was a way into the gay community. A way of saying 'look ... here, I'm one of you, I want to be part of that'.

This idea was echoed, though in much stronger terms, by a young man who was interviewed by a journalist carrying out street interviews in London for *The Independent*, in 1996 (the same year the interviewee donned the red ribbon):

> I'm gay, but this is the first time I've worn a ribbon. I've only recently come out and I've never felt confident enough to wear one before because people assume you're gay if you wear one. Now I'm proud to walk around proclaiming my sexuality on my chest. I suppose it's my allegiance to the gay community.
>
> (*The Independent*, 1 December 1996, p. 10)

It seems reasonable to suggest from this that, for some at least, the red ribbon has served as a means of marking (or 'proclaiming') their entry to the 'gay community'. Not only this, it becomes a means of asserting one's identity as a person who is homosexual. In this respect the red ribbon is a statement of self as much as a sign that one belongs to a specific social group (it allows one to proclaim something about oneself as much as it constitutes a show of allegiance to a group).

Today, however, the red ribbon's usefulness as a symbol of group membership has declined significantly. After all, the vast majority of those I observed at Manchester Pride were not sporting the red ribbon. As the participant who took part in the in-depth interview told me, the red ribbon is no longer synonymous with homosexuality:

> [n]owadays, I definitely wouldn't say that someone who wears a red ribbon is necessarily gay but maybe I would still look at them twice and see if there are any other signifiers ... *maybe* ... but I'm not even sure I would do that ... and definitely, if I saw someone

wearing a red AIDS ribbon and there weren't any other signifiers, I wouldn't think they were gay.

For this woman, the red ribbon is so frequently worn by those who are not homosexual that the symbol can not be straightforwardly 'read' as an indication of the wearer's membership to this social group. Once a symbol of group membership is co-opted by another social group, its effectiveness as an identifying and unifying feature of group conduct is lessened, and this is surely especially true of symbols used by a minority group that are co-opted by the mainstream culture. Red-ribbon wearing might remain popular amongst certain groups of committed gay activists, but outside of such groups it seems that the ribbon is not as widely used as a means of symbolising belonging to the 'gay community' as it was during the mid-1990s.

This development is in keeping with the steady acceptance of AIDS as a syndrome that can affect anybody, not just homosexual men. Indeed, it has become politically incorrect to associate these health problems with homosexuality (Weeks, 1993, p. 32). Nonetheless, the red ribbon continues to be linked with homosexuality in the culture, even if the symbol is no longer widely used by homosexuals as a means of asserting identity. Indeed, the symbol's association with a suddenly fashionable social minority, coupled with the widespread belief that AIDS was a legitimate social problem that could affect anyone, was precisely what ensured the red ribbon's popularity in mainstream society.

The ribbon as a resource in community-action campaigns

The use of the ribbon in community-action campaigns first came to my attention after an Internet search revealed several groups had launched ribbon campaigns to protest particular government directives and initiatives. Community-action campaigns are often difficult to track down and research, as they tend to be small-scale, informal and have a relatively short lifespan. Nonetheless, I managed to contact and interview the organiser of one of these campaigns, and the summary of my findings is presented below. The following discussion also looks at several Internet-based campaigns, including two groups that have launched ribbon campaigns to support freedom of speech on the Internet and 'Traffic Lights 4 Peace', a group that encourages people to tie green ribbons to traffic lights to protest against Britain's involvement in the conflict in Iraq. Though not communities in the traditional sense of the word, these groups make use of the ribbon in a similar way to those campaigns that involve a geographically-based community.

As part of my research, I interviewed the chairperson of, a group that launched a campaign in 2002 to protect local green belt land that the local council planned to destroy. The campaign lasted roughly three months, and approximately two hundred local people tied or wore green ribbons as part of this community action. The green ribbon, I was told, was chosen as a symbol of solidarity; its chief function was to symbolise unity and to 'bring people together'. We might add here, following Goffman, that the symbol helped maintain 'the main line' taken by the group, in that it articulated a certain message and was used to give an impression of the group's collective aims (Goffman, 1969, pp. 90–5). The ribbons were tied around car antennas, trees, and worn on lapels (the latter means of displaying the ribbon was particularly popular amongst the younger members of the group who 'just turned up at a meeting wearing them'). In this context, the ribbon is clearly an important resource; it provided the group with an easily recognisable symbol that could be used in a variety of ways to reiterate a shared vision, and could thereby be easily reused in future campaigns launched by the community.

Interestingly, a councillor who backed the community's campaign won a substantial increase in votes at that year's local election. My interviewee postulated that this was because the councillor's support for the campaign had made him appear more 'in touch' with the local community. It had, in other words, given him a certain integrity. More generally speaking, grass-roots campaigns are often viewed as a more authentic means of protest than organised, formal groups; they are frequently seen as non-hierarchical, spontaneous, communally oriented campaigns that enable a more personal protest (Melluci, 1989, p. 49). This pattern is evident elsewhere in today's society: whilst participation in political groups and political activities has dwindled, interest in a more personalised form of protest seems to have grown;[3] and whilst organised religion has become increasingly unpopular, we have seen the proliferation of personalised, private forms of 'religion' (Davie, 2000).

At the heart of this trend is a two-way process in which people's scepticism about social institutions and the government is galvanised by a desire for autonomy and self-expression. This general distrust of social forces is surely exacerbated by the decline of the nation state. As Zygmunt Bauman comments, people in today's society 'are unlikely to send their complaints and stipulations' to the state government, which has come to seem increasingly ineffectual in a globalised world of international organisations, laws, and markets (Bauman, 2004, p. 46):

> [a]ll in all, the meaning of 'citizenship' has been emptied of much of its past, genuine or postulated, contents, while the state-operated or state-endorsed institutions that sustained the credibility of that meaning have been progressively dismantled. The nation-state ... is no longer the natural depository for people's trust.
>
> (Bauman, 2004, p. 45)

The emergence of what we might call small-scale activism, including community-action campaigns and 'life-politics', may be seen as means of bringing about change in a society in which other means of enacting change seem unreliable or unappealing.

Not only do social forces appear to be uncontrollable to many, they are also frequently judged to curtail individual freedoms and limit self-expression. Indeed, community-action campaigns tend to see social forces as basically antithetical to, if not actively working against, personal freedom, peace, and environmental harmony. Both the blue- and black-ribbon online campaigns are involved in fighting government initiatives that they believe lead inexorably to the over-regulation of the Internet. For those involved in the anarchist black-ribbon campaign, it is the entire framework of capitalist society that is seen to restrict individual freedom:

> what people value most about the Internet comes from its *anarchistic* character: the free exchange of information and ideas among people around the world, without the intervention of a governing body. Capitalists and other authoritarians would like to end this: they want nothing more than attempt to carve up the Internet into an array of corporate/government fiefdoms, to make it just another commodity.[4]

In many community-action campaigns, society appears to exert an impersonal force, one that is incongruous with the interests of the individual. It is protecting the individual from anonymous social forces that preoccupy many such groups. As the website for 'Traffic Lights 4 Peace' states,

> [h]uman life is precious, but frail, easily snuffed out by vast military force as brandished indiscriminately by the Bush Administration. The Bush Administration and its political allies don't count civilian lives lost, they regard them as insignificant, or in their terminology, the sickeningly inadequate and disrespectful, 'collateral damage'. If you tie a ribbon you recognise that every life is precious, something the Bush and Blair Administrations do not appear to have grasped.[5]

Such campaigns recommend us to position ourselves against state governments, with their intergovernmental alliances, immense military might, and lack of care for individual human life. Their power is vast, indiscriminate, sickening, disrespectful, 'Traffic Lights 4 Peace' tells us. In contrast, community action is seen to engender a sense of autonomy, a feeling of self-determination in a society which is perceived to strip individual humans of their freedom, rights, and individuality. This is evident not just from the stated objectives of such campaigns, but also from their structure and tone. Campaigns frequently emphasise the possibility of personalising or customising acts of protest; ribbons used in such campaigns are often tied to a range of objects specifically chosen by the individual (trees, car antennas, etc.). Similarly, Internet-based protest groups encourage members to personalise their ribbons and 'post a picture of [their] interpretation' on the campaign home page.[6] Though such online groups recommend a particular, *common* course of action for group members, they essentially promote *individual* lines of action, rather than *collective* action.

On the other hand, the ribbon is also viewed as a symbol of togetherness in community-action campaigns. The emblem symbolises the sense of solidarity experienced by a group of people who share a particular point of view, even if this sense of togetherness is conceived of in rather loose, unofficial terms. In this context, it is interesting to note that the ribbon is more often tied than worn in community-action campaigns. This suggests a desire to lay claim to a particular locale, to call attention to the community's sense of self-possession in the face of what may seem like overwhelming, external social forces, such as local-government initiatives. The desire for group solidarity, on the one hand, and the desire to express individuality, on the other, are significant elements of many contemporary social practices; it was evident in the use of the ribbon as a symbol of solidarity with homosexuals and, as we shall see below, it is also an important feature of the use of the ribbon as a commemorative symbol.

The ribbon as a mourning symbol

Out of the 20 people who took part in the in-depth interviews for this project, three wore an awareness ribbon as a means of mourning for and commemorating dead loved ones.[7] Not only this, but two of the interviewees who wore the ribbon as a symbol of remembrance and mourning did so as part of a family network of mourners. Even before the interviews, I had developed a sense of this being an important use of the ribbon. During my preliminary research, before I had carried out the fieldwork, I came across the following article from a local British newspaper:

> Linda Rogerson and her sister Teresa Monk decided to pay a permanent tribute to their sister-in-law Corinne Fay, who died of breast cancer in August this year, by each having a pink ribbon tattoo. They had the breast cancer awareness emblem etched on to their arms ... on Saturday, which would have been Corinne's 48th birthday.
>
> (*Essex Chronicle*, 27 November 2003, p. 45)

What is striking about this story is the rather ritualistic use of a public symbol in a decidedly personal act of remembrance. These women had chosen to have the pink ribbon indelibly inscribed onto their bodies as a personal tribute. Though this act borrows the gravitas of ceremony, it is not, of course, a socially prescribed ritual: there is no social code of behaviour that is being adhered to, there are no spectators to this act, and it is unlikely that the tattoo's intended meaning will be recognised and acknowledged by others. The ribbon is used here as a commemorative symbol endowed with personal meaning, as part of what we might describe as a private mourning ritual.

More generally speaking, we might view ribbon wearing as participating in a recent trend towards the personalisation of mourning practices. This development includes the adaptation of religious ceremonies to better reflect the personality of the lost loved one (the playing of a favourite song at a funeral, for example), the publishing of personal memorial messages in newspapers, and the creation of memorial Internet sites that commemorate the deceased. As Tony Walter comments,

> [m]any now feel [that] funerals and bereavement must become more personal. The dying person must cease to be a medical embarrassment, and set his or her own agenda. The funeral must no longer be driven by commercial interests or bureaucratic convenience, and must honour the unique life of the deceased ... Private experience must become part of public discourse.
>
> (Walter, 2002, p. 24)

In this context, the awareness ribbon constitutes a secular symbol of mourning that is charged with personal meaning; certainly, and as we will see below, it is an emblem that provides mourners with the means of 'honouring the unique life of the deceased'.

Certain awareness campaigns are specifically aimed at fulfilling a commemorative function, such as, the 'Babyloss Awareness Campaign'. This is an international campaign that makes use of the Internet to provide support for bereaved parents around the world. The pink-and-blue awareness ribbon that accompanies this campaign is used as a symbol of remembrance by bereaved parents, though it is commonly understood to fulfil further functions, such as raising public awareness of childhood illnesses. Charlotte Forder, the founder of the British baby loss campaign, told me that

> [b]ereaved parents wear their ribbons primarily as a commemoration of their babies, and many wear them all year round, not just during the Awareness Campaign. However they also find that as it is a less well-known design, it acts as a conversation-opener and an opportunity for them to discuss with friends, family and olleagues what is often, unfortunately, considered a taboo subject.

It definitely has a therapeutic function as it provides a tangible symbol of their loss and of their support for all families affected by the death of a baby during pregnancy, birth or the first few weeks of life.

The Babyloss awareness ribbon is simply one of the numerous aids to memorialisation offered by the organisation – the babyloss.com website provides bereaved parents with message boards, dedication pages, and a forum through which parents might discuss their grief and commemorate their lost loved ones. The campaign also invites bereaved parents to participate in a 'Wave of Light' ceremony, an event organised online to mark the end of 'Babyloss Awareness Week', in September. This ceremony involves bereaved parents around the world lighting candles at an appointed time in memory of their children. The event is strikingly reminiscent of the practice of lighting votive candles in a place of worship in memory of a lost loved one. There are, however, important and instructive differences between these two acts. For example, those participating in the Wave of Light event are united in time, but not in space, whereas those lighting candles in a place of worship are united in space *and* in time. (Whilst mourners do not carry out this practice simultaneously, as in the Wave of Light event, they exist within a common time frame; the practice confirms that others are, at a particular point in time, grieving for lost loved ones). There is no visible 'wave of light' in the Wave of Light event, but rather thousands of individual, separate rays of light that represent thousands of individual, separate mourners. We might picture, in contrast to this, the blaze of light that greets us when we enter a church and see the rows of candles that people have lit that day in memory of their loved ones. In this practice, mourners add their candles to those that are already on display, using the flames of others' candles to light their own. This act invokes a sense of commonality and continuity. Indeed, it is the conception of death as something of a fundamental human experience – a shared problem that requires a collective response – that informs this social practice.

Whilst those taking part in the Wave of Light ceremony may be comforted by the thought that other parents are, exactly at that point in time, experiencing something similar to them, they are also seeking to affirm the personal, private nature of their grief. Focussed on a single candle, holding the ceremony in a personal space, bereaved parents involved in this ceremony are, we might postulate, primarily engaged in consideration of their particular loss. Whilst those involved in the baby-loss campaign might wish others to recognise their grief, it is surely the desire to affirm the particularity of their feelings and the singularity of their loss that takes precedence.

Although it may seem like something of a detour in our discussion, this analysis of the Wave of Light ceremony brings us to a rather useful point of departure for consideration of the use of the awareness ribbon as a commemorative symbol. This ceremony gives us a fascinating insight into the nature of contemporary mourning practices. In particular, it shows up a number of tensions that exist in many such rituals. At the heart of these practices is a contradiction between achieving a sense of solidarity with other mourners *and* affirming the uniqueness of one's grief. To put it in more general terms, there is a fundamental tension between the desire to be a unique individual, essentially *different* to others, and, on the other hand, the desire to receive validation from others, something that requires a subordination to conventions and norms that render the individual essentially *similar* to others.

This tension was also evident in the mourning practices developed by at least two of the three interviewees who used the ribbon as a commemorative symbol. One interviewee, a woman in her early forties and the eldest participant in the study, explained how she and her family used the pink breast cancer awareness ribbon as a means of commemorating her sister. The ribbon, she told me, was

> sort of a symbol, you know, it became really, *really* important ... and the same with my family as well, and at the funeral, it was actually coming up to awareness week and we all went out and bought one ... and it was sort of a symbol that, you know, we were all united in our grief.

First adopted as a mourning practice at the funeral, ribbon wearing has become an annual ritual of remembrance for this family, female and male members alike, and one that they do not make known to those outside of the family group. Family members sometimes give one another the ribbon, an act that is symbolic of their shared memory and grief. My interviewee's sister, who had died from breast cancer, had herself worn the pink ribbon and campaigned for an improvement in breast cancer services before her death from the disease. Whilst her sister was involved in breast cancer charities, however, my interviewee had no interest in such pursuits. Indeed, none of the family viewed the ribbon as a means of raising awareness or making money for charity (in fact, my interviewee explained that her mother believed that cancer charities received too much funding relative to other worthy causes). It was only after this interviewee's sister died that the family started wearing the ribbon themselves, as a fitting symbol of their loss, as something that reminded them of her.

Particularly affected by her aunt's death, my interviewee's daughter wears the pink ribbon at all times, because 'it makes her feel comforted'. In this instance, the ribbon stands in for an absent loved one, it enables this particular ribbon wearer to feel as though the 'spirit' of her aunt is with her at all times. This conception of the ribbon is perhaps reminiscent of the earlier usage of the yellow ribbon in the USA, during the Iranian hostage situation of 1979. Penne Laingen, the woman who initiated this campaign, tied a ribbon round a tree with the assertion that she would only remove it once her husband, a captive in Iran, returned home (Parsons, 1991, p. 10). The ribbon, then, came to stand in for Laingen's husband for the period of time that he was absent.

There is, however, an important distinction to be made between the meanings my interviewee's daughter attaches to the pink ribbon and Penne Laingen's conception of the yellow ribbon. For my interviewee's daughter there is an evident desire to *constantly remember* the deceased, to retain an ongoing, everyday connection to her aunt. Laingen left her ribbon to fray and get dirty whilst her husband was absent and, we might hypothesise, if he had never returned to undo it, the ribbon would have further deteriorated, signalling the lapsing of time and grief. In contrast to this, my interviewee's daughter replaces her ribbon when it becomes worn; she maintains a certain state of mourning over time, and her ribbon remains as new as the first day she wore it. Similarly, the women with pink-ribbon tattoos, mentioned at the start of this section, exhibit a certain desire to permanently remember their loss. Having transformed their bodies into sites of remembrance, these individuals make memorialisation an aspect of their physical makeup, a part of their very beings, even. In a society in which there is no official mourning period, the desire to remain in an ongoing state of mourning and remembrance may suggest a heightened interest in finding some means of resolving a sense of loss. Lacking official outlets to express and resolve grief, people may seek to accentuate their connection to a loved one, or to somehow subsume memorialisation practices into their everyday lives.

It is also important to recognise that whilst the awareness ribbon serves a purpose as a personal symbol of commemoration, it is not readily understood and viewed in this way by others. Whereas a black armband serves as an easily recognisable sign of loss in our society, the ribbon does not usually suggest to others that the wearer is in mourning. When I asked the interviewee mentioned above whether she tells people that the ribbon is in fact a symbol of remembrance, she replied emphatically, 'oh no, I wouldn't want to tell people that'. Like the candles lit during the Wave of Light ceremony, the awareness ribbon is used as a private commemorative symbol, and not one that can be recognised and acknowledged by others outside of the network of close family members.

Similarly, another interviewee described how she wore the red AIDS-awareness ribbon to show her involvement in a familial mourning ritual. Less intimately connected to the deceased than the interviewee mentioned above, this 21-year-old woman expressed a wish to affirm her closeness to the bereaved, her step-mother:

> [i]t's out of respect for her really ... I didn't know him, I never met him ... and it hasn't really affected me, but, you know, it has affected *her*, and I care about *her* ... I wear the ribbon so that *she* knows I do think about him.

Other family members, including the interviewee's step-mother, wear the red ribbon as a commemorative symbol, and my interviewee clearly felt a desire to signal her affiliation to this intimate group of mourners. As we might expect, the interviewee conceives of the bereaved, rather than the sufferer himself, as the victim. It is the interviewee's relationship with her step-mother, her desire to cement this relationship, and thereby validate her position in the familial group, that informs this ribbon wearer's behaviour.

For another interviewee it was not the desire to affirm his place within a familial group, but rather a wish to personally commemorate the death of his grandfather that informed his decision to wear a pink ribbon. His personal expression of loss was not one that he shared with a group of mourners, in fact, he actively kept this act of commemoration hidden. This 27-year-old man wore his ribbon under the fold of his pocket and, in this way, it remained unseen by others. Interestingly, when I asked him why he wore a pink ribbon, a symbol usually sold and worn for breast cancer awareness, it became clear that he had no idea of the emblem's official meaning.[8] As with the woman who wore a pink ribbon to commemorate her sister's death, this man has invested the awareness ribbon with personal meaning and maintains a high degree of privacy in his mourning practices.

Whilst ribbon wearing may indicate a personal expression of loss or an affiliation to an intimate, exclusive group of mourners, it can also suggest an involvement in much more wide-ranging, public mourning rituals. One of the most prominent examples of this use of the ribbon was the adoption of the black-ribbon motif as a symbol of public mourning after a terrorist organisation bombed a train in Madrid, in May 2004. Printed on people's palms and faces, painted on banners and walls, the black-ribbon motif came to be symbolic of a collective tragedy, a collective desire to mourn and to express outrage (*The Daily Telegraph*, 13 March 2004, Front Page).

In fact, the awareness ribbon has been used in public mourning rituals since its emergence in the early 1990s; the red ribbon, for example, was launched in the UK at a memorial concert for Freddie Mercury (Garfield, 1995, p. 257). The awareness ribbon has become an increasingly popular symbol of collective remembrance, as is evidenced by the number of ribbons that have been launched to specifically fulfil this function, such as the 9/11 ribbon, the Pope John Paul II memorial ribbon, and the Tsunami ribbon. The ribbon's ascendancy as a public mourning symbol is coterminous with the increased interest the public has shown in such rituals over the last decade (West, 2004, Chapter 2). Though it might at first seem contradictory, this enthusiasm for public mourning rituals is interpreted by some commentators as evidence of the decline of a sense of belonging to the wider society:

[p]articularly for the intense emotions evoked at 'moments of life and death', when there is an urge to share them with as large a we-group as possible, no such large we-group seems to be available. This feeling of lack, of an insecure and even a threatened

> we-feeling ... may have stimulated the rise of many large instantly
> formed 'communities of mourning'
>
> (Wouters, 2004, p. 20)

It is, then, at times of tragedy that a weak sense of social solidarity is
amplified and people are impelled to affirm, often in exaggerated
ways, their sense of belonging to the wider society. Zygmunt Bauman
makes a similar claim in his book *Identity*, about the rise of 'cloak-
room communities', groups 'patched together for the duration of the
spectacle' (Bauman, 2004, p. 31). According to Bauman, such groups
are attractive because they constitute makeshift communities that do
not tie the individual down to any serious group affiliation. In this
context, it is interesting to note that a significant number of those
who posted tributes to Pope John Paul II on a message board set up
by *BBC Online* clearly felt impelled to join in the public commemorative practices even though they were not Catholic. As one characteristic tribute commented,[9]

> I am not a Catholic, but I am a Christian ... Pope John Paul II was
> MY pope, truly a man of god, and whilst I do not agree with all
> aspects of Catholic teaching, he profoundly affected me.[10]

Lacking any deep commitment to the group, any shared worldview,
such 'communities of mourning' are likely to be temporary. The
crowd disperses as quickly as the shared sense of compassion, the
group's only point of commonality, subsides. For Bauman this means
that a sense of authentic solidarity eludes those taking part in such
'communities of mourning', though for good reason: the wished-for
warmth of genuine community remains inferior to the desire for
easy, interchangeable commitments that seem to affirm the individual's autonomy. In this context, it is perhaps unsurprising that those
within 'communities of mourning' commonly seek to validate the
uniqueness and personal nature of the bond between mourner and
deceased, and so assert the singularity of their emotions. We might,
for example, notice that the individual who posted the tribute above
feels personally affected by the Pope's death (he was, the writer
asserts, 'MY pope'). As another contributor to the message board puts
it, 'what is clear from these tributes is just how much Pope John Paul II
touched everybody'. A sense of personal, emotional connection to

the deceased characterises many of these tributes, though it is often expressed as a vague feeling (of being 'touched', or being 'affected', for example). As we shall see below, 'showing awareness' constitutes a similarly nebulous emotional response.

The ribbon as a symbol of self-awareness

Amongst my research subjects, the most commonly articulated reason for wearing a ribbon was to 'show awareness' of a particular cause or disease. Interestingly, far fewer interviewees claimed to spread awareness, a motivation that is frequently cited in charity literature and media reports. In a number of interviews I asked my participants directly what they thought of the idea that the ribbon enabled them to spread awareness, a question which more often than not received a polite and self-conscious concession that this was (of course) important, but that it by no means constituted a central motivation for wearing a ribbon. 'Ye-aah', one interviewee replied hesitatingly to my question, and then, more confidently, 'and it's the whole thing of AIDS awareness, of, you know, *me* being aware of it'. 'I think it's more that you yourself are aware', another interviewee told me, whilst yet another replied that '[raising awareness is important] to an extent' but, ultimately, 'it's about increasing awareness *for me*'.

It was my initial surprise at such responses that prompted me to launch the questionnaire. This allowed me to obtain responses from 70 more ribbon wearers and to ascertain whether the trend I had seen in the in-depth interviews was evident across a wider range of people. Out of the 70 ribbon wearers who filled in questionnaires, 86 per cent claimed that a central reason why they wore or had worn the ribbon was in order to show their awareness and 55 per cent claimed to wear or have worn a ribbon in order to spread awareness.[11] A high proportion of interviewees also claimed that they wore their ribbons to show that they were aware (14 participants, or 75 per cent cited this reason for wearing the ribbon), but far fewer mentioned spreading awareness (only two, or 20 per cent, pointed this out as a key motivation for wearing the ribbon). Overall, then, 81 per cent of the research participants claimed to wear or have worn a ribbon to *show* their awareness, and 37.5 per cent claimed to wear or have worn a ribbon to *spread* awareness.[12]

'Showing awareness' and its connection to other uses of the ribbon

'Showing awareness' shares certain characteristics with the various other uses of the ribbon discussed above. In a similar fashion to those who wear the red ribbon to express solidarity with homosexuals, for example, those who 'show awareness' tend to believe that they are supporting a group whose interests have not been fully attended to (in the culture or in medical research, for example). Most interviewees who wore the red ribbon to 'show awareness' spoke of the continued stigmatisation of those who suffer from AIDS and pink-ribbon wearers frequently suggested the need for 'more research' into breast cancer. However, whilst many claimed that they were supporting a vulnerable group, none were interested in political protest *per se* (just as the young woman mentioned in the first section of this chapter wore the red ribbon simply to make a 'statement about supporting homosexuals'). In this context, it is telling that none of the interviewees expressed any solid expectations of the state government. In fact, very few of those who filled in questionnaires (6 per cent) indicated that they were interested in government funding of scientific research. When I asked one interviewee what kind of protest his red-ribbon wearing constituted, he replied that he was interested in challenging stigmatisation. His protest was, he told me, 'more of a social thing', although it was altogether unclear exactly what 'the social' constituted in this instance. When I pushed him further to explain what he meant by this, he told me,

> [p]eople should be *aware* of it ... People should be able to talk about it and understand what it's about. And I think, yes, funding is important, but it's not the main reason behind [me wearing the ribbon].

Whilst other participants saw research funding as an important issue, most of them took umbrage at the idea that the state should play any role in financing scientific research. 'Research *must* continue', one pink-ribbon wearer told me adamantly, but when I asked her what she thought about the government's role in this she replied,

> the problem with that is that if we pushed the government to give to cancer research other people start pushing and saying we need

more money for AIDS research, we need more money for this and that ... And it would get to the point where the government wouldn't have any money left.

Whilst this participant viewed cancer as a central health concern, one that affected most people at some point in their lives, she strongly disagreed with the idea that the state should provide funding for research. She believed that the state provides (or constitutes, perhaps) an exhaustible fund that is meted out to groups that demand money, irrespective of the relative benefits that meeting these demands would have for the general population. In other words, for this interviewee, there is no moral impetus or sense of the social good behind the state's allocation of money, and far from being angered or even disappointed by this, she accepts it as an incontrovertible truth about state government.

Rather than having explicit political aims, those who wear a ribbon to 'show awareness' are interested in rather intangible improvements, at the level of the culture, or in terms of people's attitudes or scientific research. Indeed, these desired improvements are frequently conceived of in very general terms, as entailing either 'more visibility' in the culture, 'more tolerance', or 'more funding'. Concrete or precise conceptions of the social – of the social good, of state provisions, for example – were markedly absent in my discussions with ribbon wearers. Instead, 'showing awareness' is a personal expression of annoyance, one that is generally very vague and always apolitical. The interest in displays of personal awareness reflects the decline of more traditional forms of political protest. When we explored the use of the ribbon in community-action campaigns, we found that small-scale, personal activism has come to be seen as a more suitable and appealing response to social problems than more formal types of political protest. This method of protest reflects a sense of antipathy towards what we might loosely refer to as social forces (from local government to intergovernmental alliances), which lies at the heart of many community-action campaigns. It is a similar sense of frustration with formal social movements and organisations (the government, organised protest, and social institutions) and a similar desire for self-expression that shape the drive to 'show awareness'.

'Showing awareness' also has much in common with the use of the ribbon as a mourning symbol. Most obviously, perhaps, those who wear a ribbon to 'show awareness', like those who wear the ribbon as a mourning symbol, seek to recognise those who have died or are dying from a particular illness (though they very rarely have any personal relationship with sufferers). Several of my interviewees showed compassion for those suffering; one interviewee, for example, spoke about the need to recognise those 'who die young' from cancer, others expressed a sense of sympathy for women who fall ill with breast cancer. However, these expressions of sympathy tended to be rather vague, partly because those suffering are distant and anonymous, but, as I discuss below, also because 'showing awareness' is often more oriented towards self-expression than compassion for others. In this context it is interesting that many of my interviewees seemed more concerned about the possibility of either themselves or their loved ones falling ill and dying, than about those who suffered from a particular illness already. In fact, many of those who 'show awareness' are convinced of their susceptibility to ill health, and the precariousness of life more generally, a point of argument that I return to in Chapter 7. Whilst those who wear the ribbon as a symbol of mourning do so for specific loved ones, it seems that many of those who show awareness use the ribbon as an anticipatory, pre-emptive mourning symbol for the self.[13] Indeed, for a significant number of interviewees the possibility of imminent death was clearly something that preoccupied them. A 21-year-old interviewee, for example, mistakenly described giving money for the ribbon as 'funeral insurance'.[14] For this interviewee, ribbon wearing, just like funeral insurance, constitutes a means of preparing herself for death – and it is an imminent death, rather than a distant death in old age, that this young woman is readying herself for.

There is one further shared characteristic between 'showing awareness' and the use of the ribbon as a mourning symbol that deserves our attention here, and that is a particular tension that lies at the heart of both motivations for wearing a ribbon. As I discussed above, as a mourning symbol, the ribbon is used to invoke a sense of ceremony and solidarity between mourners, and, at the same time, emphasise the singularity of the lost loved one and the mourner's grief. These aims seem to run counter to one another, and the resulting tension suggests a more general inability to reconcile our sense of individuality with our desire for affirmation in today's society. Interestingly, there seems to be a similar tension at work in the use of the ribbon as a symbol of awareness. 'Showing awareness' is meant to suggest support for a particular group of sufferers and, at the same time, it is seen as a means of expressing ribbon wearers' personal, differentiated feelings. It is, of course, possible for an emblem to successfully symbolise both of these. However, there is good reason to believe that 'showing awareness' in fact prioritises the latter. None of my interviewees did voluntary work for the causes they wore ribbons for, and only one of them had any meaningful contact with any sufferers of the disease for which she wore a ribbon. Only two interviewees had any significant amount of knowledge about the illnesses they wore ribbons for (and this was because they had helped set up awareness campaigns at work and in college, respectively). Most telling was the fact that a significant proportion of interviewees who claimed to 'show awareness' could not remember which cause their ribbon represented.

As a symbol of awareness, the ribbon is oriented more towards self-expression than group solidarity. Whilst the ribbon's use as a mourning symbol might reflect a similar desire to affirm the singularity of both mourner and lost loved one, a desire that is fundamentally at odds with the need for communally prescribed rituals and meaning, those who use the ribbon in this way have a connection to the loved ones they mourn and are members of small mourning communities. 'Showing awareness', however, enables only a very loose sense of affiliation to a particular group of sufferers, and this provides the basis for an expression of personal awareness. With this in mind, I turn now to a more focussed discussion of what it means to 'show awareness'.

The meaning of 'showing awareness'

Whilst 'showing awareness' was the most frequently-cited motivation for wearing a ribbon, many of my interviewees struggled to explain exactly what they meant by this phrase. 'It's difficult ... how are you aware of anything?', one interviewee asked rhetorically. Another interviewee, who wore the pink breast cancer awareness ribbon, answered more confidently: 'It's about recognising the problems that need to be addressed'. In the course of the interview, though, it transpired that she herself had very little idea of 'the problems that need to be addressed'. She told me,

> [t]he only thing I'd say I know about breast cancer is what you see
> on adverts. You know, you've got those adverts with the children
> and their parents sitting behind them. And they really ... I don't
> like those adverts ... they're chilling.

It is perhaps tempting to view talk of 'showing awareness' as just glib
patter, picked up from the slick marketing campaigns launched by
companies and charities. It may well be the case that my research
subjects were making use of such a discourse; certainly, their incapacity to adequately explain this motivation for wearing a ribbon
suggests this.

The assumption that the drive to 'show awareness' is simply empty
rhetoric, however, fails to recognise that this motivation for wearing
a ribbon reveals much about how we conceive of the self in contemporary society. 'Showing awareness' centres on a desire to feel and
show a sense of self-possession; after all, 'showing awareness' is, first
and foremost, about showing that one is aware. As Frank Furedi comments, '[t]he statement 'I am aware' is really meant as an object-free
proposition. Awareness exists in a state of indifference to the public
world at large and implies a state of enlightenment about one's emotion' (Furedi, 2004, p. 73).

Indeed, in many cases 'showing awareness' means being *self-aware*,
aware of one's own personal feelings or beliefs, or aware of one's own
risk of falling ill with a disease, for example. In this context it is
telling that those who seek to show their awareness tend to wear the
ribbon on their lapel, suggesting a desire to exhibit ownership of a
secure sense of self, a possession of self-awareness (just as the tying of
ribbons round trees, car antennas, or traffic lights in community-action
campaigns revealed a desire to lay claim to a particular community
or locale). Such behaviour is aimed at conveying certain aspects of
one's identity to others, and, in this respect, 'communicative acts are
translated into moral ones' (Goffman, 1974, p. 242). People develop
expectations of us, in other words, on the basis of the impressions we
give or give off, and therefore we are likely to adopt techniques of
'impression management' (ibid., p. 85). We might see 'showing
awareness' as a type of impression management, one that says much
about a ribbon wearer's consciousness of appropriate conduct and
the formulae of emotional disclosure – and, of course, the effect these
have in conveying the self. Ironically, an intimate understanding of

such things by no means entails a deep level of self-awareness. As Goffman puts it, even though 'our day is given over to intimate contact with the goods we display and our minds are filled with intimate understandings of them ... it may well be that the more attention we give to these goods, then the more distant we feel from them and from those who are believing enough to buy them' (Goffman, 1974, p. 243). Just as a consummate tour guide who has acted out every exclamation, rare discovery, quip, and anecdote might struggle to explain the allure of a city, so ribbon wearers well-versed in 'showing awareness' can not tell us what their awareness actually *is*.

This idea was really brought home to me when I struck up a conversation with a young wristband wearer in a supermarket one Sunday afternoon. This teenager actually *collected* wristbands and, like any connosieur, was particularly interested in rare finds. He took great pleasure in describing to me his various acquisitions, including an 'England' band (a wristband with a red cross) and a gold anti-poverty band, a particularly rare wristband that he had given to his girlfriend as a present. When I asked him whether he thought it a little contradictory that an anti-poverty wristband should be gold, he was genuinely surprised at the observation; absorbed in the task of locating rare bands, choosing which to display and which to give as gifts, he hadn't given consideration to the *meaning* of the objects he collected.

In summary, awareness, as it is conceived of by ribbon wearers, consists of neither knowledge nor experience of an illness or cause. Rather it refers to a ribbon wearer's wish to demonstrate that he is conscious that a particular illness exists and causes suffering. For the majority of my research subjects, this is what their awareness constituted, and this was even true of the few interviewees who described their awareness in terms of an active engagement with the world. One interviewee, for example, who had started wearing a red ribbon when he had first left home to attend university, described 'showing awareness' as a means of affirming a sense of autonomy and individuality. Nonetheless, he struggled to give a concrete idea of what he had gained from his new-found freedom. He told me that going to university had had a big impact on his life because it had led to him 'knowing more about causes', and then, more deliberately, he said, 'no, that's the wrong word ... I became more *aware of stuff*'. Others openly spoke of their awareness in terms of a passive consciousness of a particular cause. One female red-ribbon wearer told me that '[the red ribbon] doesn't make me as aware as it used to'; just like a tired advertising campaign, the ribbon no longer pricks her conscience in the way it did five years ago. Another participant explained that his 'awareness of it [AIDS] has ... faded over the last few years', though he was at a loss to explain exactly why this was the case.

It would seem, then, that being aware constitutes a decidedly passive state of consciousness, one that can inexplicably fade, one that requires frequent and novel prompts, one that is based on a vague feeling rather than knowledge. Being conscious of a particular cause or illness is the sole aim for ribbon wearers who have only the vaguest sense of what social change might constitute. Conceived of in this way, it is difficult to see how 'showing awareness' could lead to any significant improvements in the living conditions or treatment of those who suffer from AIDS and breast cancer. Moreover, if 'showing awareness' entails a passive consciousness of illness, it is likely to engender a sense of disempowerment, and, in turn, this sense of powerlessness may well accentuate ribbon wearers' worry about the apparent risks posed by certain illnesses (I discuss this further in Chapter 7).

Portrayed by many research subjects as a state of consciousness, awareness was seen by others as a means of expressing personal belief. One interviewee, for example, repeatedly emphasised that, 'I will only give to a charity that *I believe* in'. Adamant that her sponsorship of certain charities was down to her personal beliefs, this young female interviewee was at pains to stress that each person had his or her own particular set of charities that accorded with his or her own personal beliefs. (Her boyfriend, she told me, 'would believe in different causes', for example). Similarly, another participant described awareness as 'sort of your own personal beliefs', and went on to list the various charities which she personally 'believed in'. In this context, belief refers to a deeply personal conviction that certain causes are worthy and deserve sponsorship and support. The interviewees' comments suggest that they view such beliefs as quasi-religious; they *believe in* charity, they are convinced of the unquestionable rightfulness and moral value of charity.

In a society in which ready-made, officially sanctioned religious and political beliefs seem to have become increasingly unpopular, the idea of a personalised belief system seems to have gained salience (and the two trends are, of course, inextricably linked). This is evident in the rise of the New Age, a collection of quasi-religious beliefs and practices in which 'the individual serves as his or her own source of guidance' (Heelas, 1996a, p. 23). Grace Davie suggests that, overall, religious belief has become more 'individualised, detached, undisciplined and heterogeneous' (Davie, 2000, p. 120). Davie argues that whilst few of us belong to religious groups anymore, this does not mean that people no longer hold religious beliefs: '[as religious] practice declines, belief drifts further from Christian norms *but belief itself does not disappear*' (Davie, 2000, p. 116. Italics added.). It is, she suggests, a more personal religious belief system that takes the place of officially sanctioned religious beliefs.

Whilst people might continue to articulate beliefs, however, (and in this sense 'belief itself does not disappear') we should carefully consider exactly what these beliefs consist of and what they entail in terms of meaningful action. It is, I think, important to question whether claiming to believe in a 'higher being' or leaving flowers at a church during periods of collective mourning constitute examples of the continued salience of religious belief. As Richard Sennett points out, it is crucial that sociologists recognise the distinction between belief and other aspects of human thought, such as values, opinion, and ideology. I would add that it is important to acknowledge that just because people *describe* their thoughts as beliefs does not logically entail that sociologists should see them as such. Belief, Sennett comments, is 'an activation of ideology':[15]

> [I]deology becomes belief at the point at which it becomes consciously involved in the behaviour of the person who holds it ... Much of the opinion which people hold about social life never touches on or strongly influences their behaviour. Ideology of this passive sort often shows up in modern opinion polls; people tell a pollster what they think about urban deficit or the inferiority of blacks, the pollster thinks he has arrived at a truth about their feelings ... and then the people involved behave in a way at odds with what they have professed to the pollster.
>
> (Sennett, 1993, p. 33)

Those research subjects who described their awareness as belief, did, to an extent, act on the belief that the particular causes they supported were worthy – they had, after all, bought ribbons to show that this was the case (and, I should also point out that one interviewee had also participated in several charity events). However, all three of them wore their awareness ribbons on a temporary basis (and for two participants their decision to wear the ribbon was dependent on the coat or clothes that they were wearing). There were other ways in which these research subjects' beliefs seemed rather flimsy. Firstly, other than believing that certain causes deserved their money and time, none of these interviewees were able to articulate exactly what their beliefs consisted of (flummoxed by the question, one interviewee responded that her belief was based on the idea that 'you *should* give to this charity, and show that you have done so'). Most revealing, however, was their difficulty in remembering exactly what causes they supported (I had to remind two of these three interviewees which causes their ribbons represented).

On reflection, I would argue that it is in fact erroneous to view these ribbon wearers' awareness as belief and, I would add, it is possible that other so-called 'personal beliefs' are likely to be just as flimsy and unsystematic. It is difficult to maintain a coherent belief system in the absence of collective beliefs and practices. Those interviewees who viewed their awareness as belief did not have anything that resembled a worldview, one that might have provided them with a point of departure, a set of ideas or aims. None of my interviewees, for example, had a political outlook, one that might have guided their beliefs on the aims of research or the nature of treatment. Of course, charities do offer some guidance, but this generally consists of the instruction to 'be more aware'. Whilst 'showing awareness' is a common practice, it by no means constitutes a collective one, and it is certainly not one that provides ribbon wearers with any substantial or formulated set of aims or principles that might guide their behaviour or shape their ideas. Ultimately, there is no meaningful, exterior point of reference for those 'showing awareness'. Indeed, the only source of authority for ribbon wearers is the self, the site of awareness, and the origin of 'personal belief'.

In this context it is telling that 'showing awareness' is articulated as a belief in the need to prevent illness, suffering, and death, experiences that involve the limitation or eradication of the self. To be precise, 'showing awareness' is not so much a belief in life, but a desire to guard against death; it is a sense of vulnerability – a desire to 'ward off' the seemingly all-pervasive threat of ill health – that characterises ribbon wearers' desire for awareness. At the heart of this practice is a conception of the self that is decidedly narrow; after all, we are surely more than bodies that need to be maintained. Not only this, but it is an understanding of the self that is more likely to engender a sense of worry and limited agency than genuine awareness. Before we turn to this argument, however, we need to consider the cultural-historical origin of the contemporary project of 'showing awareness'.

6
'Showing Awareness' and the 1960s Counter-culture: Breaking Rules and Finding the Self

> Nike shoes are sold to the accompaniment of words delivered by William S. Burroughs and songs by The Beatles, Iggy Pop, and Gil Scott Heron ('the revolution will not be televised'); peace symbols decorate a line of cigarettes manufactured by R.J. Reynolds and the walls and windows of Starbucks coffee shops nationwide; the products of Apple, IBM, and Microsoft are touted as devices of liberation; and advertising across the product-category spectrum calls upon consumers to break rules and find themselves.
>
> (Frank, 1997, p. 4)

'Showing awareness' constitutes a deeply personal statement of recognition that a particular illness exists and causes suffering. It is also a practice that reflects a faintly oppositional stance towards mainstream society, often involving a condemnation of the treatment of certain minority groups (AIDS patients or female breast cancer sufferers, for example), or a rather solipsistic ethic of awareness and compassion. This chapter suggests that we see 'showing awareness' in the context of a wider cultural-historical shift in which a heightened interest in personal authenticity has developed alongside a distrust of social institutions. I suggest that the countercultural period of the 1960s and 1970s was particularly important in the development of this cultural milieu in the USA and the UK, and laid the basis for the contemporary interest in 'showing awareness'.[1] It is not my purpose, however, to transport the reader back to the 1960s, to place a flag in this period's cultural soil, and claim it as the precise point at which 'showing awareness' emerged. It is clear that the contemporary drive to 'show awareness' does not straightforwardly reproduce the ideals of the 1960s, but rather *extends* and *develops* the original countercultural ethos. Nor is it my purpose to deny the existence of a certain anti-authority cultural current prior to the 1960s. I simply wish to emphasise that the 1960s counter-culture, a period when interest in 'breaking rules' and 'finding the self' became particularly widespread, provided the cultural impetus for today's project of 'showing awareness'.

The notion that the 1960s counter-culture was absorbed into the mainstream culture is not, of course, entirely original. Indeed, this process of assimilation was noted by numerous cultural commentators during the late 1960s. For example, in an article in *Ramparts*, Warren Hinckle suggested that the hippy residents of Haight-Ashbury had been willingly subsumed into the capitalist mainstream, describing them as 'brand name conscious' and 'frantic consumers' (Hinckle, 1967, p. 226). Taking a rather different stance, Ralph Gleason, a writer for *Rolling Stone* magazine, suggested that the mainstream culture had managed to temper and dilute the once subversive counterculture by a process of co-optation: 'one of the ways in which this society has managed to frustrate all the predictions of its failure', he wrote, 'has been its ability to co-opt or to absorb its enemies' (Gleason, 1968, p. 409). Central to both accounts is the idea that the assimilation of countercultural ideals into the mainstream lead to a vulgarisation or distortion of the original countercultural ethos. Such approaches tend to sideline any consideration of the impact the counterculture might have had on mainstream society.[2] There are in fact very few analyses of the 1960s counter-culture that enable an understanding of the manner in which countercultural attitudes and ideals might have informed – and might continue to inform – people's actions and values within the wider society.

This chapter seeks to capture the nature, the extent and the ongoing influence of the counterculture that emerged in the 1960s and 1970s. The first part of the chapter looks at the emergence and diffusion of anti-establishment values and attitudes. The second part examines self-expression and self-fulfilment as central countercultural ideals. Each of these sections ends with a comparison of the

1960s counter-culture with contemporary culture, and in particular 'showing awareness'.

Breaking rules

> Don't follow Leaders.
> > (Bob Dylan, 'Subterranean Homesick Blues', 1965)
>
> Fuck leaders!
> > (Participant in the Woodstock Census, Weiner and Stillman, 1979, p. 76)

The 1960s counter-culture is widely perceived to have involved a turn away from mainstream social authorities and institutions. Recognising the emergence of a 'new sensibility' – a new way of seeing things – some commentators of the 1960s considered the counterculture to be evidence of a new revolutionary spirit ('The Great Refusal', as Marcuse described it [Marcuse, 1972, p. xii]). Indeed, certain aspects of the counterculture hinged upon sustained attacks on what were conceived to be the ills of capitalist, bourgeois society. The students involved in the up-rising in Paris in May 1968, for example, suggested that

> [t]he revolution which is beginning will call in question not only capitalist society but industrial society ... The society of alienation must disappear from history. We are inventing a new and original world. Imagination is seizing power.
> > (Manifesto pinned to the entrance of the Sorbonne during the student rebellion in Paris, 1968, in Roszak, 1970, p. 22)

The counterculture under review here, however, does not only, or even fundamentally, consist of the social groups actively protesting against mainstream society. It is not simply the counterculture as the concerted and ideological repudiation of capitalist bourgeois society that I am interested in, for that is perhaps only a small aspect of what the 1960s counterculture involved. Rather, it is the more general and widespread influence of countercultural values and attitudes that concerns us here – the diffusion of the counterculture into the mainstream, the steady acceptance of nonconformity.

Certainly, we can see the influence of countercultural values across social classes during the 1960s. A British government report published in 1960 notes the increased spending power of working-class youths, and claims that this group, like their middle-class counterparts, had become particularly interested in 'goods designed to impress other teenagers (e.g. dressing up) or on gregarious pursuits (e.g. coffee-bar snacks)'. 'This is spending', the report commented, 'which is, to an unusually high degree, charged with an emotional content – it helps to provide an identity or to give status or to assist in the sense of belonging to a group of contemporaries' (The Findings of the Albernale Committee, 1960, in Marwick, 1998, p. 61). For the historian Arthur Marwick, this 'sense of belonging' was to a youth movement that went a long way towards dissolving class boundaries to produce a 'generational consciousness' (Hebdige, 1979, p. 74).

To believe that the counterculture was the preserve of the young, however, is to ignore a much more widespread interest in what was to become a dominant cultural current. 'The meaning of the sixties', Thomas Frank notes, 'can not be considered apart from the enthusiasm of ordinary, suburban Americans for cultural revolution' (Frank, 1997, p. 13). Indeed, according to the results of an attitudinal survey carried out in the mid-1970s, most US citizens saw themselves as having participated in the 1960s counterculture: 89 per cent of respondents claimed to have flashed the 'peace sign' to strangers, 90 per cent of women wore a miniskirt, and 62 per cent of participants believed that they were hippies during the 1960s.[3]

Growing dissatisfaction with the mainstream was in fact evident at every turn in a society swiftly giving way to the orthodoxy of the counterculture. Indeed, the anti-authority ethos is apparent in a wide range of cultural endeavours and artefacts of the period. Protest movements emerged to challenge the status quo, the anti-establishment beat and then hippy culture developed (and influenced music, fashion, and art), and people grew their hair long or wore it 'natural' in opposition to prescribed social roles. The underground press flourished, Susan Sontag sought to reveal the artificiality of conventional art criticism, and the Pop Art movement emerged, decrying the superficiality of US culture.[4] Involvement in organised religion sharply declined (Bellah, 1976), the naturalistic 'anti-acting' of James Dean and Marlon Brando captured the imagination of millions of cinema goers, and Ossie Clark popularised the leather jacket (an item associated with the anger and nonconformity of the rockers).

In some instances dissatisfaction with mainstream social values, norms, and roles provoked an interest in previously marginalised social groups. As Paul Willis comments in his ethnographic study of hippies living in London during the 1960s, 'oppressed cultures were used as a set of forms, a milieu, within which to express criticism of the rational-technical order' (Willis, 1978, p. 93). We see the celebration of minority groups within the wider culture too. Working class accents, fashions and values were lauded, from Michael Caine's cheeky and deeply fashionable Alfie, to the interest in clothes previously associated with work, such as denim jeans (Jones 1980, p. 85). Similarly, feminine expressiveness and the assumed 'naturalness' and authenticity of 'black culture' (and, in the USA, the culture of Native Americans) were given a certain credence. Characteristically antagonistic towards the white, masculine mainstream society, Jack Kerouac, in *On the Road*, writes,

> [a]t lilac evening I walked with every muscle aching among the lights of 27th and Walton in the Denver colored section, wishing I were a Negro, feeling that the best the white world had offered was not enough ecstasy for me, not enough life, joy, kicks, darkness, music, not enough night. I wished I were a Denver Mexican, or even a poor overworked Jap, anything but what I so drearily was, a 'white man' disillusioned.
> (Kerouac, 1991 [original, 1953], p. 67)[5]

Indeed, those involved in the counterculture frequently represented minority groups as the antithesis – and the antidote – to the cold, calculating impersonality of capitalist society. In doing so they reinforced the idea that those within minority groups were inherently different to the 'straights' that inhabited the mainstream. Women, the working class, ethnic minorities – those, in short, who existed on the peripheries of society – were seen to embody a pure articulation of countercultural ideals. They represented, as Todd Gitlin puts it, 'the animal spirit now reviving from beneath the fraudulent surface of American life' (Gitlin, 1993, p. 216).

More generally speaking, scratching the 'fraudulent surface' of life became a central motif of the 1960s counter-culture. It was frequently suggested that individuals ought to strive to grasp a more profound reality, one that lay beyond the 'surface phenomena' of mainstream society. 'The sixties', the US sociologist Jeffrey Alexander writes, 'marked a great outbreak of the social unconscious' (Alexander, forthcoming, p. 3). Indeed, evident in many of the countercultural endeavours is the assumption that there was something beyond 'all this', something natural, spontaneous, and real, something latent that could be made manifest. Uncovering the real essence of things was a task that deserved serious, everyday attention because it was the self – its emotional well-being, its authenticity, even – that was perceived to be at stake. As the Beat poet Allen Ginsberg asks his generation with characteristic frustration, '[a]re you going to let your emotional life be run by / Time magazine?' ('America', 1956, lines 48–9).

This countercultural attitude is also evident in Joseph Heller's *Catch-22* (1960) and Ken Kesey's *One Flew Over The Cuckoo's Nest* (1963), two of the most prominent novels of the 1960s. These books present the individual as trapped inside nullifying social institutions: Heller's anti-hero, Yossarian, can not escape the military, just as Kesey's protagonist MacMurphy is unable to escape an institute for the mentally ill. MacMurphy, with his sideburns and his 'real' laugh (ibid., p. 15), his work-shy attitude and his love of sex and fighting, is ultimately made subordinate to the mechanisms of the institute. Having undergone an involuntary lobotomy, MacMurphy is put on show to demonstrate to the others what happens if 'you buck the system' (ibid., p. 253). Horrified to see his friend in such a state, the Chief suffocates MacMurphy at the end of the novel, thus restoring some of his dignity. In *Catch-22*, having found authority difficult to accept, Yossarian strikes a deal with some military officials to be dismissed early from the air force on honourable discharge, as long as he never raises the fact that his fellow servicemen fly more missions than they officially should. At the last moment he decides that the only truly self-affirming course of action is to desert his post and to go on the run from the military. For Yossarian the cost of this action – the constant fear of being found and court-marshalled – is far outweighed by the possibility of regaining agency by rejecting the system entirely.

Interestingly, both novels focus on the small confines of particular institutions, unlike comparable novels written earlier in the twentieth century, such as Orwell's *Nineteen Eighty-Four* (1949) or Huxley's *Brave New World* (1952), which look at the social structure as a whole.

Frank Parkin noted an equivalent attitude in his study of middle-class radicals of the 1960s. He suggests that these groups, which became increasingly prevalent during the 1960s, advance

> an approach which does not require, and may even be inimical to, any coherent ideology which purports to explain all social ills as epiphenomena of one major evil – such as the oppressive power of the state, or private property relationships. The approach of the middle class radical movement, unlike its working class counter-part, is to treat each evil *sui generis*, and not as reducible to some greater underlying malady which throws into question the legiti-macy of the existing order.
>
> (Parkin, 1968, p. 54)

Similarly, whilst Heller's and Kesey's books may lead the reader to question the worth of social institutions and authorities, they pre-clude her from imagining the origins of social control and power (What kind of society uses mental health institutes as places to imprison troublemakers? What kind of society allows bureaucrats and officials to become corrupt?) Denied a broader view of the social structure, the reader learns that the only way of dealing with overly constraining social institutions is to attempt to place one-self beyond their reach (and, we might note, this aim is shown in both novels to be practically impossible). It is perhaps unsurprising that these novels provide such a narrow idea of how we might counter impersonal social institutions, given that it is the preser-vation of individual subjectivity, rather than the protection of social or political freedom, that concerns Yossarian and MacMurphy. It is not, that is to say, the overturning of a corrupt social system that interests these characters, rather it is the preservation of a sense of self. As a result, discussions of reform or revolution and the origin of power or conflict are rendered superfluous. 'The cultural and politi-cal radicalism of the sixties', Jeffrey Alexander comments, 'focused on emotions and morality, on the structuring and restructuring of internal life. *Subjectivity was everything'* (Alexander, forthcoming, p. 7. Italics added.). The lack of a more thoroughgoing social critique in *One Flew Over The Cuckoo's Nest* and *Catch-22* is partly due to the overriding interest in protecting subjectivity in these two novels. This outlook suggests a certain attitude towards the relationship between the self and society, one that foregrounds the former and acknowledges the latter only in so much as it places unspeakable demands upon the self.

In this context, the repudiation of social authorities becomes a corollary of the desire for self-possession. Both *One Flew Over The Cuckoo's Nest* and *Catch-22*, for example, contest the highly impersonal ways in which the self is understood and discussed within social institutions. In particular, the novels conceive of madness as merely a label applied by those groups with power to those who are relatively powerless. Interestingly, this idea had gained real salience with the work of R.D. Laing, another key figure in the 1960s counter-culture. In his highly influential book, *The Divided Self* (originally published in 1960), Laing suggests that the anxiety experienced by schizophrenics is an extension of the fears felt by 'normal' people. He argues that 'schizophrenia' and 'madness' are socially produced labels that wrongly imply a break from, rather than an extension of, 'normal' psychological difficulties concerning ontological security. By 1967, Laing had developed his thesis to argue that sanity requires a capacity and willingness to subordinate oneself to social controls (Laing, 1967, p. 116). Social restraints, he argues, invariably impinge upon and diminish a sense of self (ibid., p. 80). However, Laing's work – illuminating as it might be as a philosophical tract about experience – gives few clues as to the mechanisms or origin of such deadening social constraints. For Laing society is simply 'the external world', or anything that is outside of the self (ibid., p. 116).

The lack of social critique in such texts was noted by a number of commentators during the 1960s and 1970s, who believed that the counterculture lacked direction and ideological impetus. Warren Hinckle, for example, described the countercultural attitude as an empty rhetoric of defiance, or, as he put it, a 'political posture of unrelenting quietism' (Hinckle, 1967, p. 232). This is not, of course, to deny the existence of political groups and political action during the 1960s. After all, this period saw the emergence of the civil rights movement, second wave feminism, the radical student group, the S.D.S, and C.N.D. Nonetheless, we should acknowledge that, as a cultural movement, the counterculture often manifested itself as a rather innocuous *anti-mainstream* attitude. As Roszak conceded, the counterculture was 'much more a flight from than toward' (Roszak, 1970, p. 34). This is perhaps most clear in the rise of so-called 'anti-art', and the emergence of various counter-institutions, including the 'anti-university', founded in London in 1968 (ibid., pp. 43–4). Even Herbert Marcuse, one of the most prominent and vocal intellectuals of the period, suggested that the counterculture was 'still the simple, elementary negation, the antithesis ... the immediate denial', though he hoped that it would be the precursor to a much more concerted struggle (Marcuse, 1972, pp. 46–7).

'What was most evident in the 1960s, Daniel Bell writes, 'was the scale and intensity of feeling that was not only anti-government, but almost entirely anti-institution and ultimately antinomian as well' (Bell, 1976, p. 123). For Bell, the counterculture's 'attack on reason itself' (ibid., p. 143) should be seen as part of a major historical shift that started during the mid-nineteenth century. During this period the 'surge of modernity' brought about significant changes in both the social and cultural spheres, the former as a consequence of the bourgeoisie's revolutionising of the means of production, and the latter as a result of the rise of modernism within the arts (ibid., p. 17). Ultimately, Bell argues, these developments created a rupture between the two spheres. Running to the tune of the market, the social sphere demanded that workers be efficient, orderly, compliant, and focussed on achieving set goals. Outside of the social sphere, however, individuals were urged to be pleasure-seeking and to develop a sense of individuality:

> [the social structure] is ruled by an economic principle defined in terms of efficiency and functional rationality, the organisation of production through the ordering of things, including men as things. [The culture] is prodigal, promiscuous, dominated by an anti-rational, anti-intellectual temper in which the self is taken as the touchstone of cultural judgements.
>
> (ibid., p. 37)

As a result, '[t]he principles of the economic realm and those of the culture [came to] lead people in contrary directions' (ibid., p. 15). The tension between the two spheres grew more acute as culture came to play an increasingly dominant role in shaping values and lifestyles in economically advanced societies, a development aided by the rise of mass consumerism during the second quarter of the twentieth century (ibid., pp. 65–72). By the mid-twentieth century,

Bell argues, the culture had 'become supreme' (ibid., p. 33) to the extent that a radical impulse came to be expressed through the culture, rather than through political debate. This development was surely compounded by the emergence of the counterculture during the 1960s, a primarily cultural movement that re-articulated the earlier modernist disparagement of mainstream society.

There is much to suggest the continued dominance in today's society of the cultural impulse identified by Bell. Expressing dissatisfaction with mainstream society has become something of an imperative, to the extent that attitudes and values that were once deemed dangerously countercultural are now widely accepted. Protesters, as Freeman points out, are no longer viewed as subversive (Freeman, 1983, p. xv), and scepticism about government agencies, politicians, scientists, and religious authorities is seen to constitute a healthy distrust of social institutions. In their study of political participation in Britain, Parry et al. point out that during the late 1980s,

> almost as many people had signed a petition (68.8%) as had voted in local elections (68.8%); almost twice as many had attended a protest meeting (14.6%) as had attended a rally organised by a mainstream political party (8.6%); and as many people had been on a protest march (5.2%) as had participated in fund-raising (5.2%), canvassing (3.5%) or clerical work (3.5%) on behalf of political parties.
>
> (Parry et al., 1992, p. 5)

As John Bell suggests, since the countercultural period of the 1960s and 1970s, expressing dissatisfaction with the mainstream has itself become a mainstream activity (Bell, 1999, pp. 68–3). Possibly the most obvious example of this is the number and range of advertising campaigns in today's society that seek to prompt countercultural sentiments: advertisements make reference to 'the real' (Coca-Cola), play countercultural music (Nike), and use ethnic minority groups as evidence of their anti-establishment credentials (Benetton). We might also note other, perhaps less immediately perceptible, ways in which distancing oneself from the mainstream has gained salience in contemporary culture: irony, for example, has become a central feature of many prime-time US sit-coms (*Friends; Will and Grace*) suggesting a desire to demonstrate a knowing detachment from shared, social meanings.

The desire to establish one's distance from the mainstream is also evident in the contemporary drive to 'show awareness'. This practice involves expressing support for groups of sufferers whose interests have historically been neglected, such as AIDS sufferers or female breast-cancer patients. Affiliation with such groups seems to enable ribbon wearers, like those involved in the earlier counterculture, to locate themselves in opposition to mainstream society. 'When you're seventeen or eighteen', one female interviewee told me, 'and wearing a red ribbon for AIDS awareness, you're trying to prove a point to everybody who wouldn't be seen *dead* in it'. For this woman, such an attitude is bound up with youthful rebellion and disaffection though, interestingly, the responses from other participants indicated that ribbon wearing is still seen as a mildly rebellious act by those well past their teenage years. A 31-year-old-interviewee, for example, commented that he had experienced renewed enthusiasm for wearing the red ribbon after being asked unfriendly questions about his motivation for wearing the symbol during a trip to the USA. He 'want[ed] to make a statement and ... to be seen as somehow in support of an issue', though he also conceded that it was maybe something that he 'wanted to be *seen* to be in favour of'.

Other interviewees complained that ribbon wearing has become too mainstream, a surprising reaction considering ribbon campaigns' emphasis on the need to spread awareness. Once we begin to see ribbon wearing as a self-affirming (rather than socially oriented) practice that is aimed at expressing a sense of detachment from the mainstream, however, such responses become easier to comprehend. 'It just isn't shocking anymore – the ribbons are everywhere', one interviewee told me, a sentiment that was echoed by another participant who was concerned that the ribbon 'doesn't shock' most people today. 'It's too similar, it's spreading ...', she said later in the interview, vaguely agitated by her inability to find the right words to express her growing disillusion with ribbon wearing. Both of these women had stopped wearing their awareness ribbons, though both also claimed that they would start wearing a ribbon again, 'if a campaign touched me', as one put it mysteriously. For some, stressing an emotional connection to a cause offers a means of reasserting the singularity of their motivation for wearing an awareness ribbon.

For those less concerned (or less reflexive) about the ubiquity of the symbol, the awareness ribbon remains vaguely risqué, a means of singling oneself out from all those who 'wouldn't be seen dead' wearing one.

It is in this context that the awareness ribbon might be viewed as something like a protest symbol. Certainly, this was how the symbol was widely viewed during the early 1990s. The red AIDS-awareness ribbon, for example, was described as the '1990s' version of the peace-symbol button of the Vietnam War' (Fleury, 1992; see also Garfield, 1995, p. 255). Of course, there are significant differences between these two symbols. For instance, whereas the peace-symbol badge worn during the 1960s and 1970s was symbolic of people's wish for specific, concrete changes, such as the removal of troops from Vietnam, the red ribbon symbolises the rather less tangible aim of increasing awareness about AIDS and HIV. Nonetheless, the comparison between the peace symbol and the ribbon is an interesting and instructive one, not least of all because both symbols have been used to indicate a broad sense of dissatisfaction with social authorities.

We might also note that both the peace symbol and the red AIDS-awareness ribbon have been used as fashion accessories.[6] Indeed, more generally speaking, both the 1960s counterculture and the awareness ribbon campaigns of the 1990s have enjoyed significant commercial success. Just as the counterculture was embodied in various consumerist items – records and clothes, for example – the awareness ribbon campaigns have been sponsored by the film, television, fashion and beauty industries. However, the process of commodification, evident in the earlier countercultural period, has reached further in the awareness campaigns of the 1990s. Financial support from companies – from Estée Lauder to Calvin Klein, from MacDonalds to BMW – has transformed the awareness ribbon into a slick corporate symbol, and the campaigns into vehicles for marketing empathy and commercialising dissent.

One effect of this has been to render awareness campaigns politically neutral. Awareness ribbon campaigns are devoid of any discussion of politics or inequalities of class, gender, sexuality, or ethnicity. Even the red AIDS-awareness campaign lacks any political objectives; though frustrated at the lack of government interest in HIV/AIDS, the AIDS activist group that launched the red ribbon did not wish to make an overtly political statement with the symbol (Fleury, 1992, pp. 14–16). Illness itself is the focus of contemporary awareness campaigns – not, to be clear, because it is the point at which social inequalities become most marked, but because it is deemed to be a scourge that makes victims of us all in one way or another.

This attitude is most evident in the breast cancer awareness campaign, which implies that all women – regardless of age, class, or ethnicity – are at serious risk of developing breast cancer (see Chapter 7). As was argued in Chapter 4, the pink-ribbon campaign makes use of a rhetoric similar to that employed by the feminist movement that emerged in the late 1960s. Whilst this might be taken as further evidence of the continued salience of the counter-cultural ethos in today's society, there are important differences between second-wave feminism and the contemporary pink-ribbon campaign. Most notable is the latter's lack of political impetus. Unlike the earlier feminist movement, the pink-ribbon campaign is uninterested in addressing socially produced inequalities. Indeed, the campaign engenders a desire to protect oneself from illness, rather than a wish for social betterment. It is this overriding concern with the self – also a feature of the 1960s counter-culture – that I turn to in the next section.

Finding the self

> I'll never finish saying everything I feel, but I'll be doing my part to make some sense out of the way we're living, and not living, now. All I'm doing is saying what's on my mind the best way I know how. And whatever else you say about me, everything I do and sing and write comes out of me.
> (Bob Dylan, album sleeve for *The Freewheelin' Bob Dylan*, 1963)

> I just believe in me / Yoko and Me / and that's reality.
> (John Lennon, *Let It Be*, 1970, in Foss and Larkin, 1976, p. 57)

In the counterculture of the 1960s and 1970s, the self was viewed as the point from which all effective actions and values issue, as the source of revolution, the arbiter of truth. In particular, self-expression was frequently – and often dogmatically – presented as a crucial component of social movements, cultural artefacts, and personal identities. The Beat artists, for example, claimed the need for direct self-expression (hence their stream of consciousness style of writing), hippies sought means of communicating freely and fully, and psychedelic music was seen as an articulation of the irrational, formless, unconscious self. Self-expression was recurrently viewed as a means of protest: 'being yourself' was generally conceived of as a repudiation of impersonal social authorities, feminists 'spoke bitterness', and the underground press was often full of praise for the 'subjective dimension of revolution; the importance of imagination, self-development and flexible-mindedness' (*Oz*, January 1971, in Nelson, 1989, p. 91).

In turn, many of the countercultural protests point to – and indeed are premised upon – a fundamental belief in the need for greater freedom to act in accordance with one's personal beliefs and feelings.[7] We have already seen how the importance of obtaining autonomy in two of the main novels of the countercultural period, *One Flew Over The Cuckoo's Nest* and *Catch-22*, worked towards a protest against the constraining nature of social institutions. We see a similar attitude elsewhere in the 1960s counter-culture. 'The main pay-off for middle class radicals', Frank Parkin noted in his work on the rise of middle-class disaffection in the UK during the 1960s, 'is that of a psychological or emotional kind – in satisfactions derived from expressing personal values in action' (Parkin, 1968, p. 2).

The interest in self-expression was itself tied up with a desire for personal authenticity. The literary critic Lionel Trilling notes that by the mid-twentieth century, authenticity – being true to oneself – had come to be seen as a more 'strenuous moral experience than sincerity', an attribute that involves being true to oneself in order to avoid misleading others (Trilling, 1972, p. 11). Certainly, during the 1960s counter-culture, showing oneself to be authentic became something of a moral imperative. '[W]hatever else you say about me', Bob Dylan writes, 'everything I do and sing and write comes out of me'. His statement implies that, regardless of the content of an argument, the sheer fact of having expressed it oneself is what matters most.

An interest in the self was by no means an unchanging feature of the period. The counterculture underwent an important transformation towards the end of the 1960s, whereby the development and protection of the self became virtues *in themselves*. During the early and mid-1960s, the desire for self-expression and authenticity was often (though by no means always) combined with a belief in the possibility of social change. A rather more solipsistic attitude emerged in the late 1960s, a development noted by numerous writers and cultural commentators (see Foss and Larkin, 1976; Gitlin, 1993; Stein, 1985; Weiner and Stillman, 1979). As idealistic radicalism gave way to embittered, often insular protest and high rates of overseas and domestic volunteerism gave way to communes and self-help, self-preservation became a more explicit and primary aim. This shift was underpinned by a sense of apathy and self-absorption, a scepticism about collective responses to social problems, and a growing inclination to view self-development as the only possible and worthwhile area in which advance could be made. Growing distrust of the government and the assassination of several key countercultural figures (Martin Luther King, Malcolm X, John F. Kennedy, and Robert Kennedy) contributed to this outlook.

The covers of *MAD* magazine during the late 1960s, satirised the growing sense of apathy. The magazine cover for December 1967, for example, showed a massive pin with the words 'We don't try very hard!', an image mocking the scores of people wearing protest pins as much as the writers' own sense of ennui (The Usual Gang of Idiots, 1996). In other instances, disillusion with society – including the counterculture's attempts at social change – was articulated as a desire for absolute freedom from social constraints. In a lecture delivered at Birbeck College in London in 1972, the distinguished scientist Freeman J. Dyson presented his vision for the future, a vision that reflected his desire to escape modern social life. In years to come, he hypothesised, the solar system would be split into two spheres, an inner domain where men will be organised into giant bureaucracies and an outer sphere where,

> men will live in smaller communities, isolated from each other by huge distances. Here men will find once again the wilderness that they have lost on Earth. Groups of people will be free to live as they please independent of governmental authorities.
>
> (Dyson, 1972)

Dyson's solipsistic wish for absolute freedom from social authorities suggests a frustration with other strategies for social change, including, we might postulate, those put forward by the counterculture. More explicitly contemptuous of the ideals of the early counterculture, the participants in a survey carried out in the late 1970s in the USA described how they had come to see self-development as a more attractive and realistic aim. 'I now realize that the individual can only act successfully for himself. I am now totally apolitical', one participant commented. 'Today I have no hope of being instrumental in making any change and even wonder about the possibility of change ... I'm more selfish and concerned with my own survival', another reported. 'I'm into the human condition in a smaller, more personal way', explained another, adding, 'I've turned my focus from the "solid" realm to more spiritual concerns' (Weiner and Stillman, 1979, p. 151).[8]

Commenting on a similar movement towards solipsism in the music of the late 1960s, Foss and Larkin point to a perceptible change in John Lennon and Bob Dylan's song lyrics around this time. Three years after he had written the protest song 'Day In The Life', Lennon's outlook had changed substantially enough for him to claim, 'I just believe in me / Yoko and Me / And that's reality' (Lennon, 1970, in Foss and Larkin, 1976, p. 57). Similarly, by the start of the 1970s Dylan's lyrics reflected a desire for the privacy of domestic life: 'Build me a cabin in Utah / Marry me a wife and catch rainbow trout / Have a bunch of kids who call me Pa / That must be what it's all about (Dylan, 1971, in Foss and Larkin, 1976, p. 57).

The increased interest in self-development towards the end of the 1960s is also reflected in the rise of a wide range of therapies around this time, including Primal Scream therapy, The Self-Awareness Movement (later to become 'est'), and Esalen (Foss and Larkin, 1976, p. 56). More generally speaking, a 'rhetoric of authenticity and awareness' had come to be adopted by a significant number of social movements and groups (Lasch, 1979, p. 30). The self-help movement, for example, became particularly prominent in the 1970s. Therapeutic in tone, the movement promoted the idea that greater self-awareness was an integral aspect of personal development. Interestingly, Irene Taviss Thomson, in her study of self-help literature in the USA from the 1920s onwards, suggests that there was an evident shift in the self-help movement during the 1970s whereby 'autonomy came to mean protection of the inner self' (Thomson, 1997, p. 641). Becoming self-sufficient, in other words, was seen as a primarily emotional and spiritual process, rather than in terms of material or moral betterment.

It is perhaps unsurprising, therefore, that, during this period, self-help groups 'attained a new importance as people use[d] them for open self-expression and as a vehicle of self-discovery' (ibid., p. 651).

Foss and Larkin point to a comparable development in the various US-based youth protest groups at the turn of the 1970s. Around this time, such groups undertook a 'revaluation of the self and its capacities', which resulted in 'movement participants engag[ing] in what amount[ed] to mass therapy' (Foss and Larkin, 1976, p. 47). Similarly, Marlene Dixon argues that the feminist movement that emerged during the late 1960s, ostensibly a protest movement, also served an important therapeutic function. 'For many new recruits', Dixon suggests, 'consciousness raising was the end-all and be-all of the early movement, a mystical method to self-realized and personal liberation' (Dixon, 1977).

The increased popularity of a therapeutic approach and rhetoric is also evident in a comparison of the US presidential speeches of 1960 and 1969, given by John F. Kennedy and Richard Nixon respectively. Kennedy's rousing inaugural speech in 1960, suggestive of the potential of individual action (most memorably in his instruction to 'think not what your country can do for you, but what you can do for your country'), was to be mirrored almost a decade later with Nixon's inaugural address that, on the surface, urged a similar stance:

> what has to be done, has to be done by government and people together or will not be done at all. The lesson of past agony is that without people we can do nothing; with people we can do everything.

This appeal, however, was sharply interposed with the assertion that spiritual fulfilment was central to the project of participatory democracy:

> [s]tanding in this same place a third of a century ago, Franklin Delano Roosevelt addressed a Nation ravaged by depression and gripped in fear. He could say in surveying the Nation's troubles: 'They concern, thank God, only material things'. Our crisis today is the reverse. We have found ourselves rich in goods, but ragged in spirit; reaching with magnificent precision for the moon, but falling into raucous discord on earth. We are caught in war,

wanting peace. We are torn by division, wanting unity. *We see around us empty lives, wanting fulfillment.* We see tasks that need doing, waiting for hands to do them. *To a crisis of the spirit, we need an answer of the spirit. To find that answer, we need only look within ourselves.* (Italics added.)

Nixon's speech reveals the individual's psychological well-being to be of utter importance – it at least implies that the therapeutic discourse appealed to the electorate. Interestingly, and somewhat problematically, obtaining self-fulfilment is represented here as both an end-goal and as a means to an end. The eminent psychologist, Abraham Maslow, in his work on self-actualization, comes across the very same irregularity:

> I wish to underscore one main paradox ... which we must face even if we don't understand it. The goal of identity (self-actualization, autonomy, individuation ... authenticity) seems to be simultaneously an end-goal in itself, and also a transitional-goal, a rite of passage, a step along the path to the transcendence of identity.
>
> (Maslow, 1964, p. 161)

If there is no way of distinguishing between the means and the end-goal of a particular practice, how might we determine that the aim has been achieved? At what point, in other words, is an individual able to declare that she has obtained self-fulfilment?

This 'paradox' was made more problematic by the popular countercultural idea that the self constituted an ongoing, end-less project, so aptly summed up in Bob Dylan's comment that, 'I'll never finish saying everything I feel' (Bob Dylan, album sleeve for *The Freewheelin' Bob Dylan*, 1963). As a result, the desire for self-fulfilment was continually off-set by the wish for an unbounded self, one that was never quite complete or fully realisable. Instead, self-fulfilment became an unending task in which the self was to be continually brought to the surface and made imminent through acts of instantaneous, unhindered self-expression. 'The effect of immediacy, impact, simultaneity and sensation as the mode of aesthetic – and psychological experience', Daniel Bell writes, 'is to dramatize each moment, to increase our tensions to a fever pitch, and yet to leave us without a resolution, reconciliation, or transforming moment, which is the catharsis of a ritual' (Bell, 1976, p. 118). Derisory of modernity's tele-ological impulse, the counterculture recommended a perpetual process of becoming more fully oneself.

Perhaps the real paradox of the countercultural desire for self-fulfilment, however, lay in the belief that self-realisation could be achieved on one's own, 'by looking within ourselves', as Nixon put it. Desirous of pure self-expression and full self-awareness, the counter-cultural individual eschewed any obviously shared, social meanings, norms and rules. Those determined to express themselves independ-ently of socially prescribed meanings adopted esoteric practices, behavioural codes from other cultures, or sought more direct ways of expressing the self. There are various examples of such attempts at self-expression during the countercultural period, particularly towards the end of the 1960s: numerous therapies encouraged inchoate self-expression (primal scream therapy, for example); John Lennon and Yoko Ono took to their bed in an eccentric, personal act of protest; Action art – Jackson Pollock's drip paintings, for example – was lauded for making the artistic gesture itself the subject of artwork (Eco, 1999). 'My painting is direct', Pollock wrote, adding, 'I want to express my feelings, rather than illustrate them' (Pollock, in Ferrier, 1999, p. 492).

What the 1960s counter-culture failed to acknowledge was that a common language and shared behavioural code are *prerequisites*, rather than impediments, to self-expression and self-development. Social frames of meaning furnish us with the means of articulating intense feelings and complex ideas – indeed, without such frames of meaning, our range of emotional expressions and thought processes would be seriously limited. As Wittgenstein argued, a 'private lan-guage' does not and can not exist (Wittgenstein, 2003, Paras 243, 261, and 262). Unhindered self-expression is a false and particularly pernicious fantasy, the pursuit of which often entails a real lack of autonomy. The popular self-help movement and therapies of the countercultural period, for example, *prescribed* particular ways of expressing the self. Clothes that seemed to speak of new-found free-dom were worn by millions – the miniskirt, for example, a sign of sexual liberation, was worn by 90 per cent of women in the USA (Weiner and Stillman, 1979, p. 37). In short, the emphasis on 'keep-ing it real' helped produce a group of uniformly 'real' individuals.

David Riesman, in *The Lonely Crowd* (1957, updated 1969), also noted a strong level of conformity in the countercultural generation, though his line of argument is markedly different to the one presented above. Riesman argued that as parental controls over the child's development declined during the second quarter of the twentieth century (due, in part, to the emergence of more permissive child-rearing practices), the child's peer group took on a more important role in passing on values and norms (Riesman, 1957, pp. 14–24). Riesman suggested that the resulting 'other-directedness' 'permitted a close behavioural conformity … through [the promotion of] an exceptional sensitivity to the actions and wishes of others', a conformity that he believed would become a central trait of those living in western societies (ibid., pp. 21–2).

Richard Sennett, in his highly influential book, *The Fall of Public Man* (1977), also points to an increased interest in developing close relationships with others during the second half of the twentieth century. 'The reigning belief today', he writes, 'is that closeness between persons is a moral good. The reigning aspiration today is to develop individual personality through experiences of closeness and warmth with others' (Sennett, 1993, p. 259). For Sennett, however, this emergent 'intimate society' was based primarily on the desire to develop a full sense of self, rather than a desire for acceptance from others. Indeed, he viewed his study as a critique of Riesman's thesis, arguing that he erroneously 'believed American society, and in its wake Western Europe, was moving from an inner- to an outer-directed condition. The sequence should be reversed' (ibid., p. 5).

Sennett's argument that an interest in the self has become increasingly pronounced in late modern societies is convincing. This development does not, however, preclude conformist behaviour. As noted above, activities that seem individualistic and personally motivated might in fact involve conformity to certain patterns of behaviour or adherence to particular discourses. This seeming contradiction is easily explained. The desire for unhindered self-expression may prompt a repudiation of social frames of meaning that seem to hinder 'real' self-expression. For most, however, the desire to communicate something about the self and the difficulty in developing independent means of self-expression create a need for socially produced norms and conventions. This need, however, is rarely acknowledged, primarily because it seems to undermine the search for pure, direct self-expression. It may, as a result, produce an unreflexive conformity to practices and discourses that *seem* to be highly individualistic. Those taking part in the aerobics events organised by breast cancer charities, for example, might enjoy a separateness from fellow exercisers as they dance away anonymously, but their autonomy is, of course, illusory. The dance, every week the same, has been choreographed by an instructor who keeps the group stepping in unison to the equally predictable beats of a contemporary pop song.

A similar illusion of individuality is apparent in the social practice of ribbon wearing. Like earlier countercultural pursuits, ribbon wearing is often viewed as a means of expressing a deeply personal sense of awareness and empathy. Launched as a 'grass-roots expression of compassion', the red AIDS-awareness ribbon, for example, is commonly seen as a spontaneous, personal display of the wearer's awareness and empathy (O'Connell, director of Visual AIDS, in *The Los Angeles Times*, 24 March 1993, F6). As in the 1960s counter-culture, such expressions of compassion are primarily directed towards achieving self-expression; after all, ribbon wearers are more interested in *showing*, than spreading, their awareness.

On closer inspection, however, we find that the ribbon encapsulates a highly uniform statement of empathy and awareness. Compassion for numerous groups of victims – from sufferers of diabetes to those killed in church fires – is represented in the same looped-ribbon motif. Ribbon campaigns repeat the rhetoric of awareness to the point of abstraction (just as tag lines in advertisements become nothing more than verbal cues). As a result, ascertaining precisely what awareness consists of and how it manifests itself is a rather tricky task, one that is comparable to understanding the place a particular brand name has in our consciousness. Few of the ribbon wearers I interviewed could explain what they meant when they described the ribbon as a symbol of their awareness. 'How are you aware of anything?', one woman asked me rhetorically, rather flustered by the question. 'It's a *good* thing that people are wearing the ribbons', another interviewee told me eagerly, 'I couldn't pinpoint exactly *why* I think that ...', she added, tailing off. Another interviewee spent some time considering exactly why he showed awareness of AIDS, but ended up simply stating that 'people *should* be aware of it'. Similarly convinced of the unquestionable efficacy of awareness, the pop star Ronan Keating was unruffled by questions from a presenter on the British television show GMTV about his motivation for running a marathon to raise awareness of cancer. 'The money is secondary', Keating said, '[the event is] really about making people aware of cancer'. The presenter pointed out that people are already aware that they need to self-examine and visit a GP if they find a lump on their bodies, to which Keating, undeterred, replied, 'well, that's obviously a *good* thing'.

The benefits of raising awareness are regularly taken to be obvious, yet when we ask those involved in 'showing awareness' what this practice consists of, or what it achieves, we are greeted with confusion and incredulity. Awareness and compassion are deemed to be of indisputable moral worth in today's society. Even the discovery that the white Make Poverty History wristbands were made in Chinese factories accused of using forced labour did not shore up the public's enthusiasm for wearing the symbol (*The Independent*, 30 May 2005, p. 6). As long as the worth of awareness remains unquestioned, discussions of political ideology, economic policy, and the social good will be judged unimportant.

It is, of course, deeply ironic that a personal gesture of awareness requires such little reflection. This lack of contemplation is surely a consequence of the apolitical nature of the ribbon campaigns and the lack of any definable aims. Like 'self-actualization' and self-fulfilment, 'showing awareness' is in fact an endless pursuit of an unreachable goal. If ribbon wearers find it difficult to explain the purpose of 'showing awareness', this is partly due to the fact that this practice simply isn't directed towards achieving anything specific.

Conclusion

In this chapter I have argued that the countercultural ethos of the 1960s and 1970s continues to influence contemporary culture. It has been suggested that the anti-mainstream attitude fostered by the counterculture remains prominent today. Similarly, the prioritisation of self-expression, self-awareness and self-fulfilment in the counterculture is also evident in today's society. Ribbon wearing, a social practice that involves disassociating oneself from the mainstream and expressing a sense of personal awareness, was taken to be exemplary of the extant influence of the 1960s counter-culture.

Properly speaking, we see the *extension* and *transfiguration* of the countercultural impulse in the contemporary culture, and the awareness campaigns of the 1990s more specifically. Whilst the counter-culture found expression through various consumerist items, for example, the awareness ribbon campaigns are more wholly commercial enterprises, popularising dissent and compassion through slick marketing campaigns. In addition, we see the normalisation of self-awareness in the ribbon campaigns of the 1990s, its transformation, that is to say, into an unquestionably beneficial attribute. The unquestioned acceptance of the need for ever-greater awareness has transformed awareness into a standard response to illness, tragedies, and social problems, one of seemingly undeniable efficacy. Most importantly, perhaps, cynicism during the late stages of the counter-culture about the possibility of bringing about social change has been transformed into a wholesale rejection of social critique in the politically neutral awareness campaigns of the 1990s. As mentioned in the previous chapter, we see a widespread scepticism concerning the government and social institutions in the contemporary awareness campaigns, an attitude that is bolstered by the notion that the self is the only level at which meaningful changes can be made.

7
Worry as a Manifestation of Awareness: The Implications of 'Thinking Pink'

As we saw in Chapter 5, 'showing awareness' requires neither concerted action nor knowledge of an illness. Rather, it is an expression of *self*-awareness, one that reflects the belief that the self is the most meaningful and viable site for improvement. In this respect, 'showing awareness' might be seen to embody the type of self-reflexivity that Giddens (1991) believes has become a core characteristic feature of the late-modern individual. However, my research suggests that ribbon wearers' sense of awareness often manifests itself as worry, rather than a process of rational evaluation. This is not to suggest that all research subjects expressed worry about the illnesses for which they wore a ribbon. Those participants who wore the red AIDS-awareness ribbon, for example, were generally unworried about the possibility of either themselves or their loved ones falling ill with the syndrome. Only one out of the 12 interviewees who wore the red AIDS-awareness ribbon expressed fear about contracting HIV:

> I know that sometimes it's got a stigma attached to it, that you have to be a certain sort of person to ... but that is not the truth, you know. Anyone could get it. I mean God, you know, I might be at work, someone falls down, they start bleeding, and I've got a cut and then I end up with it. And that's nothing to do with me ... You know, that wouldn't be my fault whatsoever. And so it could happen to anyone. And then I might get really ill you know. I would want the treatment if it was there. And so, therefore, I'm quite happy to give money to it, because I think that ... anyone could be attacked.

Though uncharacteristic of red-ribbon wearers' responses, this woman's concerns about HIV closely resemble those expressed by pink-ribbon wearers about breast cancer. Indeed, most pink-ribbon wearers who took part in this study exhibited a significant level of worry about breast cancer, and the vast majority of these ribbon wearers were female.[1]

The relationship between gender and the emotions is an area of study that has received substantial attention from sociologists (Charles and Walters, 1998; Simon and Nath, 2004; Thoits, 1989, pp. 321–2). Those working in this field generally point out that there are particular, socially constructed rules that govern emotional expression, and that these rules are closely bound up with notions of appropriate gendered behaviour. Women, for example, are generally held to be 'both more emotional and more emotionally expressive than men' (Simon and Nath, 2004, p. 1138). That women are more likely to express their experiences in emotional terms may partly explain female pink-ribbon wearers' worry about breast cancer. Of course, the symbolic importance of breasts in our culture – the association of breasts with sexual attractiveness and mothering – may well also heighten a sense of fear about breast cancer and the potential of this illness to strip women of their femininity.

Nonetheless, the increasing popularity of the breast cancer awareness campaign over the past 15 years – at exactly the same time as the mortality rate for breast cancer has sharply dropped – suggests that there is something distinctly new about women's worry about breast cancer. Indeed, it is possible to see women's fear about breast cancer in a broader context, as characteristic of the health panics that have become so pervasive since the early 1990s. From toxic shock syndrome triggered by tampons to deep vein thrombosis brought on by use of the contraceptive pill, health panics have become a staple of contemporary society. More generally speaking, the constant body monitoring recommended by health care literature and certain sections of the media can easily become an anxiety-inducing process, not least of all because of the inconsistencies in the information we receive. '[A]t any one time there is substantial, sometimes radical, disagreement within the medical profession about risk factors' (Giddens, 1991, p. 121), Giddens notes, though he believes that such expert advice can also be empowering (ibid., p. 141). Of course, it is not simply medical advice about health that is confusing. We are faced with a bewildering range of information about health risks on an almost daily basis. A recent segment on Channel Five's weekday morning programme, *The Wright Stuff*, for example, made use of spiritual, therapeutic, and medical language to discuss a dizzying range of risk factors for breast cancer, including emotional upheaval, harmful chemicals emitted by televisions, using certain deodorants, taking vitamin pills, and even bad luck.

Health care advice, as Nettleton and Bunton point out, penetrates 'virtually all aspects of modern life from additives in the food we eat to the state of our psyche', and thereby helps produce an all-encompassing concern with ill-health (Nettleton and Bunton, 1995, p. 47). Such concern is accentuated by a widespread belief that personally monitoring one's health is something akin to a moral imperative. In an individualised society, Beck and Beck-Gernsheim argue, health 'is not so much a gift from God as a task and achievement of the responsible citizen, who must protect and look after it or face the consequences' (Beck and Beck-Gernsheim, 2002, p. 140).

This 'new morality of health' (ibid.) may well be particularly applicable to women. Not only do they tend to be more concerned about health issues than men (Miles, 1991, p. 59), but health consciousness is often associated with femininity in our culture. The breast cancer awareness campaign is a pertinent example of this. The practices recommended by the campaign to guard against breast cancer — developing self-awareness and body consciousness — are, as Desiderio points out, 'the same kinds of body projects used to achieve and maintain the ideal of feminine beauty' (Desiderio, 2004, p. 14). For Desiderio, the campaign's reiteration of gender norms is one important way in which the breast cancer awareness movement helps to maintain the patriarchal social structure (ibid.). In a similar vein, she argues that the campaign's employment of 'a rhetoric of risk' persuades women to medicalise their bodies and thereby submit to a system of patriarchal regulation (ibid., p. 2).

Desiderio's work focusses on the US breast cancer campaign and involves an analysis of a range of secondary data (ibid., Chapter 4). This chapter employs a similar approach to analyse the British breast cancer awareness campaign, though, unlike Desiderio, I also discuss ribbon wearers' feelings about breast cancer. To be clear, it is not my purpose to infer a causal relationship between pink-ribbon wearers' worry about breast cancer and the breast cancer awareness campaign, for my research was not aimed at providing such a conclusion. Rather, I present a detailed account of pink-ribbon wearers' fears about breast cancer, and suggest that the campaign is more likely to have amplified, rather than allayed, their concerns about the illness.

Worrying about breast cancer

More women than ever before are surviving breast cancer and going on to lead healthy lives, and yet many women express fear about the disease. Most of the young women I interviewed, for example, were inordinately worried about breast cancer. Research carried out recently by Macmillan Cancer Relief shows that these women's responses are not unusual: 'women are still afraid of the Big C', the charity commented, 'despite the fact that 76 per cent of women now survive five years after a breast cancer diagnosis and that figure is rising'.[2] In the very first interview for this research, my 20-year-old female interviewee told me that she was *scared* of getting breast cancer. I was really interested by this comment, and particularly her choice of words; to be scared of something is a rather childlike response, it suggests sudden, irrepressible alarm and fear. Moreover, this young woman's fear of breast cancer interested me because it was so disproportionate to her actual risk of getting the disease: young women under the age of 25 currently have a 1 in 15,000 chance of getting breast cancer in the UK.[3] In addition to this, breast cancer has one of the best survival rates of all cancers: 77 per cent of those who suffer from breast cancer survive five years or more.[4]

This young woman's fear becomes easier to understand once we begin to look more closely at the breast cancer awareness campaign. It was with the launch of the pink ribbon in the UK, in 1993, that the breast cancer awareness campaign became a highly visible movement in this country. Since the ribbon's emergence, the campaign has developed to include a wide range of events, groups, charities, and companies (and in this respect has come to closely resemble the pink-ribbon campaign in the USA). Today, we can, for example, participate in a 'stride for life', a series of marathons organised by Cancer Research UK, or join other women for the 'aerobics in the park' event, organised by Breast Cancer Care. There is also a dizzying array of breast cancer awareness products, including earrings, cosmetics, teddy bears, children's clothes, and underwear. We are now greeted by adverts for breast cancer awareness and the related products *everywhere*: when we travel on the tube, when we do our shopping, in magazines, on people's T-shirts, in doctor's surgeries, and in charities' mail-shots. Indeed, the breast cancer awareness campaign has been cannily marketed: the pink-ribbon logo has gained the recognisability and kudos of a Nike swoosh.

However, whilst extensive marketing and advertising might improve the visibility of the campaign, it is unlikely that it promotes anything beyond an increased consciousness that breast cancer is prevalent and that it is something to be feared. After all, marketing strategies are designed to do little more than gain consumers' attention and encourage spending. In this way, many of my interviewees made reference to advertisements and slogans, but knew very little about breast cancer (their likelihood of falling ill and their chances of recovery should they do so; the range of possible symptoms and the likely nature of consultations; the government provisions for treatment and what precisely their charitable donations were being used for). One of the interviewees who wore a breast cancer awareness ribbon, for example, commented that all she knew about the illness was what she'd 'seen on adverts'. The television advertisements to which she referred, produced by the charity Cancer Research UK, show images of seemingly healthy people suddenly fading from view whilst in the midst of everyday interaction with friends and family. A child appears bereft after his mother vanishes before his very eyes. For those convinced of the necessity of raising people's awareness of breast cancer, my interviewee's mere consciousness of the illness is perhaps a heartening example of the predominance of breast cancer in the social consciousness. However, I believe that it is crucial to consider more carefully the worth – and indeed the price – of breast cancer awareness.

For most of the female pink-ribbon wearers I interviewed, awareness of breast cancer manifested itself as worry about the illness. Worry is similar to anxiety in the sense that it stirs up feelings of uncertainty, fear, and helplessness. It is, in the first instance, difficult to discern major differences between the two terms, though there are good reasons why I have chosen to describe ribbon wearers' feelings about breast cancer as worry rather than anxiety. Anxiety is a medical term and is often used to refer to a rather unfathomable sense of unease and jumpiness (this is what Freud described as 'neurotic anxiety' [Freud, 1974, pp. 440–60]). In contrast to this, my research subjects could detect the root cause of their worry, even if at times they were unwilling or unable to express this clearly and fully. Interviewees experienced an *everyday, nagging* fear that is disproportionate to the actual threat, a *painful consciousness* of their assumed susceptibility to breast cancer – this is what I mean by the term 'worry'.

It seems that many of those who have donned a pink ribbon to show their awareness of breast cancer are in fact worried about the disease. Out of the 52 pink-ribbon wearers who responded to my questionnaire, 78 per cent claimed to feel scared at the prospect of either themselves or their loved ones falling ill with breast cancer. In-depth interviews carried out with pink-ribbon wearers highlighted further women's apprehension about this illness. The interviewee who discussed the Cancer Research UK adverts with me, for example, was clearly deeply troubled by the prospect of falling ill. 'I don't like them ... they're chilling ...' was her final comment on the adverts, her only source of information about breast cancer.

A few ribbon wearers explicitly described the pink ribbon as a symbol of their fear about breast cancer. These interviewees exhibited a heightened sense of worry about the illness. Indeed, at times they appeared anxious about breast cancer. When I asked one interviewee, a 26-year-old teacher, why she wore the pink ribbon, she answered abruptly, '[b]ecause it's your worst fear, to have breast cancer'. This woman was often reticent and frequently spoke in a whispered tone. Another interviewee, whose mother had recently recovered from breast cancer, described wearing the pink ribbon as a means of reminding herself of the risks associated with the disease:

> [e]very time I put my coat on [and see the ribbon] I'm remembering that this thing's going to be in my mum's body for the rest of her life. And it could happen to me. You've got to be aware that it could happen to you ... I obviously don't sit there everyday thinking, 'Oh, I could have breast cancer. I could get breast cancer'. It's just one of those subconscious things that rushes across your mind in a matter of seconds when you put your coat on and see the ribbon.

What is interesting, and rather worrying, about this statement is this young woman's sense of pessimism about her state of health.

The popular saying 'don't worry, it may never happen' has become defunct for many of those who are painfully aware that *it could happen to me*. In this respect, pink-ribbon wearers' worry about breast cancer is something that refuses to be 'worked through' and resolved, it is, as I described it before, a nagging fear. It is telling that many of the women I interviewed were on their third or fourth ribbons; they maintain a constant, niggling sense of worry about this illness, and the ribbon remains as new as the first day it was bought.

The psychoanalyst Adam Phillips neatly describes worries as 'emotional constipation' (Phillips, 1994, p. 47), thought processes which refuse to be fully 'digested', to continue the metaphor. Worriers are unable to reconcile their concerns, they are in a state of emotional stasis. These characteristics of worry were clearly evident in many of my interviewees. A number of women, for example, spoke in meandering monologues which belied their inability to work through their worries, to draw to a conclusion. Similarly, some interviewees repeated certain phrases; they continually returned to their most central worries about breast cancer (one interviewee repeated the phrase 'you have to accept that it could be you [who gets breast cancer]' six times in a 40-minute interview, another repeated the phrase 'it could happen to anybody' three times).

Of course, cancer has, historically, invoked what Susan Sontag refers to as a 'thoroughly old-fashioned kind of dread' (Sontag, 1987, p. 10). Sontag shows that, since the nineteenth century, a range of metaphors have been employed in representations of cancer; this illness has been seen as, for example, an invasion, a plague, a contamination, and a 'demonic possession' (Sontag, 1987, pp. 72-3). As Sontag rightly suggests, this use of metaphors belies an inability to speak plainly about cancer, and, in turn, an inability to reconcile fears about the disease. In today's society it is quite evident that we remain unable to adequately discuss, represent, and understand cancer, and breast cancer in particular. Magazine articles and charities, for example, describe breast cancer euphemistically as the 'Big C'.[5] Similarly, the adverts produced by Cancer Research UK depict cancer as a hidden menace; victims disappear suddenly, leaving painful confusion and emptiness. Indeed, many of my interviewees found it difficult to articulate their worry about this illness. They used words like 'attack' and 'threatened' to describe their sense of vulnerability to the disease.

Some interviewees' sentences tailed-off, or they found themselves struggling for words. One interviewee, whose apprehension was quite characteristic, could barely finish her sentences:

> With breast cancer, you know, you've got much more of a chance of picking it up maybe, than some of the other ... I know you might go blind, but you don't think like that. Whereas you think 'oh, breast cancer ... scary'.

Similarly, one woman who had filled in a questionnaire simply wrote 'sorry – would rather not answer' next to the question 'How do you feel about breast cancer?' For many of my research subjects words and even metaphors escape them – they are simply unable to articulate their concern about this illness. With this in mind, it is important to understand that worry about breast cancer is, in many respects, a thoroughly *contemporary* kind of dread.

In what sociologists describe as a risk society, or a culture of fear we may come to view ourselves as peculiarly susceptible to seemingly all-pervasive threats and hidden risks.[6] Risk is surely felt to be even more pernicious and alienating when it is perceived to issue from one's own body. As a 21-year-old interviewee explained,

> [e]very time you get a headache you're like 'oh, what's wrong?' I think everybody's like that these days. Ev-ery-time you read a magazine it's like symptoms of this, symptoms of that. What to do if you get migraines. And you've got a brain tumour and you're going to die. And it's just scaring you. You hear stories, you know 'I didn't have symptoms then a prawn sandwich nearly killed me'. *Everywhere you go you're threatened by it.* (Emphasis added.)

Whilst this young woman feels scared (that word again) about a range of apparently unavoidable diseases, she also feels threatened by the various scare stories she has heard or read about which seem to face her, as she says, everywhere she goes. (And, as something of an aside here, we might also note that it is not merely the constant stream of scare stories which troubles this woman, but also her apparent inability to discount any of these stories, and her related inability to discern which expert is telling her the truth). For this interviewee, and several others besides, glossy women's magazines constitute a central source of information about breast cancer – she remarks on the exhausting range of symptoms ('symptoms of this, symptoms of that') presented to her in these magazines. It would seem that this particular type of media has played an important role in stirring up young women's worry about breast cancer (see Desiderio, 2004, Chapter 4; Furedi, 1997; Giddens, 1991; and Lupton, 1999 for discussions on the media's role in promoting a risk consciousness).

This interviewee was in fact so alarmed by magazine articles about the possible link between the contraceptive pill and breast cancer, that she consulted a leaflet produced by a breast cancer charity. Indeed, literature produced by cancer charities is another important source of advice about breast cancer; it can be accessed on the Internet and may well seem to be more reliable and accurate than media reports. Unfortunately, in many instances, the literature produced by cancer charities is more likely to increase, rather than alleviate, women's fear about breast cancer. Cancer Research UK, for example, provides information on 18 'definite risk' factors for breast cancer as well as a large number of unproven risk factors.[7] These 'definite risks' include getting older, drinking too much alcohol, being overweight and post-menopausal, underweight and pre-menopausal, and being tall. This dizzying and confusing list of risk factors also includes the possible effects of radiation emitted during mammogram procedures. It is reasonable to suggest that women who are already acutely aware of their vulnerability might take this as a disincentive to attend screenings. More generally speaking, it seems unlikely that those caught up in an emotive campaign would be able to keep a sense of proportion about these threats to their health, to be able to judge the relative risk of these factors objectively.

Indeed, it is primarily the tenor of media articles and charities' reports, rather than the accumulation and dissemination of scientific data, that has stirred up a sense of worry about breast cancer in today's society. Confusing scientific evidence may add to women's consternation, but it is the *tone* of reports, in particular, the inference that breast cancer is inescapable, which has fostered a sense of dread about the disease. This representation of breast cancer as an unavoidable threat should be seen in terms of the wider cultural context, one that makes many acutely aware that they are always *potential victims*. As Ulrich Beck puts it, in the risk society, 'one is no longer concerned with attaining something good, but rather with preventing the worst'

(Beck, 1992, p. 49). In this cultural context, the breast cancer awareness campaign speaks of a more general perception that the world in which we live is somehow dangerous, that it poses considerable and inescapable threats to our individual existence. Nancy D. Vineburgh inadvertently implies this in a recent article in which she proposes that the pink-ribbon campaign serves as a model for a terrorism-awareness campaign (Vineburgh, 2004). Vineburgh sees the pink-ribbon campaign as wholly successful as a means of alerting the public to hidden dangers. Vineburgh's supposition that the structure, tone, and ethos of the pink ribbon campaign would be easily transposed into a terrorist awareness campaign is entirely understandable; the breast cancer awareness campaign recommends constant vigilance, preparation for a sudden, indiscriminate attack, and awareness that 'it could easily be me'.

Women are, for example, frequently informed that they or their loved ones are likely to fall ill sometime soon. A report by Action Cancer describes the breast cancer death toll as equivalent to 'a family losing a mum, or a sister, or a wife on an almost daily basis'. A recent mail-shot sent out by Cancer Research UK addresses the reader with the suggestion that, 'we all know of someone's mother, daughter, sister or close friend whose life has been touched by this disease'. Overall, the main message of the campaign is that breast cancer affects 'people just like you', as one leaflet produced by Cancer Research UK put it.[8] Bearing in mind that the breast cancer awareness campaign is aimed at young women, this is a particularly misleading and pernicious message: none of the interviewees I spoke to realised that the vast majority of those suffering from breast cancer are post-menopausal women. Though none had developed breast cancer themselves, and only one had known anybody who had developed the illness, they were convinced that the illness was pervasive and indiscriminately affected young and old. '*Everybody* knows someone who's either had [breast] cancer or died from it', one woman commented, a sentiment that echoes Cancer Research UK's claim that 'we all know of someone' who has been affected by breast cancer. Another interviewee claimed that 'almost everyone is affected' by breast cancer at some point, whilst another suggested that there would be 'two or three people who have been affected by breast cancer' in each of her university seminar groups. It is perhaps unsurprising, given such comments, that most of my research participants believed breast cancer to be far more prevalent than is actually the case. For example, 77 per cent of my research subjects overestimated, often grossly, the number of deaths from breast cancer every year in the UK; 37 per cent put the figure at more than one hundred thousand; and 10 per cent (worryingly) put the figure at two million or more.[9]

Femininity in the breast cancer awareness campaign

The breast cancer awareness campaign's suggestion that women ought to be constantly conscious of their bodies and supposedly impending illness reiterates a deeply conventional view of women as inherently sickly. This conception of femininity has been widely criticised by feminists,[10] not least of all by those involved in the Women's Health Movement (Bass and Howes, 1992, p. 3). Breast cancer has received attention from feminists seeking to criticise the medicalisation of women's bodies and to challenge the conception of women as inherently sickly beings. Ann Oakley, for example, has argued that the prescription of the drug tamoxifen to healthy women at genetic risk of developing breast cancer is a further example of the medical establishment's attempt to regulate women's bodies[11] (Oakley, 1993, Chapter 15). Wilkinson and Kitzinger have criticised the self-help resources available to breast cancer sufferers, suggesting that this literature represents women as 'passive victims' (Wilkinson and Kitzinger, 1994, p. 128). These authors also highlight that, 'the experience of breast cancer is clearly influenced by the cultural emphasis on breasts as objects of male sexual interest and male sexual pleasure' (ibid., p. 125). Indeed, when discussing breast cancer we are also discussing notions of female beauty and femininity; as Susan Garfinkel puts it, 'ideas about breast cancer' are, by virtue of the cultural connotations of breasts in our culture, 'ideas about ... femaleness' (Garfinkel, 1999, p. 82).

Surprisingly few of these feminist critiques have discussed the breast cancer awareness campaign, one of the most influential sources of 'ideas about breast cancer' in today's society is an exception (Desiderio, 2004, is an exception to this). Yet the campaign offers fascinating insights into the treatment of the disease in the culture and, more generally, ideas about femininity in contemporary society. We might note, for example, that the campaign encourages women to see their potential victimhood as giving them access to a private language of suffering. Breast cancer is often represented in the campaign as 'the cross women have to bear' (charities' mail-shots, for example, are addressed knowingly to 'the woman of the house', and articles suggest that 'breast cancer should be close to every woman's heart'[12]).

In other ways, too, the breast cancer awareness campaign represents women as distinctly mystical and unknowable. In an article for the 2003 edition of *Pink Ribbon* magazine, for example, Sarah Parkinson urges doctors to be 'more aware that, as women we live with the cycles of our bodies, month in month out – and that, just maybe, we might be right'. However legitimate Parkinson's criticism of medical practitioners is, her assumption that 'as women' we possess a self-awareness that makes us unknowable to doctors underscores the notion that 'we' are simply different from 'them'. It is difficult to see how the concretisation of this binary opposition helps to expel essentialist assumptions about women from medical practices. Moreover, this conception encourages women to celebrate their apparently superior skills of self-awareness, and to enjoy and cherish their position outside of the public sphere of medical knowledge.

In fact, there are a number of ways in which the breast cancer awareness campaign perpetuates a curiously conventional notion of femininity. Even a cursory glance at the campaign reveals this. We can buy make-up, sexy underwear, jewellery, and low-fat chocolates to show our awareness of breast cancer (and, of course, adhere to the norms of femininity). Companies' advertisements for breast cancer awareness products advise women to 'flaunt [their] femininity', 'look sensational' and suggest that their products will 'leave you feeling like the most beautiful person in the world'.[13] In the glossy women's magazines produced for the campaign, advertisements for skin creams, clothes, shampoos, bras, and make-up feature alongside articles on the most fashionable breast cancer awareness products. Overall, the inference readers of these magazines are likely to draw is that breast cancer is a thoroughly feminine disease, a point that the cultural critic Barbara Ehrenreich also makes (see Ehrenreich in *The Times*, 8 December 2001, Features). Interestingly, several interviewees viewed the disease in this way. Breast cancer is a 'womanly thing' one told me, a sentiment that was echoed by another interviewee who suggested that breast cancer is 'very feminine'. 'The word [cancer] is a very soft sounding name', she went on to tell me, 'I always associate cancer with women. I can accept women getting it, it just doesn't seem right for men to get such ...'. The worrying implication of this is that breast cancer may come to be seen as an integral aspect of 'what it means to be a woman'. Indeed, it is significant that a number of my interviewees had been given their pink ribbons by their mothers and viewed this act as something akin to a rite of passage, as a means of gaining access to femininity.

In this context, it is perhaps unsurprising that the breast cancer awareness campaign often celebrates the shapely female form, and in particular, breasts. Charities' posters use images of women's (in-tact, shapely) chests as focal-points and articles in magazines devoted to breast cancer awareness discuss the power and pleasure gained from having big breasts. In a particularly thoughtless move, Breast Cancer Care decided to allow the sports bra company, LessBounce to sponsor its 'Pink Aerobics in the Park' event. Leaflets and posters sent out for the event show a cartoon of a buxom young woman looking down and smiling at her secured breasts as she carries out her exercises.

Of course, breast cancer patients are unlikely to feel cheered by the breast cancer awareness campaign's emphasis on beauty, breasts, fitness, and feminine charms. Indeed, instead of challenging the notion that women with breast cancer become asexual and unfeminine, the campaign helps to perpetuate the assumption that 'real' women look pretty, dress up, and have a full cleavage. Possibly the most worried pink-ribbon wearer I interviewed told me 'I do worry about getting breast cancer, you know ... I wouldn't want to lose my ... you know'. The irony is that, once again, the breast cancer awareness campaign probably increases this interviewee's fear of the disease, rather than allaying it. By playing on the fears women have of being stripped of their femininity, the breast cancer awareness campaign helps create a climate of nagging worry.

Conclusion

This chapter has attempted to provide a critical evaluation of the British breast cancer awareness campaign. I have suggested that the campaign is likely to stir up and accentuate women's worry about breast cancer, and pointed to the wider cultural context out of which this fear has emerged. I also argued that the campaign promotes a particular conception of femininity, one that represents women as sickly, body conscious, beautiful, and buxom. This is a rather pernicious element of the campaign, considering breast cancer sufferers' incapacity to adhere to conventional norms of femininity. Moreover, it is possible that the climate of nagging worry about breast cancer may in fact deter women from obtaining medical attention for a suspected tumour. In a recent study in which women were questioned about their reasons for seeking medical help for breast cancer symptoms, 5.3 per cent of the participants cited fear as a barrier to seeking care (Lauver, 1995, p. 31). Another piece of research explores mammography-related anxiety amongst women, apparently now a key reason for women missing appointments for this procedure. According to the authors of this report, anxiety about breast cancer has risen steadily in recent years, and 'the fear of discovering breast cancer generates most mammography-related anxiety' (Baukje and Schapps, 2001, pp. 10–14).

It is also unlikely that cultivating a sense of worry about the illness is particularly health promoting for those women who do not have breast cancer. The practice of worrying has come to be subsumed into young female pink-ribbon wearers' everyday lives in ways that are at once fascinating and deeply troubling. These women's fear has manifested itself in burdensome routines and gestures (compulsive self-examination or wearing a pink ribbon, for example) which speak of a nagging, everyday sense of worry which refuses to be resolved.

8
The Commercialisation of Charity and the Commodification of Compassion

Ribbon wearers' attitudes towards charity

Bearing in mind that many pink-ribbon wearers feel worried about breast cancer, it is unsurprising that they see their charitable donations as contributing to a fund that they are likely to make use of themselves in the future. Over a quarter of the interviewees, all of whom wore the pink ribbon, saw charity in this way. 'Some people don't really believe in what they're investin' ... 'I mean *giving* to', one female teacher in her mid-20s told me, her slip revealing that she sees charity as a way of saving for future medical needs. Another female interviewee was emphatic that she 'believed in' charity, because 'everyone needs help at some point'. She wore both the pink and the red ribbons, and believed that she was at significant risk of developing HIV and breast cancer. Speaking about the possibility of contracting HIV herself, she told me, '*I* would want treatment if it was there. And so, therefore, I'm quite happy to give money to it [the AIDS awareness campaign], because I think that ... anyone could be attacked'. Another interviewee was similarly motivated by a belief that she would need to rely upon charity-funded services and research in the future. There is no point, she said, in thinking 'it will never happen to me', because, 'what if it *did* happen to you and you always passed that box and never put money in? And now it's happening to you. Before you didn't care, and *now* it's happening to you'. This interviewee described her donations as 'funeral insurance', a slip of the tongue that not only revealed a deep sense of pessimism about her health, but also echoed other interviewees' suggestions that charity constitutes a kind of insurance scheme.

137

Expressing high levels of self-interestedness, these three female interviewees also reported the deepest and most consistent involvement in charitable organisations. Two had participated in a number of charitable events and had done voluntary work, and all three gave generously and frequently to charities. These women were actively involved in charity work to a degree that seemed to contradict their rather sterile conception of charity as a personal investment fund. This was one of the particularly engaging riddles thrown up by my research, one that I saw at first in terms of the cultural contradictions of femininity: in our culture the 'good' woman is both self-interested (concerned about her appearance, health, body) *and* selfless (willing to put others' needs before her own). Did this gender double-bind explain these female interviewees' behaviour? On closer inspection of their accounts, I came across a further clue. All of these women expressed significant fear of falling ill: could their involvement in charity, I wondered, be explained in terms of a displaced desire to guard against ill-health?

Standard typologies of donor motives are not able to pick up on such ambiguous features of human behaviour, nor do they take into account the socio-political context in which acts of charity take place. Interviewees' comments about insurance and private investment in health might be seen to reflect a particular social context in which the state plays an increasingly limited role in providing welfare services. It was the charity sector, rather than the state, that was seen as the ideal provider of welfare by interviewees, though they were by no means acritical of charities. Indeed, what was particularly striking was that research participants (both red- and pink-ribbon wearers) regularly compared charities to companies, often so as to highlight the unfavourable techniques employed by the former. Underpinning such comments was a belief that charities should attempt to resemble companies, a view that reflects institutional pressures on charities to become more commercially oriented. As we saw in Chapter 2, the so-called contract culture which emerged in the 1980s, a situation in which charities were forced to compete with other charities and service providers from the private sector, was fundamentally oriented towards making charities subject to market forces. The various marketing techniques developed by charities around this time have demonstrated (not least of all to those in charge of charities' fundraising operations) that effective branding and stylish advertising campaigns garner support and, of course, donations. Such techniques also encourage the conflation of charity and big business; this was clearly the case for the young female ribbon wearer I interviewed who used the words 'charity' and 'company' interchangeably.

In this respect, a strenuous marketing campaign can help a charity to acquire the gloss and cachet of a commercial organisation, which in turn helps to deflect the distrust many express about charities. Indeed, half of the ribbon wearers I interviewed expressed a lack of trust in charities, and only two expressed positive views about charitable organisations. 'I give to my church', one young woman told me when I asked her which charities she gave to apart from the AIDS awareness campaign, 'and then I'd rather interact with a homeless guy on the street than give to a charity where I don't know where my money's going'. Expressing a similarly pessimistic view of charitable organisations, another young female interviewee commented that 'you see people on the street and you think maybe you'd give them money ... [but] you're never actually sure if they are giving the money back [to the charity they are collecting for]'. This ribbon wearer suggested that she felt far more comfortable buying products from a well-known company, such as ASDA, a supermarket chain that sells breast cancer awareness products. 'I'd [have more of an intention] if I'm in ASDA and it's their pink week', she told me, "cos I know at least part of it is going to ... at least some of it's going to [the charity]'.

Several interviewees also criticised charities' street collectors whom they felt to be 'intrusive', as one 31-year-old male participant put it. 'When people are shaking their cans, you just feel like ... "go away" ...' another interviewee told me. This sentiment was echoed by four other interviewees, one of whom told me that

> if you give some money it gets rid of these people. Because they sort of stand there shaking their cans at you as if to say 'come on, cough up!' ... It's sometimes quite intimidating. People sometimes feel as though they have to give.

For this interviewee street collecting constituted 'begging'; charity, she told me 'should be an optional thing', instead, she feels that it's an 'obligation'.

In contrast to this, several participants viewed the awareness ribbon as an effective fund-raising tool. A central reason for this positive attitude to the ribbon is that it is sold in high-street stores and there-fore the ribbon wearer does not feel as though she is pressurised into buying one. As one interviewee put it, 'there's no pressure to do any-thing. There's a choice whether you want to [buy a ribbon or not]'. Sold in shops, rather than touted by street collectors, the awareness ribbon seems less like a charity token and more like a product. In this context, it is telling that a significant number of interviewees could not remember which charities they had bought their ribbons from, though most could remember the store they purchased the ribbon in. At times more akin to a fashion accessory than a charity token, the awareness ribbon is as susceptible to shifts in trends as women's bags and hairstyles. The red ribbon was supplanted by the pink ribbon during the late 1990s as 'the ribbon of the moment', just as the recent trend for empathy wristbands suggests a further shift in the deeply fashionable practice of showing compassion. In this way, ribbon wearing allows for a very fleeting expression of empathy for a partic-ular group of sufferers. I asked one interviewee, who had worn a number of ribbons and charitable tokens, whether she saw herself as a supporter of the causes for which she wore tokens. 'I wouldn't go that far', she replied.

This attitude to charity was also evident at a Pink Aerobics event I attended. Pink Aerobics is a series of aerobics classes held across the UK to raise money for Breast Cancer Care. I attended the session held in Canterbury in late September 2004, with the aim of gaining a better understanding of why people participate in these events. The partic-ipants, the vast majority of whom were women, had been asked to dress in pink, presumably in order to create a sense of togetherness. However, one of my first impressions of this event was that there was a distinct lack of solidarity between the women: people arrived and stayed in small groups, and the instructor who led the aerobics ses-sion rarely made mention of the breast cancer awareness campaign, the cause we had all (ostensibly) come together to raise money for. This isolation was compounded by the fact that aerobics is a highly individualised activity that limits contact between fellow exercisers.

A lack of fellow feeling was also evident in the participants' attitude towards me. Even before they knew I was a social researcher, they seemed distinctly unfriendly; throughout the course of the event I attempted to strike up conversations with them, but to no avail. When, at the end of the session, I was identified as a social researcher by one of the aerobics instructors, I found it even harder to gain the participants' attention. Many of them seemed more interested in buying merchandise from the stall set up in the hall by the sport's bra company sponsoring the event than speaking to me about the causes of breast cancer, the treatment of patients, or government-funding for research. One group of women refused to take part in a (short) interview because they wanted to buy something from the stall (the queue for breast cancer awareness products had become so long at this point that they were worried they might not get to buy the t-shirts they wanted).

Whilst the commercialisation of charity is welcomed by many − surely the money these women spent on their t-shirts contributed to important research? −it does little to actually increase understanding and knowledge about particular causes. Participants at the Pink Aerobics event were handed plastic bags full of free gifts and advertising from companies. The bag contained a pack of vitamins from Wellwoman, a fruit and nut bar from Frumba, a handful of chocolates from Swiss Delice, a small can of deodorant from Nivea, promotional literature from the sport's bra company Lessbounce (the sponsors of the event), an offer for free day membership at an LA Fitness gym − and one small leaflet from Breast Cancer Care which contained information on the services they provided.

Overall, the Pink Aerobics event seemed to be aimed primarily at encouraging participants to buy merchandise. Interestingly, the woman on the stall selling Lessbounce's wares told me that it was in fact the company that had come up with the idea for the event. It certainly seemed as though Breast Cancer Care was sponsoring an event organised by Lessbounce, rather than the other way round. In a society in which charitable organisations are seen as untrustworthy 'beggars', company sponsorship may well effectively gloss over the apparently unappealing characteristics of charity. However, company sponsorship has also helped transform charity into nothing more than a profit-seeking exercise. Companies, as we might expect, have no real inclination to improve breast cancer services or treatment − their primary aim is to find and sponsor a charity that shares a particular 'marketing territory'.

Feelings of compassion

The backdrop to such developments in the charity sector is a culture of compassion that has emerged in the last quarter of a century

(Nolan, 1998; Wagner, 2000; Furedi, 2004; West, 2004). For some commentators the increased interest in charity over the past decade is a result of a rising tide of empathy. I would emphasise the importance of examining the *cultural meaning* of compassion, in order to ascertain the nature of this relationship. Of particular interest is the way in which compassion has come to signify emotional authenticity, 'realness', humanness even – not as a means of proving one's religious worth or standing in the community, but *as a means of affirming one's self-identity*. Displaying compassion is no longer a mere attribute, it is an expression of one's identity, one that has become inextricably bound up with fashion, consumerism, and celebrity – aspects of the culture more commonly used for self-identification. 'You can come here and you can see causes that mean something to celebrities and if you wish to you can donate directly to that cause', Kevin Bacon tells us on his *Six Degrees of Separation* website. 'Or', he adds, 'you can become a celebrity for your cause and create a celebrity badge for yourself'. Launched in early 2007, the website allows us to click on images of individual celebrities (self-created or otherwise) and read a list of charities they support, along with an explanation of why they support these causes. We are directly invited to self-identify with the celebrities on this site – from Ricky Gervais to Nicole Kidman – or become celebrities for our own causes; carve out, in other words, an identity for ourselves based on our support for certain charitable causes. The injunction to 'show you care' is everywhere in our culture. 'Denimstrate you care' urges the Jeans for Genes appeal, a campaign seeking to help children with genetic disorders. 'Caring girls are proud to give support' claims Breakthrough Breast Cancer. 'Prince Charles has a caring heart', Ivan Corea comments in an article on the National Autistic Society's website about the Prince's interest in Autism Awareness Year.[1]

It is hardly surprising, then, that the vast majority of those who filled in questionnaires for this research (92 per cent) viewed other ribbon wearers as compassionate and caring. By extension, of course, respondents were implying that they themselves were to be seen as compassionate individuals. For some, being compassionate has become an integral aspect of their identities. One interviewee, for example, had worn a red ribbon for 12 years, and felt a strong sense of commitment to the AIDS awareness campaign:

> I've supported that cause [AIDS] for a long time and I want to continue supporting that. I feel almost as if chopping and changing

from one to [another cause] would send the wrong message ...
I think the reason I kept with the AIDS ribbon is for the fact that it
kind of signifies something that I started doing ... I wanted to show
some degree of solidarity, rather than chopping and changing.

This 31-year-old man saw the symbol as something that confirms the
underlying continuity in his identity as a person who is deeply concerned about certain causes. Originally, however, this expression of
compassion helped bolster a sense of individuality. 'Choosing to wear
the ribbon was something I did for myself' he told me, and added that,
as a young man, wearing the ribbon had been one of the first such
decisions he had made: 'It becomes an individual choice, rather than
something you do in groups – you know, growing up you do things
in groups. And this suggests something that I chose to do myself'.

For others too, showing compassion is a conscious act of self-
identification. 'I'm into charity', a wristband wearer I met on the bus
told me, as if caring about others' suffering was comparable to being
'into' a pop group or television series. She went on to tell me that she
would wear wristbands 'up her arm' if she could, and that she 'had
her eye on' the NSPCC wristband. Although rarely expressed in
such fatuous terms, showing oneself to be compassionate was clearly
important for a number of ribbon wearers. One of my interviewees,
a 21-year-old woman, told me that her family 'always call [her] the
caring one':

[a]nd at Christmas they always ask me, 'oh ... what have you done
this year?' And I'll be like 'well, I went to America to work with
some kids for eight weeks over the summer and, you know, I came
back and did this and that ...'.

Heavily involved in voluntary work, planning a career as a carer, this
young woman's identity revolves around her sense of compassion for
others. Indeed, she was most animated during our interview when
she was telling stories about the voluntary work she has done, recount-
ing with pleasure the ways in which she became involved with certain groups or charities. It is particularly telling that she saw ribbon
wearing in terms of, 'trying to help ... in my own way, in the biggest
way that I can, really'.

Most, however, had no such stories to tell about their involvement in charitable organisations, though they nonetheless spoke of

themselves and their relationship to particular causes in emotional terms. Interviewees spoke of the need to be 'touched' or 'reached' by a campaign and frequently referred to the ribbon as a symbol that elicited emotional responses ('it's a powerful symbol', one young woman told me, whilst others spoke of the ribbon 'affecting' them). Interestingly, these emotional responses to awareness campaigns were rarely directed towards specific sufferers. Instead, ribbon wearers voiced a generalised expression of empathy for such amorphous groups as breast cancer patients or those who 'die young'.

The vagueness of these expressions of compassion was not simply due to ribbon wearers' lack of contact with sufferers of a given illness (after all, we would not wish to deny the human capacity to empathise with people we have never met). A much more important obstacle was participants' lack of knowledge and understanding about the illnesses for which they wore a ribbon. It is difficult, we might reasonably surmise, to offer a sustained and precise expression of compassion if one has no understanding of the suffering endured by, for example, breast cancer or AIDS patients.

It is also interesting to note that a significant number of ribbon wearers are given their ribbons by others. In this respect, the ribbon wearer's sense of compassion may not have developed organically, and, indeed, may not be forthcoming. Out of the 20 ribbon wearers I interviewed, four had been given ribbons by friends or family members, two had been required to wear a ribbon as part of a work uniform, two had received free ribbons (one through the post from a breast cancer charity and one at a concert), and one had worn a ribbon because she was part of a school campaign. Overall, only 11 out of the 20 interviewees had personally chosen to buy and wear a ribbon.

Of particular interest were the two women who had been required to wear a pink ribbon as part of their work uniform. One even described the ribbon as 'part of the work dress' for breast cancer awareness week. The other interviewee told me that her participation in a work-sponsored breast cancer awareness event had initially been half-hearted, but that over time she had begun to feel that it was her moral duty to support the campaign:

> [y]ou have to all get involved with raising the money, you know for the breast cancer awareness ... And it's just like a natural progression. And I guess that probably came first and then you get to

thinking, actually, you really should be helping. Whereas first and foremost it's like 'you've got to help out' and you think 'oh right, ok, great', it's like part of your job or what have you [*sic*].

Less obviously coerced into wearing the ribbon, the four interviewees who had been given the ribbon by friends and family felt a rather different sense of obligation. Interestingly, three interviewees who were given ribbons had received pink ribbons as gifts from their mothers. 'My mum's *always* worn the ribbon', one young woman told me; 'I think she was the one who got me my first one'. Another told me within one minute of starting the interview that the pink ribbon pin she wore was given by her mother ('she's a Macmillan nurse', she added proudly). When I asked her why it was particularly special for a mother to give a daughter a pink ribbon, she replied, 'it's because it's breast cancer, it's a womanly thing', and added that she saw charity giving, in general, as a deeply feminine gesture:

[w]omen like to pride themselves on being good people. (Adopts squeaky voice) 'Look at me ... Like me! You've got to like me, I give to charity and everything, I'm nice!'

In this context, we might see the pink ribbon as a symbol of femininity, and the act of giving the pink ribbon as a means of passing on feminine values (of course, it is particularly telling that it is mothers who give their daughters the ribbon). In his study of gift giving, Marcel Mauss argues that a gift is given with the expectation that the receiver will be obliged to make some kind of return on that gift. 'In theory', Mauss writes, gifts are 'voluntary'. 'In reality, they are given and reciprocated obligatorily' (Mauss, 2004, p. 3). Criticising Malinowski's argument that a gift from a husband to his wife is an example of a 'pure gift' in which no return gift is expected, Mauss points out that 'precisely one of the most important facts reported by Malinowski ... consists of comparing the *mapula*, the 'constant' payment made by the man to his wife, as a kind of salary for sexual services rendered' (ibid., p. 93). Similarly, we might reasonably suggest that a mother's gift of a pink ribbon contains the implicit expectation that her daughter will foster certain feminine attributes associated with the symbol (such as health- and body-consciousness, self-awareness, compassion).

There are other ways in which ribbon wearers might feel compelled to wear a ribbon, even if they seem to have freely chosen to buy and wear the symbol. A significant number of interviewees who had bought the ribbon themselves nonetheless expressed a sense of obligation to do so. 'I was in a pub and everyone was wearing one', one interviewee told me. Two others bought the ribbon to distinguish their sense of belonging to groups of mourners. Several spoke of wanting to show family members that they had 'done the right thing' and given to charity: 'if I've got the ribbon on', one young woman told me, 'my mum already knows I've done it [given to charity]. My aunt knows I've done it. My cousin knows I've done it. My granddad knows I've done it'. Others expressed a similar desire to fit in. Asked what she thought of other ribbon wearers, one interviewee replied that if she was wearing a ribbon, she would think, 'oh cool, I'm part of something'. Another replied that 'if I wasn't wearing one, I'd probably think, "oh, I'll have to find out where they are"'. 'I do think you have peer pressure', another interviewee conceded when I asked her whether she felt obliged to wear the ribbon, 'you know, where *everyone's* wearing it'.

Indeed, showing compassion seems to have become something of a moral imperative in today's society. The UN's World AIDS campaign in 2001, for example, used the tag line 'I Care ... Do You?' in a bid to shame people into adopting a compassionate outlook. Even academics studying charitable behaviour reinforce the idea that not giving to charity is immoral behaviour that needs to be corrected wherever possible. Sally Hibbert, for example, argues that those who 'argue about whether it is an individual's responsibility to help, rather than that of the government', or suggest that charity should be the preserve of 'older people or others with more money' are adopting 'a technique known as denial of responsibility'.[2] Such people have undergone a process of 'neutralisation', Hibbert explains, a term 'used ... to explain how juvenile delinquents insulate themselves from self-blame and the condemnation of others'.[3] In a culture of compassion, those who choose not to be charitable are judged to be deviant, maladjusted human beings.

The consequence of refusing to show compassion was represented to comic effect in a 1995 episode of *Seinfeld*, the hit US television comedy, in which Kramer is mobbed for refusing to wear a red ribbon during an AIDS rally.[4] Such an over-blown response to a refusal to wear a ribbon is by no means unusual. Celebrities who would not wear the red ribbon at awards ceremonies during the mid-1990s were 'actively harassed and even menaced', as a reporter for *The Mail on Sunday* put it:

> Deidre Hall, star of the daily soap opera Days of Our Lives, says that at one recent awards ceremony the ribbon-wielding zealots hounded her from the pre-show reception to the post-show Press conference. She says that one magazine even threatened to write about her ribbonless ways.
>
> (*The Mail on Sunday*, 11 July 1993, p. 9)

For the majority of ribbon wearers who aren't celebrities, the pressure to show themselves to be compassionate works in more subtle ways, through, for example, the rhetoric employed by charities, peer pressure, or the persistent suggestions in the culture that demonstrating compassion makes one a more 'real' human being. Placing oneself outside of this culture of compassion is tremendously difficult: ribbons are sent through the post, sold in shops, clubs, pubs, schools, colleges, given away with newspapers, and even incorporated into work uniforms. Unable to ignore the ribbon and its related marketing, accepting the legitimacy of the ribbon as a symbol of compassion seems like a 'natural progression', as one of my interviewees put it.

Yet, ribbon campaigns tend to promote a very narrow conception of compassion, one in which, paradoxically, sufferers are rarely given much consideration. Indeed, the ribbon does not necessitate any reciprocal relationship with any identifiable person or group. 'When one pays money one is completely quits', Simmel noted some one hundred years ago (Simmel, 'Prostitution', 1971, p. 121). He was writing about prostitution, but his observations about monetary transactions also bear upon ribbon wearing. Whilst we might not want to suggest that ribbon wearers pay to ensure that their relationship to sufferers remains impersonal, as a man might pay a prostitute for a 'no strings attached' sexual relationship, buying a ribbon does appear to be an act curiously devoid of genuine empathy for others. The commodification of the ribbon − and the commercialisation of charity more generally − has surely contributed to this.[5] Charities in contemporary society have cashed in on the selling power of compassion, as have the numerous companies that sponsor ribbon campaigns. In so doing, they have transformed compassion itself into a commodity.

Conclusion

This chapter opened with the observation that many pink-ribbon wearers see their donations as contributions to a fund which they themselves will benefit from at some point in the future. For these participants, charity was something akin to a personal investment scheme or health insurance. They were not, however, acritical about charity. Indeed, participants (both red- and pink-ribbon wearers) regularly expressed more trust in companies than charities, and believed that the latter would be improved if they simply let donors choose to make donations freely, as companies appear to let us choose products.

The second half of the chapter looked more deeply at ribbon wearers' sense of compassion. Here I argued that my participants' expressions of empathy tended to be rather vague and insubstantial, which may be due to their distance from sufferers of a given illness and their lack of knowledge about certain diseases. We should also note that a significant number of ribbon wearers do not personally choose to wear the symbol, but are given ribbons as gifts, and for this reason a feeling of compassion may not have developed organically. Many ribbon wearers are given ribbons by friends and family members, or are required to wear a ribbon as part of a campaign at school or at work.

Indeed, it is hard to ignore or avoid ribbon campaigns. Not only this, but a refusal to wear a ribbon is often seen to be a deeply suggestive of a lack of humanity or authenticity. In this respect, showing compassion has become something of a moral imperative in contemporary society. This by no means entails ribbon wearers' steadfast commitment to a particular cause. Indeed, most ribbon wearers reported a fleeting involvement in particular ribbon campaigns. As a consequence, ribbon wearers' support is rarely fixed to one particular cause long enough to transform into a focussed interest in a particular group of sufferers. As Bauman points out, whilst our search for identity in contemporary society speaks of a desire for stability and security,

> a fixed position amidst the infinity of possibilities is not an attractive prospect ... In our liquid modern times, when the free-floating, unencumbered individual is the popular hero, 'being fixed' − being 'identified' inflexibly and without retreat − gets an increasingly bad press.
>
> (Bauman, 2004, p. 29)

Showing compassion is a means of navigating the gap between a fixed identity and a fluid identity; nebulous, spontaneous, and deeply personal, emotions such as compassion obtain a more solid form when directed towards a specific campaign, though the level of commitment required does not extend much beyond a fleeting period of ribbon wearing.

What is surprising about this practice, directed as it is towards emotional authenticity, is that ribbon wearers' expressions of compassion are highly standardised. Like the aerobics and marathon fundraising events set up by breast cancer charities, ribbon wearing is an activity that seems highly individualised, but in fact requires adherence to a very specific code of behaviour and discourse. An important reason for this is that the discourse of compassion that accompanies the ribbon, a rhetoric that is so compelling as to make a refusal to accept its legitimacy tantamount to inhumanity, has transformed this emotion into a neat, marketable commodity, easily translated into pat phrases and easy gestures.

9
Conclusion

Ribbon wearing has a short but contested history. The practice originated in the USA, where the yellow ribbon, a symbol used to show
support for troops fighting in conflicts, is often seen as the symbol
that started the ribbon-wearing craze. Though various media accounts
trace the yellow ribbon back to the American Civil War, the first official
ribbon campaign involved the tying of yellow ribbons round trees in
1979, after 52 US embassy workers were captured in Iran. The yellow
ribbon re-emerged in the USA in 1991, during the conflict in the Gulf,
and it was the success of this campaign that prompted the emergence
of awareness ribbons, such as those worn for AIDS and breast cancer.
The yellow ribbon is a fundamentally conservative symbol in that it
suggests an acceptance of, if not support for, the nation's involvement in a given conflict. In this respect the yellow ribbon resembles
early British flag day tokens, such as those worn during the First
World War or the Armistice Day Poppy. Just as the yellow ribbon promotes support for the 'hard fought for' status quo, flag days promoted
a sense of belonging and a shared belief in the 'British way of life'. It
is especially striking that both the social practice of yellow-ribbon
tying and the early flag day events reiterated decidedly conventional
gender norms. In the former, women passively await the return of
their absent male loved ones who are fighting foreign aggressors, and
in the latter, women are conceived of as the repositories of national
virtue whilst men are represented as the active protectors of the nation.

In contrast, the descendents of the yellow ribbon – most notably the
red and pink awareness ribbons – symbolise a faintly oppositional
stance to mainstream society, rather than support for the status

quo; ribbon wearers are often interested in supporting groups that have been marginalised (AIDS patients, or female breast cancer sufferers, for example). In this respect, whilst flag day tokens and the yellow ribbon are, to use Rubinstein's terminology, *pro-social* tie-symbols, the later awareness ribbons are *anti-social* tie-symbols.

Whilst a comparison of early flag days and ribbon campaigns helps us to understand the development of charitable behaviour during the twentieth century, a comparison of the yellow-, red-, and pink-ribbon campaigns is also instructive. Taken together, these three campaigns show up an interesting trajectory in ribbon wearing practices. Of particular importance is the shift from using the ribbon to recognise particular loved ones to the use of the ribbon to express the wearer's personal, emotional meanings. This development occurred during the 1991 yellow-ribbon campaign and became increasingly prominent with the emergence of the red and then the pink ribbons. The changing meaning of the ribbon is underscored by the shifting site in which the symbolic meaning of the ribbon is created, and in particular the move away from tying the ribbon (as 'around the ole oak tree') to wearing the ribbon on the lapel. This reiterates the movement away from using the ribbon in an act that is ostensibly directed towards recognising, remembering or celebrating a particular loved one, to using the ribbon as an exhibition of the self and the emotions. The notion that the ribbon represents the wearer's awareness, particularly prominent after the emergence of the red-ribbon campaign, confirms the symbol's transformation into a repository of personal sentiments. The empathy wristband is a further step in this process. Unlike the ribbon, the wristband is worn on the body (rather than on clothes) and it is more obviously a personal belonging (like a piece of jewellery). The emergence of the wristband, in other words, is a further indication that 'showing awareness' is widely deemed to be a deeply personal gesture of self-awareness.

The personalisation of the ribbon's meaning might be seen in the context of a more general socio-historical process in which shared sources of symbolic meaning have become obsolete (see Chapter 2). Certainly, my research highlighted that ribbon wearers do not see the ribbon as inferring any shared worldview or belief system, but rather see the symbol as an expression of personal feelings of compassion and self-awareness. Even for those who used the ribbon for reasons other than to 'show awareness', the ribbon was seen to invoke deeply personal meanings. In its use as a commemorative symbol, for example, the ribbon is a private mourning symbol used by small family groups. In its use in public mourning rituals, the ribbon is often deemed to articulate a distinctive emotional response. Similarly, as a symbol of solidarity with homosexuals, the red ribbon not only serves as a means of affirming one's sense of belonging to the 'gay community', it is also deemed to be a gesture that constitutes a form of personal protest through self-identification. Even as a resource in community-action campaigns, tying a ribbon at once reinforces a collective ethos and constitutes personal action against government directives and policies.

However personal these uses of the ribbon seem, they are all shaped by social norms, codes of behaviour, and frames of meaning. Following Goffman, I have argued that we should recognise that even seemingly private acts of self-expression adhere to certain rules of self-presentation. We should also be alert to the ways in which gestures that appear distinctively individualistic might reflect social trends and cultural currents. Each of the uses of the ribbon mentioned above point to a wider socio-cultural context in which the desire for personal authenticity is underscored by the widespread distrust and repudiation of social authorities, from religious rituals to local government, from international organisations to formal protest movements. This socio-cultural context has fostered a certain attitude towards the relationship between the self and society, one that foregrounds the former and acknowledges the latter only in so much as it places unspeakable demands upon the self. In fact, despite the emphasis on private emotions and personal identity in our society, expressions of individuality are often strangely uniform. An instruction to 'just be yourself' – part of what Beck and Beck-Gernsheim see as a dominant social impulse towards individualisation – does not in itself ensure individuality. It may simply obscure the *standardisation* of expressions of the self. The contemporary project of 'showing awareness' is one of the most pertinent examples of this.

Amongst my research subjects, the most commonly articulated motivation for wearing a ribbon was to 'show awareness' of a given cause or disease (81 per cent of participants claimed to wear or have worn a ribbon for this reason). Yet, it is unclear what ribbon wearers' sense of awareness actually consists of: it does not constitute knowledge of a particular cause, nor does it necessitate any reciprocal relationship with those who suffer from a given illness or tragedy. Furthermore, 'showing awareness' does not entail any concerted action, nor does it require any consideration of the relationship between health and social, economic, and political factors. Indeed, illness itself tends to be the focus of awareness campaigns, not because it is the point at which social inequalities become most marked, but because it is believed to make victims of us all in one way or another. Nonetheless, interviewees sometimes spoke of ribbon wearing as something akin to an act of protest, though they found it difficult to articulate the aim of this gesture. Where they did speak of 'showing awareness' in terms of specific goals, they generally spoke of rather intangible, vague improvements, such as 'more visibility' for certain social groups or 'more funding'. In most cases, their sense of awareness constituted a rather vague and passive consciousness that a particular illness exists and causes suffering.

'Showing awareness' is often perceived by ribbon wearers to be a very personal gesture. Wearing a ribbon, a number of interviewees commented, is a matter of 'personal belief' in the validity of particular causes and, more generally speaking, the need to eliminate certain illnesses. Moreover, ribbon wearers often referred to their particular emotional responses to a given campaign (some spoke of the need to be 'touched' or 'reached' by a campaign, another described the ribbon as a 'powerful' symbol, others spoke about their sense of empathy for others). Such responses seem to confirm the existence of what Furedi refers to as 'feeling-based identities' (Furedi, 2004, p. 144). Indeed, the very idea of 'showing awareness' suggests an affective response: the practice is a demonstration of the ribbon wearer's sense of compassion, her sensitivity to certain causes and, more generally speaking, emotional authenticity. The compassionate identity adopted by ribbon wearers is shaped by a socially produced discourse of compassion, in which the exhibition of concern for others is represented as an integral aspect of emotional maturity. Regardless of frequent claims to the contrary, this identity is by no means freely chosen or individually created. Roughly a quarter of all participants (and nearly half of the interviewees) were given their ribbons by others, a gesture that contains the expectation of adherence to certain norms and a certain identity.

Another common feature of the identity adopted by those 'showing awareness' is a vague distrust of mainstream society (especially what is seen to be an impersonal, ineffective state government) and a lack of faith in overtly political means of bringing about social change. This aspect of 'showing awareness', along with other features of this practice, can be traced back to the countercultural period of the 1960s and 1970s. Following Daniel Bell's (1976) suggestion that a hedonistic, anti-rational cultural impulse became increasingly dominant during the twentieth century, it is reasonable to suggest that anti-authority values became particularly widespread during the 1960s counter-culture. During this period, the wish to distance the self from seemingly corrupting social institutions and the desire to obtain full and pure self-expression became especially pronounced. Contemporary society does not simply rearticulate countercultural values; my work suggests that we see the *extension* and *transfiguration* of the countercultural impulse in the contemporary culture, and the awareness campaigns of the 1990s, more specifically. Self-awareness, a celebrated trait during the counterculture, has come to be seen as a natural, unquestionably proper response to any disease, tragedy or social problem. Most importantly, perhaps, cynicism during the late stages of the counterculture about the possibility of bringing about social change has been transformed into a wholesale rejection of social critique in the politically neutral awareness campaigns of the 1990s. This might partially account for the fact that both the AIDS and the breast cancer awareness ribbons became popular *after* the UK and the US governments had accepted the need to tackle these health problems. Certainly, in the absence of political objectives, the awareness ribbon campaigns lack direction, focus, and impetus.

The rejection of a political framework reflects a more general attitude that lies behind ribbon wearing, in which a widespread distrust of social institutions is coupled with a belief that the self is the only level at which meaningful changes can be made. 'Showing awareness', after all, is an expression of *self*-awareness, one that might seem to typify the type of self-reflexivity that Giddens (1991) sees as a central trait of those living in late-modern societies. However, I have argued that awareness often manifests itself as worry about an illness, rather than rational self-scrutiny. Young women who wear the pink breast-cancer awareness ribbon exhibit particularly high levels of worry about the illness for which they wear a ribbon. These women experienced a nagging sense of worry that manifested itself in burdensome routines and gestures.

There are a number of possible explanations for these women's responses. We might see their fear of breast cancer in terms of a more general perception that our lives are fraught with inescapable dangers and hidden threats (as part of what sociologists refer to as a 'risk consciousness'). Young women are likely to be particularly susceptible to health scares; not only do women seem to be more concerned about health issues than men (Miles, 1991, p. 59), but femininity is widely associated with health-consciousness in our culture. Women should care about their bodies and health, the culture instructs us, even young women who are perfectly healthy. As a pink-wristband-wearing teenager I met on the train put it, 'it's a *good* thing that women are worried about their bodies'. The orthodox view that women are morally obliged to care about their health is difficult to resist, and this may well partly explain why the women I interviewed expressed such high levels of worry about their health.

We should also recognise that the British breast cancer awareness campaign is likely to have an important impact on women's perception of the disease. The campaign's lack of political objectives, for example, may well accentuate women's sense of powerlessness, leaving them without any clear course of action for tackling breast cancer. The ways in which the campaign represents illness and femininity may also contribute to feelings of worry about breast cancer. The campaign frequently suggests that young women – the target group of its corporate sponsors, but by no means the group most affected by breast cancer – should be constantly aware that they are at significant risk of developing the illness. Also of note is the breast cancer awareness campaign's promotion of a particular conception of femininity, one that represents women as sickly, body-conscious, beautiful and buxom. The campaign thus stirs up, rather than allays, fears that breast cancer strips women of their femininity.

Considering that many pink-ribbon wearers feel worried about breast cancer, it is unsurprising that they view their charitable donations as contributing to a fund which they themselves are likely to benefit from in the future. This is in keeping with a more general social climate in which welfare provision is increasingly seen as the individual's responsibility, charity has become a commercial enterprise, and the principle of consumer choice has come to dominate government policy. In such a social context, charities become increasingly interested in marketing their wares and services. In a certain sense, charities are simply responding to their market: the ribbon wearers I interviewed often expressed a greater level of trust in companies than in charities. Recognising the benefits of adopting a commercial orientation, charities have taken on corporate sponsors eager to develop a cause-related profile, adopted marketing tactics pioneered by companies, and launched themselves as brands. In this respect, the ribbon is a canny marketing tool that promotes recognition of a particular cause. In fact, the ribbon does little *beyond* promoting brand-name consciousness: pink-ribbon wearers, for example, know very little about breast cancer, but are often able to repeat advertising slogans.

Nonetheless, an incredible range of charities and groups make use of the ribbon, eager to benefit from the recognisability and kudos of the symbol. Indeed, compassion for numerous groups of victims – from AIDS sufferers to missing children – is represented in the same looped-ribbon motif. The ribbon's colour is the only point of variation in what has become a highly uniform symbol of personal sentiments. Similarly, compassion and awareness have been transformed into standardised responses in the awareness ribbon campaigns. Amongst the ribbon wearers I interviewed, awareness and compassion were regularly invoked, but rarely substantiated. Very few participants were able to tell me what their sense of awareness consisted of, though they nonetheless remained convinced of the efficacy of 'showing awareness'.

The ribbon's uniformity and the fixity of its meaning point to an underlying tension between the desire to obtain unhindered self-expression and the necessity of making the self knowable to others. By donning a ribbon, the wearer is first and foremost seeking to *demonstrate* her self and emotions. Yet, the fixity and broadness of the ribbon's meaning preclude any really spontaneous, complex feelings from being expressed and instead render self-expression standardised and uniform. In this way, the ribbon has in fact become an object that articulates the self and the emotions only vaguely and dispassionately.

Just as the ribbon is unconducive to meaningful self-expression, it is a poor means of relating to others – the real bind here is that the former can not be obtained without the latter. The desire to express the self is hindered by the ribbon wearer's failure to recognise her indebtedness to others. The lack of any relationship (reciprocal or imagined) between the ribbon wearer and the sufferer seriously undermines the possibility for self-expression. In the absence of this kind of relationship, the ribbon wearer's feelings towards the suffering other are rather diluted, vague and non-specific. The search for self-fulfilment and self-expression conceals our bonds to others and their importance in enabling the self to be understood and rendered authentic. Since Freud's rendering of the self as split between a repressive Ego and an instinctive Id, our involvement in society has been typically, but erroneously, viewed as hindering the articulation of the essential self. The terms in which we currently understand the self demand its articulation in a personalised form; but with this must come the recognition that an entirely private language precludes any meaningful articulation of the self at all. Though we might try to convince ourselves otherwise, *very little* is achieved through a personal gesture of awareness and support, least of all genuine self-awareness and compassion.

Appendix: Some Brief Notes on Methodology

In-depth interviews

My main research method was in-depth interviewing, although I also carried out two formal interviews with people who had helped set up ribbon campaigns. Of the 20 in-depth interviews I carried out, 13 were with female ribbon wearers and seven were with male ribbon wearers. All interviewees were white and middle class, and their average age was 26 years (the oldest was 41 and the youngest was 19). Whilst representativeness was a concern in this project, of greater concern was producing a vivid and detailed analysis. It was therefore important to find a group of research subjects who would be willing to discuss ribbon wearing at length. For this purpose, I used a volunteer and snowball sampling procedure to make contact with interviewees. As a result, all interviewees were from the South-East or London.

The information gathered from in-depth interviews has been used extensively in the book, to support claims made about the cultural meaning of the ribbon and in my discussions on compassion and worry, for example. My findings are presented in a more systematic fashion in Chapter 5, entitled, 'Symbolic Uses of the Ribbon'. Here I seek to categorise ribbon wearers' motivations for wearing a ribbon, though it is my hope that I have also managed to capture the more subtle features of their attitudes and behaviour. The analysis is presented as a typology, a system of categorisation most often adopted by quantitative researchers dealing with large samples. Though sometimes (and often quite rightly) seen as a reductive means of presenting findings, this format is used simply as a means of focussing my discussion.

Within the parameters of the typology, there is the possibility to consider the more nuanced aspects of ribbon wearers' behaviour and beliefs. After all, in-depth interviews provide an ideal means of gathering detailed and personal information from participants. For this reason, it is an ideal method for exploring the extent to which ribbon wearing inheres in a particular identity. This method also enabled me to gain insights into ribbon wearers' motivations and aims, their understanding of 'awareness', how they view their relationship to sufferers, their attitude towards charities, and what they consider ribbon wearing to achieve. Most interviews were based on these main points of discussion, which helped to make my data relatively easy to analyse and compare. At the same time, however, the interviews were sufficiently unstructured for interviewees to influence the line of discussion. This afforded participants the possibility of raising points outside of my research agenda and, on many occasions, such admissions were tremendously illuminating. It was in this way that

I gained insights into, amongst other things, the use of the ribbon as a mourning symbol and the conception of breast cancer as a 'feminine' illness.

Making interviewees feel comfortable to speak at length about their views and actions was essential for the successful completion of this research. It was during these moments that I came to understand more clearly the basis of ribbon wearers' behaviour, their attitudes and beliefs. Some interviewees would speak, practically uninterrupted, for many minutes, and it was during these monologues that they grew confident enough to express themselves more fully and reflect upon their motivations for wearing a ribbon (a process of rationalisation that was often in itself revealing). These monologues were also often peppered with fascinating slips of the tongue. For example, having referred to a particular charity campaign throughout the interview, one participant suddenly substituted the word 'charity' with 'company'. Another interviewee intended to describe her charitable donations as medical insurance, but instead used the term 'funeral insurance', a slip that revealed a deep sense of worry about breast cancer. 'Such slips' Freud writes, are not insignificant errors, but 'derive from ideas outside what the speaker intends to say' (Freud, 2002, p. 78). Ideas that are too troublesome to deal with consciously – such as one's death – may well be repressed and revealed unintentionally in, amongst other things, linguistic slips (ibid.). Whilst the interviews carried out for this project are by no means analysed using a psychoanalytic framework, Freud's comments about the influence of the unconscious on our use of language are illuminating. It is just such attention to the more implicit, subtle aspects of interviewees' responses and behaviour that I hope to have incorporated into my analysis.

Participant observation

Sociologists often expect interviewees and questionnaire respondents to express nebulous emotions and difficult beliefs articulately and in concrete terms. Moreover, and as Hoinville comments, 'people are often poor predictors of their own behaviour, so that statements of intent often lack validity when compared with subsequent events, though they may well have been valid as statements of hopes, wishes, and aspirations. Altogether, we do not often find a one-to-one relationship between attitudes or opinions and behaviour' (Hoinville, 1978, p. 73). Participant observation offers the possibility of gaining insights into behaviour, beliefs and attitudes that participants might otherwise find difficult to articulate or predict. It also enables the researcher to study interaction between group members as well as a group's social surroundings, and thereby ascertain whether a social practice develops particular meanings when carried out as a group activity and in a particular location.

I carried out participant observation with two groups, hoping that this would give me a better insight into ribbon wearers' behaviour and beliefs. In both cases, I distributed questionnaires to group members at the end of the period of observation. The first observation was carried out at Manchester Gay Pride in late August 2004, an event which attracted some two hundred and fifty thousand people. I attended the event on the Sunday (the last day) for six hours. My purpose in carrying out this observation was to ascertain whether the red ribbon is widely used by those within the 'gay community' as a symbol of solidarity with homosexuals (see Chapter 5).

The second observation was carried out at a 'Pink Aerobics' event in Canterbury, Kent, in October 2004. Lasting four hours, the event was organised by a fitness instructor at the University of Kent's Sport's Centre to raise money for Breast Cancer Care. Held on a Saturday in place of a regular aerobics class, roughly eighty women (and four men) attended, of varying ages (some were university students, others were regular members of the fitness class). All were asked to wear pink, and many wore the pink ribbon.

Though it is customary for researchers to make use of an observation schedule, I found it difficult to create a list of expected responses and behaviour before the events I attended. Instead, I chose to relay my impressions as a narrative account (in a similar fashion to observers who keep a field diary). Though they were recorded in a rather unsystematic manner, I believe that these observations facilitated an understanding of ribbon wearing that would not have been possible using other research methods.

The questionnaire

The questionnaire was not an original feature of the research design. It was whilst I was carrying out the interviews that I decided to devise a questionnaire. There were a number of striking similarities between the interviewees' responses, and I was keen to find out whether their attitudes and beliefs were shared by a larger group of ribbon wearers. I therefore developed the questionnaire with several key questions in mind, and included words and phrases that had been used repeatedly by interviewees (for example, one question asked whether the respondent was 'scared of developing breast cancer', a phrase that numerous interviewees had used). As Courtenay writes, '[i]t is all too easy for researchers to 'create' attitudes by putting ideas into respondents' minds or words into their mouths' (Courtenay, 1978, p. 32). I hope that by using interviewees' phrases in the questionnaire I have reduced the effects of this problem.

Although I attempted to reach a range of people living in the South-East with the questionnaire, the respondents were in fact markedly similar to those who had taken part in in-depth interviews in terms of age, sex, and ethnicity. I approached people on the High Street in Canterbury, Kent, at charity events, and at Manchester Gay Pride. I left questionnaires in cafes, libraries, and work-places in the South-East and London. Some questionnaires were administered face-to-face, as structured interviews. Others were left in particular locations and collected at a later date. Whilst I realise that this choice of sampling technique renders my research unrepresentative, I would emphasise the impossibility of achieving a representative sample in this instance, not least of all because there is no applicable sampling frame from which I might have drawn my research group. In the end, 70 ribbon wearers filled in questionnaire, and I believe that this data gives some sense of the prevalence of certain attitudes amongst ribbon wearers.

Secondary data

The book makes extensive use of secondary data. My exploration of early flag days, for example, required a consideration of over a hundred articles that appeared in *The Times* from 1912 to 1931. This part of my work involved a thorough textual analysis of all articles from this period that made mention of flag days, and my findings are presented in Chapter 3. Of course, an analysis based on one sole source of data is likely to give a partial view of social reality. Nonetheless, I restricted my research to *The Times*, not only because it was the most widely read newspaper in the UK at the time, but also so as to obtain an understanding of the development of flag day events during this period, an aim better achieved through consideration of articles from a single source.

The main body of my analysis also makes frequent use of secondary data. A key premise of this study is that the ribbon *obtains* and *infers* certain meanings, and that an examination of the ribbon's cultural meanings is integral to understanding what it means to wear an awareness ribbon. As Karl Mannheim points out,

> [Sociology's] actual subject, society, exists not only in acts of sociation and the coalescence of men into structured groups. We encounter society also in meanings which likewise join or divide men. As there exists no sociation without particular understandings, so there are no shared meanings unless they are derived from and defined by given social situations. The dichotomy of the two academic realms of analysis, namely Simmel's science of the forms of sociation and the sociology of ideas, does not bespeak two such separate entities in the real world, although the necessities of academic specialization may make their thematic isolation temporarily expedient. There is no harm in such an abstraction so long as it is treated as an artifice. Ultimately, however, the duality of the ideational versus the social realm of things must resolve itself into a single view of the original subject of human reality.
>
> (Mannheim, 1956, pp. 18–19)

This is an approach that has very much shaped my research on ribbon wearing. More specifically, my work is shaped by the belief that, as Mannheim puts it, the cultural and social spheres are not 'separate entities in the real world', and that a consideration of both enables a more comprehensive understanding of the 'subject of human reality'. Alongside the primary data I have collected, I have made extensive use of secondary data to examine the socio-cultural context out of which the yellow, red and pink ribbons emerged. This part of my research examines the ribbon's development in both the UK and the USA, the country from which the yellow-, red- and pink-ribbon campaigns originated. My work involves textual analysis of media sources (newspaper articles and magazines), cultural critiques, the literature produced by charities, and folklorists' accounts. The mode of analysis employed in this area of my work depends less on formal procedures of codification, and more on attention to the stylistic tendencies of texts, the nature of the representation, and the tone of the article.

Aimed at a rich, detailed account of specific ribbon campaigns and their respective cultural contexts, this research is followed by an analysis of the cultural–historical basis of the contemporary project of 'showing awareness'. This aspect of my study is concerned with the emergence and development of a particular discourse – a certain means of discussing, understanding and representing the self – that finds its contemporary articulation in the drive to 'show awareness'. More precisely, this part of my research is given over to tracing the development of a countercultural discourse that originated in the 1960s in the USA and the UK, and swiftly became embedded in mainstream society.

Following the historian Arthur Marwick, in this thesis the countercultural period constitutes the years between 1958 and 1974 (Marwick, 1998, pp. 4–5). A wide range of artefacts and documents from this period is analysed to understand the emergence of a discourse related to 'showing awareness', including media articles, self-help books, popular psychology books, autobiographies, novels, historical documents, political speeches, and films. This analysis is then combined with a discussion of the contemporary project of 'showing awareness', a discussion that aims to highlight the ongoing influence of the countercultural discourse.

The research method used in this part of my work is discourse analysis, a type of textual analysis that uncovers transformations, ruptures, similarities and differences in texts. Discourse analysis is about peeling back layers of representation, seeking out fields of knowledge, unearthing the distinctive, socially and historically specific nature of our language and thoughts – these aims, or loosely conceived methods, are aptly referred to by Foucault as *archaeological*. Whilst a discourse refers to a common language used (this is perhaps most evident in Foucault's analysis of discourses concerning madness), it is also much more than this – study of a discourse might involve understanding representations, an ethos, ideals, ways of seeing the self, notions of normalness (and difference), accepted methodologies and instruments of learning, the nature of exchange, and notions of space. Foucault argues that the analysis of discursive practices involves tracing the emergence of new ideas and concomitantly recognising the continued influence of previously accepted ideas. Essentially, culture is a shifting, dynamic entity through which we may trace vertical lines of regularity between certain texts and artefacts; as Foucault comments, '[analysis] describes the integration of the new in the already structured field of the acquired, the progressive fall from the original into the traditional, or, again, the reappearances of the already-said, and the uncovering of the original' (Foucault, 2001, p. 142). Following on from this, a key goal of my work is to understand the gradual absorption of the ideals and ethos of the counterculture into mainstream culture and society.

The subtle complexities of this course of enquiry are made substantially less unwieldy by the application of a Foucauldian approach. Foucault recommends that analysis should aim to establish regularities between texts, in order to draw attention to the consistency of a certain discourse (ibid.). My study therefore aims to draw out regularities between texts from this period up to the present day, so as to ascertain the manner in which the countercultural discourse has been subsumed into our everyday vocabulary.

Whilst I believe that the use of secondary data is essential to obtaining a more complete understanding of ribbon wearing, it is important to acknowledge that both discourse analysis and textual analysis entail what is essentially a subjective, partial interpretation of texts. This bias is not simply evident in the actual analysis, but is also an element that influences the choosing of texts to be analysed. I have attempted to restrict this bias by including a wide range of data in my analysis and foregrounding particularly prominent or pertinent aspects of the culture. Moreover, when weighed against the various biases of much primary data, the subjectivity involved in selecting and analysing secondary data is minimal. Indeed, the use of secondary sources facilitates a level of detachment from the object of research that would otherwise be impossible with the use of primary data – the typical labelling of secondary data collection as an 'unobtrusive method' is testament to this (see Lee, 2000; Robson, 2002).

Notes

1 Introduction

1. There are no official records of ribbon campaigns. Wikipedia contains a list of ribbon campaigns (see 'Awareness Ribbons' at www.wikipedia.com) and Carolyn Gargaro, a US citizen with an expansive personal homepage, has developed a list of ribbon campaigns based on information provided by Web users (see 'Ribbon Campaigns' at www.gargaro.com).
2. This ribbon originates from Canada, rather than the USA (Yocom and Pershing, 1996 74n).
3. See 'Awareness Ribbons' at www.wikipedia.com and 'Ribbon Campaigns' at www.gargaro.com.
4. See *Times Union*, 27 April 1995, A10.

2 Ribbon Wearing: Towards a Theoretical Framework

1. In the original French: 'Elles constituent à la fois des signes de différentiation qui distinguent un groups donné, et des moyens de reconnaissance pour une communauté. C'est en fonction de cette considération que l'on peut dire que le partage des mêmes costumes, des mêmes critiques et des mêmes modes vestimentaires, crée une communication sensorial, non verbale, entre les members du groups social'.
2. See the Yellow Ribbon website set up to raise awareness of young adults' lack of Internet access and the Yellow Ribbon Teen Suicide website. Articles in *The Daily Record* (4 November 1997, p. 9) and *The Guardian* (17 June 1998, p. 5) discuss the yellow-ribbon campaign in support of the British au pair, Louise Woodward, who was accused of shaking to death a toddler in the USA.
3. Goffman, whose work influenced Butler's conception of gender identity, is subject to similar criticisms in his use of a stage metaphor to explain social action.
4. See 'UK Giving 2004/2005: Results of the 2004/2005 survey of individual charitable giving in the UK' (www.cafonline.org/default.aspx?page=7663).
5. See the National Center for Charitable Statistics 'Quick Facts' (www.nccsdataweb.urban.org/NCCS/files/quickFacts.htm).
6. See The UK Voluntary Sector Almanac 2006: The State of the Sector (www.ncvo-vol.org.uk/research/index.asp?id=2380&fID=158).
7. See Charities Aid Foundation 'General Facts and Figures'. (www.cafonline.org/research/factsandfigures.cfm).
8. See CharitiesDirect.com 'UK Charity Information' (www.charitiesdirect.com).
9. See the National Center for Charitable Statistics 'Quick Facts' (www.nccsdataweb.urban.org/NCCS/files/quickFacts.htm).

3 Flags and Poppies: Charity Tokens of the Early Twentieth Century

1. The Marie Curie Daffodil Day raises roughly three million pounds each year (a half of the charity's annual income) (Stead and Mercer, 1998, p. 216).
2. Flag days were initially (and for a short time only) known as flower days. One of the first flower days was the Alexandra Rose Day held on the 26 June 1912 (Fowler, a publication for *The Voluntary Action History Society*). This campaign was launched by Queen Alexandra, was held annually for several years, and provided funds for a number of charities, including voluntary hospitals (ibid.). There is some evidence to suggest that a number of flower days preceded this campaign; both the Blue Cross animal charity, as well as the Royal National Lifeboat Institute lay claim to the first flower day (ibid.).
3. Also see reports in *The Times*, 11 July 1916.
4. See, for example, *The Times*, 12 May 1915, p. 5; *The Times*, 15 September 1915, p. 9.
5. Men were wearing 'two or three in each buttonhole', according to a report in *The Times* (Fowler, a publication for *The Voluntary Action History Society*). See also *The Times* 12 May 1915, p. 5.
6. As Sue Corbett comments in a report for *The Times*, 'Eighty years on [from the poppy's launch], in 2001, poppies made by the legion's workforce of ex-soldiers raised a record £21, 254, 948' (12 August 2002).
7. Quotations from *The Times*, 12 August 2002, p. 10 and *The Times*, 9 November 2002 (Features Magazine) p. 98.

4 Ribbon Histories

1. See Parsons, 1991; Tuleja, 1994, p. 23; Heilbronn, 1994, p. 155.
2. See, for example, *The Economist*, 2 March 1991, p. 43 and *New York Times* 3 February 1991, F3.
3. This is mainly due to the release of the song 'Tie a Yellow Ribbon round the ole oak tree' in 1973. Although this song was about a man returning home from prison, many saw it as a reference to the soldiers returning from Vietnam (see Tuleja, 1992, p. 25).
4. There are some who argue otherwise (see Tuleja, 1992, p. 24). Nonetheless, it is reasonable to suggest that the John Ford film may well have influenced how the yellow ribbon was understood in the USA. As the historian Edward E Coffman points out, much of what constitutes the US citizens' knowledge of their military history, originates from the media, and films in particular (Coffman, 2000).
5. In Heilbronn's survey this was the most commonly cited reason for using the ribbon (Heilbronn, 1994, p. 76).
6. A number of other ribbons were launched around this time, including the white ribbon in opposition to male violence against women, a red ribbon for drug-prevention awareness, a blue ribbon in support of child-abuse victims (Yocom and Pershing, 1996, 74n, 75n).

7. The red ribbon has also been used by the US-based National Family Partnership against Alcohol and Drug Abuse since the late 1980s (see http://www.tcada.tx.us/redribbon/history.html).
8. Others point out that she took the red ribbon off to join her husband on the podium (*Los Angeles Times*, 24 March 1993, F6).
9. See *The Independent*, 1 December 1997, p. 14 and *BBC Monitoring International Reports*, 2 April 2004, for information on the Chinese campaign.
10. Red Ribbon International has since merged with the National AIDS Trust (see NAT press release September 2000).
11. The finale of a fashion show from the Italian designer Moschino in 1994 'featured dozens of children wearing red ribbons round their necks' (*The Guardian*, 24 February 1994, p. 14). The red ribbon also made it into a fashion supplement in the British newspaper *The Independent* shortly after its launch in 1992 (*The Independent*, 21 May 1992, p. 17).
12. See 'Bono Bets on Red to Battle Aids' (www.news.bbc.co.uk/2/hi/business/4650024.stm).
13. In the UK the death rate for breast cancer has declined significantly during the 1990s, though the incidence rate has increased (see National Statistics Online 'Breast Cancer: Incidence Rises as Deaths Continue To Fall', available at www.statistics.gov.uk/CCI/nugget.asp?ID=575&Pos=&ColRank=1&Rank=374). In the USA, both the death rate and the incidence rate for breast cancer has decreased since 1987 (see the American Cancer Society's 'Breast Cancer Facts and Figures' www.cancer.org/downloads/STT/CAFF2005BrF.pdf).
14. See National Statistics Online 'Breast Cancer: Incidence Rises as Deaths Continue To Fall' (www.statistics.gov.uk/CCI/nugget.asp?ID=575 &Pos=& ColRank=1&Rank=374) and the American Cancer Society's 'Breast Cancer Facts and Figures' (http://www.cancer.org/downloads/STT/CAFF2005BrF.pdf).
15. See the Breast Cancer Research Foundation's website (www.bcrfcure.org/ab_10_timeline.html).
16. See an interview with Lauder on a British television show, *This Morning* (23 October 2003).
17. Information from *Pink Ribbon* magazine (October 2002), *InThePINK* (October 2004) and Ehrenreich, *The Times*, Saturday, 8 December 2001.

5 Symbolic Uses of the Ribbon

1. See Manchester Pride press release 'Manchester Pride 2004 Hailed a Great Success' (www.manchesterpride.com/press_article.asp?id=44).
2. See Manchester Pride website (www.manchesterpride.com/qna_cat.asp?catid=7).
3. Both Giddens (1991) and Bauman (2003) refer to this as the emergence of 'life-politics', or 'self-managed politics (with a small P)' (ibid., p. 39). Following a similar line of argument, Beck and Beck-Gernsheim discuss the emergence of 'self-politics', a decidedly different type of political action

to governmental politics, which involves 'a direct and tangible link-up between private actions that may have little meaning in themselves ... and outcomes in which individuals can feel themselves to be authors of global political acts' (Beck and Beck-Gernsheim, 2003, p. 45).

4. See the anarchist black ribbon campaign's website (www.a4a.mahost.org/black.htm).

5. See the Traffic Lights 4 Peace website (www.trafficlights4peace.com).

6. See the anarchist black ribbon campaign's website (www.a4a.mahost.org/black.htm).

7. None of those who responded to the questionnaire indicated that they used the ribbon in this way, though, of course, we might postulate that this kind of motivation might not be readily admitted to in a questionnaire, a research tool that creates a certain emotional distance between researcher and research subject.

8. I should point out here that though this man's grandfather died from cancer, he did not die specifically from breast cancer.

9. In 9 per cent of the 130 tributes, people made a mention of their lack of affiliation to the Catholic church.

10. See BBC News Archive, 'Pope John Paul II: Your Tributes' (www.news.bbc.co.uk/1/hi/talking_point/2806153.stm).

11. A convincing explanation for this difference between interviewees and those who responded to the questionnaire is that the latter were offered a range of possible answers to the question 'Why do you wear a ribbon?' and may well have felt obliged to indicate that they were interested in spreading awareness. In contrast, those who were interviewed were offered no such prompts – when I did ask interviewees questions about spreading awareness, I did so towards the end of the interview in order to reduce bias.

12. I would tentatively suggest that those interested in spreading awareness are more likely to be involved in organising awareness campaigns. One of the interviewees who said he wore a ribbon to 'spread awareness' had played a central role in organising an AIDS awareness campaign at his college to help improve the students' awareness about sexually trans-mitted diseases. In his role as Welfare Officer for the college he studied at, this interviewee had been amazed by the number of people who approached him for help with a suspected sexually transmitted disease. He had, he told me, even accompanied several students to have blood tests if they felt exceptionally worried. He had also developed a broad knowledge of sexually transmitted diseases; out of all the people I inter-viewed, he was most able to provide accurate, balanced information on AIDS and HIV.

13. This idea is not as strange as it might at first seem. Kubler-Ross put forward the idea that those who learn that they are terminally ill go through a stage of mourning for the loss of the self (Kubler-Ross, 1970).

14. She meant health insurance, which is in itself interesting. Many ribbon wearers give to charity because they feel that they are likely to benefit

from the services and research they help fund. I return to this idea in Chapter 8.

15. There are, of course, other ways of understanding belief. It is important to recognise that the interviewees' conception of belief suggests that they view charity as something that they should be *involved in* (rather than something that they simply believe to be true or to exist, other possible understandings of belief).

6 'Showing Awareness' and the 1960s Counter-culture: Breaking Rules and Finding the Self

1. The phrase '1960s' counterculture' or 'the counterculture' will be used throughout to refer to the period 1957–74 (see Appendix for notes on periodisation and methodology).

2. See Roszak (1970, p. 27) and Quattrocchi (1970, pp. 214–15) for further examples of the view that the 'genuine' counterculture was vulgarised by commercial interests, and see Frank, 1997, for a rare contestation of this position.

3. See Weiner and Stillman's survey of attitudes during the 1960s (1979, pp. 41, 37, and 45, respectively).

4. In James Rosenquist's painting, *The President-Elect* (1960–1) John F. Kennedy is associated with mass-made, commercial products, such as cake and automobiles.

5. Similarly, Norman Mailer, in his influential essay the 'White Negro' suggests that the 'black culture' offered a better way of life (Mailer, 2005). Black people, Mailer argued, lived for the moment and were guided by their desire for immediate gratification.

6. Patrick O' Connell – the founding director of Visual AIDS, the organisation that created and launched the red ribbon – was awarded a fashion award by the Council of Fashion Designers of America (Garfield, 1995, p. 257). Similarly, the 1960s' peace symbol is used by many as a fashion accessory and adorns a range of clothes items, and even appears in an advertising campaign for Volkswagen.

7. The psychologist Rollo May argued that countercultural protest in fact emerged out of a prevalent feeling of powerlessness in the society. In a discussion of the origins and purpose of countercultural protest, he suggested that countercultural protest was in fact all about the self: '... the act of rebelling ... force[s] the impersonal authorities or the too systematic system to look at me, to recognize me, to admit that I *am*, to take account of my *power* ...' (May, 1967, p. 27).

8. Whilst only 9 per cent of respondents openly admitted to being 'more apathetic and selfish in the Seventies' (Weiner and Stillman, 1979, p. 151), others believed that there 'is little they can do' and many have 'found other [more peaceable] means of effecting social change' (ibid., p. 152).

7 Worry as a Manifestation of Awareness: The Implications of 'Thinking Pink'

1. Only 3 per cent of pink-ribbon wearers were male. It should be noted here that a significant proportion (39 per cent) of the female participants had worn the red AIDS-awareness ribbon: sex is not, in other words, the sole determinant of worry.
2. 'Women still not checking for breast cancer – lack of confidence to blame?' Macmillan Cancer Relief, 25 October 2004.
3. Information taken from Breakthrough Breast Cancer's leaflet 'Breast Cancer Risk Factors: The Facts'.
4. This information was taken from Cancer Research UK's web page 'Recent Progress', a site giving information on recent developments in breast cancer research.
5. See an article on Macmillan Cancer Relief's website, 'Women still not checking for breast cancer – lack of confidence to blame?' (25 October 2004).
6. The terms are, of course, Ulrich Beck's (1992) and Frank Furedi's (1996), respectively.
7. 'Definite Risks' on Cancer Research UK's website (downloaded from http://www.cancerresearchuk.org).
8. See Cancer Research UK's leaflet for their 'stride for life' event.
9. This data is based on information gathered from questionnaires filled in by 52 pink-ribbon wearers. Roughly thirteen thousand women die from breast cancer every year in the UK (according to information provided by Cancer Research UK, www.cancerresearchuk.org/aboutcancer/statistics/mortality).
10. Dijkstra's (1986) analysis of representations of women and ill-health during the mid- to late nineteenth century and Ehrenreich and English's (1979) review of medical practioners' advice to women from the mid-nineteenth century onwards highlight the salience of the idea that women were inherently sickly beings.
11. See Foster (1996, p. 16) for a similar argument about mastectomies.
12. These examples are taken from Macmillan Cancer Relief's 2004 mail-shot and an interview with the pop singer Jamelia in the October 2004 edition of the magazine *InthePINK*.
13. See adverts for the make-up company, Shiseido (in *Pink Ribbon* magazine, October 2003 edition) the designer Betty Barclay (*InthePINK*, October 2004 edition) and the luxury towel makers, Christy (in *Pink Ribbon* magazine, October 2003 edition).

8 The Commercialisation of Charity and the Commodification of Compassion

1. 'Prince Charles presented with Autism Awareness Ribbon', 22 July 2002, National Autistic Society website (http://www.autism-awareness.org.uk/news220702).

2. Hibbert (2005) 'Charitable Giving: The Research Briefing' (www. esrcsocietytoday.ac.uk/ESRCInfoCentre/about/CI/events/esrcseminar/).
3. Hibbert (2005) 'Charitable Giving: The Research Briefing' (www. esrcsocietytoday.ac.uk/ESRCInfoCentre/about/CI/events/esrcseminar/).
4. See Episode 11, 'The Sponge', aired on 7 December 1995 (available at www.seinfeldscripts.com/TheSponge.html).
5. For Marx, commodities efface the social relations between individual producers:

> the social character of men's labour appears to them as an objective characteristic, a social natural quality of the labour product itself ... consequently the relation of the producers to the sum total of their own labour is presented to them as a social relation, existing not between themselves, but between the products of their labour.
>
> (Marx, 2004, p. 473)

The products of human labour, Marx argues, come to be divorced from the essential social act of production, and, as a result, we come to treat commodities as if they have value in themselves. 'It is', Marx writes, 'simply a definite social relation between men, that assumes ... the fantastic form of a relation between things' (ibid.).

References

Books and articles

Adkins, L. 'Taking the HIV Test: Self-Surveillance and the Making of Heterosexuality', in Bashford, A. and Hooker, C. (eds) *Contagion: Historical and Cultural Studies* (London: Routledge, 2001).

Adkins, S. *Cause Related Marketing: The Cares Wins* (Oxford: Heinemann, 2005).

Alcock, N.Z. *The Emperor's New Clothes and Other Irrelevant Essays for the Seventies* (Ontario: CPRI Press, 1971).

Alexander, J.C. 'The Sixties and Me: From Cultural Revolution to Cultural Theory', in Turner, S. and Sica, A. (eds) *The Disobedient Generation* (London: University of Chicago Press, 2005).

Anderson, B. *Imagined Communities: Reflections on the Origin and Spread of Nationalism* (London: Verso, 1992).

Atkins, K. (ed.) *Self and Subjectivity: Blackwell Reading in Continental Philosophy* (Oxford: Blackwell, 2005).

Auerbach, J.D. and Figert, A.E. 'Women's Health Research: Public Policy and Sociology', *Special Review Journal of Health and Social Behavior*, 35 (1995) 115–31.

Barbalet, F. (ed.) *Emotions and Sociology*, a monograph from *The Sociological Review* (Oxford: Blackwell, 2002).

Barker-Benfield, J. *The Culture of Sensibility: Sex and Society in Eighteenth Century* (Chicago: Chicago University Press, 1992).

Bass, M. and Howes, J. 'Women's Health: The Making of a Powerful New Public Issue', *Women's Health Issues*, 2 (1) (1992) 3–5.

Bauman, Z. *Thinking Sociologically* (Oxford: Blackwell, 1991).

Bauman, Z. *Liquid Modernity* (London: Polity Press, 2000).

Bauman, Z. *Identity* (London: Polity Press, 2004).

Beck, U. *Risk Society: Towards a New Modernity* (London: Sage, 1992).

Beck, U. and Beck-Gernsheim, E. *Individualization: Institutionalized Individualism and Its Social and Political Consequences* (London: Sage, 2002).

Becker, H. *Outsiders: Studies in the Sociology of Deviance* (New York: The Free Press, 1973).

Bell, D. *The Cultural Contradictions of Capitalism* (London: Heinemann, 1976).

Bell, J. 'The End of Our Domestic Resurrection Circus: Bread and Puppet Theater and Counter-Culture Performance in the 1990s', *The Drama Review*, 43 (3) (1999) 62–8.

Bellah, R. 'New Religious Consciousness and the Crisis of Modernity', in Glock, C. and Wuthnow, R. (eds) *The New Religious Consciousness* (Berkeley: University of California Press, 1976).

Berger, J. *Ways of Seeing* (London: Penguin, 1977).

Berger, P. *Invitation to Sociology: A Humanistic Perspective* (Harmondsworth: Pelican, 1963).

Berger, P. and Luckman, T. *The Social Construction of Reality: A Treatise in the Sociology of Knowledge* (New York City: Doubleday, 1966).

Berger, P.L., Berger, B., and Kellner, H. *The Homeless Mind: Modernization and Consciousness* (Harmondsworth: Penguin, 1979).

Berlant, L. (ed.) *Compassion: The Culture and Politics of an Emotion* (London: Routledge, 2004).

Berridge, V. 'AIDS: History and Contemporary History', in Herdt, G. and Lindenbaum, S. (eds) *The Time of AIDS: Social Analysis, Theory, and Method* (London: Sage, 1992).

Berman, M. *All That is Solid* (Oxford: Blackwell, 1990).

Blumer, H. 'Symbolic Interactionism', in Calhoun, C., Gerteis, J., Moody, J., Pfaff, S. and Virk, I. (eds) *Contemporary Sociological Theory* (Oxford: Blackwell, 2002).

Boehnke, K., Schwartz, S., Stromberg, C. and Sagiv, L. 'The Structure and Dynamics of Worry: Theory, Measurement, and Cross-National Replications', *Journal of Personality*, 66 (5) (1998) 745–82.

Bourdieu, P. 'Rhetorical Illusion', in Du Gay, P., Evans, J., and Redman, P. (eds) *Identity: A Reader* (London: Sage, 2000).

Breazeale, K. 'Bringing the War Back Home: Consuming Operation Desert Storm', *Journal of American Culture*, 17 (1) (1992) 31–7.

Brooks, A. *Who Really Cares: The Surprising Truth about Compassionate Conservatism*, (USA: Basic Books, 2006).

Butler, J. *Gender Trouble: Feminism and the Subversion of Identity* (New York: Routledge, 1990).

Calhoun, C. (ed.) *Social Theory and the Politics of Identity* (Oxford: Blackwell, 1994).

Campbell, C. *The Romantic Ethic and the Spirit of Capitalism* (Oxford: Blackwell, 1987).

Campbell, C. 'Detraditionalization, Character and the Limits to Agency', in Heelas, P., Lash, S. and Morris, P. (eds) *Detraditionalization: Critical Reflections on Authority and Identity* (Oxford: Blackwell, 1996).

Cannadine, D. 'War and Death, Grief and Mourning in Modern Britain', in Whaley, J. (ed.) *Mirrors of Mortality: Studies in the Social History of Death* (London: Europa, 1981).

Capozza, D. and Brown, R. (eds) *Social Identity Processes* (London: Sage, 2000).

Carter, S. 'Boundaries of Danger and Uncertainty: An Analysis of the Technological Culture of Risk Assessment', in Gabe, J. (ed.) *Medicine, Health and Risk: Sociological Approaches* (Oxford: Blackwell, 1995).

Castells, M. *The Information Age: Economy, Society and Culture (Vol. II) The Power of Identity* (Oxford: Blackwell, 1997).

Charles, N. and Walters, V. 'Age and Gender in Women's Accounts of Their Health: Interview with Women in South Wales', *Sociology of Health and Illness*, 20 (3) (1998) 331–50.

Cherry, S. 'Before the National Health Service: Financing the Voluntary Hospitals, 1900–1939', *The Economic History Review*, 50 (2) (1997) 305–26.

Cherry, S. 'Hospital Saturday, Workplace Collections and Issues in Late Nineteenth-Century Hospital Funding', *Medical History*, 44 (4) (2000) 461–88.

Clark, C. *Misery and Company: Sympathy in Everyday Life* (Chicago: Chicago University Press, 1992).

Clary, E.G., Snyder, M., Ridge, R.D., Copeland, J. and Stukas, A.A. 'Understanding and Assessing the Motivations of Volunteers: A Funcitonal Approach', *Journal of Personality and Social Psychology*, 74 (6) (1998) 1516–30.

Clecak, P. *America's Quest for the Ideal Self: Dissent and Fulfilment in the 60s and 70s* (New York: Oxford University Press, 1983).

Coffman, E.M. 'The George C. Marshall Lecture in Military History: The Duality of the American Military Tradition', *Journal of Military History*, 64 (4) (2000) 967–80.

Cohen, A. 'Symbolic Action and the Structure of Self', in Lewis, I. (ed.) *Symbols and Sentiments: Cross-Cultural Studies in Symbolism* (London: Academic Press, 1977).

Connelly, M. *The Great War, Memory and Ritual: Commemoration in The City and East London, 1916–1939* (Suffolk: Boydell Press, 2002).

Cosgrove, A. 'Iran Hostage Anniversary', *CBS News*, 18 January 2001 (www.cbsnews.com/stories/2001/01/18/iran/main265244.shtml).

Courtenay, G. 'Questionnaire Construction', in Hoinville, G. (ed.) *Survey Research Practice* (London: Heinemann, 1978).

Craik, J. *The Face of Fashion: Cultural Studies in Fashion* (London: Routledge, 1994).

Crimp, D. (ed.) *AIDS: Cultural Analysis, Cultural Activism* (London: The MIT Press, 1991).

Csikzentmihaliyi and Rochberg-Halton *The Meaning of Things: Domestic Symbols and the Self* (Cambridge: Cambridge University Press, 1981).

Davie, G. 'Religion in Modern Britain: Changing Sociological Assumptions', *Sociology*, 34 (1) (2000) 113–28.

Denzin, N.K. *Symbolic Interactionism and Cultural Studies: The Politics of Interpretation* (Blackwell: Oxford, 1992).

Deschamps, J.C. and Devos, T. 'Social Identity and Personal Identity', in Worchel, S., Morales, J.F., Paez, D. and Deschamps, C. (eds) *Social Identity: International Perspectives* (London: Sage, 1998).

Desiderio, G. 'Protecting the Breast and Promoting Femininity: The Breast Cancer Movement's Production of Fear Through a Rhetoric of Risk', MA thesis submitted at the faculty at Virginia Polytechnic Institute and State University, 2004 (http//scholar.lib.ut.edu/theses/available/etd-05022004184942/unrestricted/ETD.PDF).

Dickstein, M. 'Black Humor and History' in Howard, G. (ed.) *The Sixties: Art, Politics and Media of Our Most Explosive Decade* (New York: Paragon House, 1991).

Dijkstra, B. *Idols of Perversity: Feminine of Feminine Evil in Fin-de-Siecle Culture* (Oxford: Oxford University Press, 1986).

Dixon, M. 'The Rise and Demise of Women's Liberation: A Class Analysis' *C.W.L.U. Herstory Archive*, 1977 (www.cw/uherstory.com/CWLArchive/dixon.html).

Douglas, J. *Why Charity?: The Case for a Third Sector* (London: Sage, 1983).
Douglas, M. *Natural Symbols: Explorations in Cosmology* (London: Routledge, 1996).
Douglas, M. *Risk and Blame: Essays in Cultural Theory* (London: Routledge, 1992).
Doyal, L. *What Makes Women Sick?: Gender and The Political Economy of Health* (London: Macmillan Press, 1995).
Durkheim, E. *The Rules of Sociological Method*, in Calhoun C., Gerteis, J., Moody, J., Pfaff, S., Schmidt, K. et al. (eds) *Classical Social Theory* (Oxford: Blackwell, 2002).
Durkheim, E. *The Division of Labour in Society* (Basingstoke: Macmillan, 1984).
Eco, U. 'The Form of the Informal', in Ferrier, J.L. (ed.) *Art of the Twentieth Century: The History of Art Year by Year 1900 to 1999* (Italy: Editions du Chene, 1999).
Ehrenreich, B. and English, D. *For Her Own Good: 150 Years of the Experts' Advice to Women* (London: Pluto Press, 1979).
Ellemers, N., Spears, R. and Doosje, B. (eds) *Social Identity: Context, Commitment, Content* (Oxford: Blackwell, 1999).
Elliott, A. *Social Theory and Psychoanalysis in Transition: Self and Society from Freud to Kristeva* (London: Free Association Books, 1999).
Elliott, A. 'Beck's Sociology of Risk: A Critical Assessment', *Sociology*, 36 (2) (2002) 293–315.
Erikson, E.H. *Identity: Youth and Crisis* (London: Faber and Faber, 1968).
Erikson, E.H. *Identity and the Life Cycle* (New York: Norton, 1980).
Farsides, T. 'Charitable Giving: The Research Briefing', 2005 (www.esrcsocietytoday.ac.uk/ESRCInfoCentre/about/CI/events/esrcseminar/).
Fee, E. (ed.) *Women and Health: The Politics of Sex in Medicine* (New York: Baywood Publishing Company Inc., 1982).
Fee, E. and Fox, D.M. (eds) *AIDS: The Burdens of History* (University of California: California, 1988).
Fernandez, P. 'Pretty in Pink' (www.thinkbeforeyoupink.org/Pages/PrettyInPink.html).
Ferrier, J.L. (ed.) *Art of the Twentieth Century: The History of Art Year by Year 1900 to 1999* (Italy: Editions du Chene, 1999).
Firth, R. *Symbols: Public and Private* (London: Allen and Unwin, 1973).
Fiske, J. *Understanding Popular Culture* (Boston: Unwin Hyman, 1989).
Foss, D.A. and Larkin, R.W. 'From "The Gates of Eden" to "Day of the Locust": An Analysis of the Dissident Youth Movement of the 1960s and Its Heirs of the Early 1970s – The Post Movement Groups', *Theory and Society*, 3 (1) (1976) 45–64.
Foster, P. *Women and The Health Care Industry: An Unhealthy Relationship?* (Buckingham: Open University Press, 1996).
Foucault, M. *The Archaeology of Knowledge* (London: Routledge, 2001).
Fowler, S. 'The Origins of Flag Days', *The Voluntary Action History Society* (www.vahs.org.uk/vahs/papers/vahs3.pdf).
Frank, T. *The Conquest of Cool: Business Culture, Counter-Culture, and the Rise of Hip Consumerism* (Chicago: University of Chicago Press, 1997).
Frankenberg, R. 'One Epidemic or Three? Cultural, Social and Historical Apects of the AIDS Pandemic' in Aggleton, P., Davies, P. and Hart, G. (eds) *AIDS: Social Representations, Social Practices* (London: Falmer Press, 1989).

Fraser, D. *The Evolution of the British Welfare State: A History of Social Policy Since the Industrial Revolution* (London: Macmillan Press, 1984).

Freeman, J. (ed.) *Social Movements of the 60s and 70s* (New York: Longman, 1983).

Freud, S. *New Introductory Lectures on Psychoanalysis* (London: Hogarth Press, 1974).

Freud, S. *The Psychopathology of Everyday Life* (London: Penguin, 2002).

Furedi, F. *Culture of Fear: Risk-Taking and the Morality of Low Expectation* (London: Cassells, 1997).

Furedi, F. *Therapy Culture* (London: Routledge, 2004).

Gabe, J. 'Health, Medicine and Risk: The Need for a Sociological Approach' in Gabe, J. (ed.) *Health, Medicine and Risk: Sociological Approaches* (Oxford: Blackwell, 1995).

Garfield, S. *The End of Innocence: Britain in the Time of AIDS* (London: Faber and Faber, 1995).

Garfinkel, S. 'This Trial Was Sent in Love and Mercy for My Refinement': A Quaker Woman's Experience of Breast Cancer Surgery in 1814' in Leavitt, Judith, W. (ed.) *Women and Health in America: Historical Readings* (USA: University of Wisconsin Press, 1999).

Geertz, C. *The Interpretation of Cultures* (New York: Fontana Press, 1993).

Gente, M. 'Family Ideology and the Charity Organization Society in Great Britain During the First World War', *Journal of Family History*, 27 (3) (2002) 255–71.

Gerth, H. and Mills, C.W. *Character and Social Structure: The Psychology of Social Institutions* (London: Routledge, 1965).

Giddens, A. *The Consequences of Modernity* (Cambridge: Polity Press, 1990).

Giddens, A. *Modernity and Self-Identity: Self and Society in the Late Modern Age* (Cambridge: Polity Press, 1991).

Gitlin, T. *The Sixties: Years of Hope, Days of Rage* (New York: Bantam Books, 1993).

Gladstone, D. (ed.) *Before Beveridge: Welfare Before the Welfare State* (London: IEA, 1999).

Goffman, E. *Asylums: Essays on the Social Situation of Mental Patients and Other Inmates* (Harmondsworth: Penguin, 1961).

Goffman, E. *The Presentation of Self in Everyday Life* (Harmondsworth: Penguin, 1969).

Goffman, E. *Relations in Public: Microstudies of the Public Order* (London: Penguin, 1972).

Goodwin, J., Jasper, J.M. and Polletta, F. *Passionate Politics: Emotions and Social Movements* (Chicago: University of Chicago Press, 2001).

Green, D.G. *Reinventing Civil Society: The Rediscovery of Welfare Without Politics* (London: IEA 1993).

Green, J. *Days in the Life: Voices from the English Underground 1961–1971* (London: Heineman, 1988).

Gregory, A. *The Silence of Memory: Armistice Day 1919–1946* (Oxford: Berg, 1994).

Gullace, N.F. 'White Feathers and Wounded Men: Female Patriotism and the Memory of the Great War', *Journal of British Studies*, 36 (April) (1997) 178–206.

Harris, D. *The Rise and Fall of Gay Culture* (USA, Ballantine Books, 1997).

Harvey, D. *The Condition of Postmodernity: An Enquiry into the Origins of Cultural Change* (Oxford: Blackwell, 1995).

Hebdige, D. *Subculture: The Meaning of Style* (London: Methuen, 1979).
Heelas, P. *New Age Movement: The Celebration of Self and the Sacralization of Modernity* (Oxford: Blackwell, 1996).
Heelas, P., Lash, S. and Morris, P. (eds) *Detraditionalization: Critical Reflections on Authority and Identity* (Cambridge: Blackwell, 1996).
Heilbronn, L.M. 'Yellow Ribbons and Remembrance: Mythic Symbols of the Gulf War', *Sociological Inquiry*, 64 (2) (1994) 151–78.
Hibbert, S. and Horne, S. 'Giving to Charity: Questioning the Donor Decision Process', *Journal of Consumer Marketing*, 13 (1) (1996) 4–13.
Hibbert, S. 'Charitable Giving: The Research Briefing', 2005 (www.esrcsocietytoday.ac.uk/ESRCInfoCentre/about/CI/events/esrcseminar/).
Hobsbawm, E. and Ranger, T. (eds) *The Invention of Tradition* (Cambridge: Cambridge University Press, 2001).
Hochschild, A.R. *The Managed Heart: Commercialization of Human Feeling* (California: University of California Press, 1983).
Hockey, J., Prendergast, D. and Kellaher, L. *Environments of Memory: New Rituals of Mourning in the UK* (www.shef.ac.uk/ashes/projoverview.html).
Hoinville, G. *Survey Research Practice* (London: Heinemann, 1978).
Hunt, A. 'When did the 60s Happen?: Searching for New Directions', *Journal of Social History*, Fall (1999) 147–61.
Jenkins, R. *Social Identity* (London: Routledge, 1996).
Jones, L.Y. *Great Expectations: America and the Baby Boom Generation* (New York City: Ballantine Books, 1980).
Jones, V. (ed.) *Women in the Eighteenth Century: Constructions of Femininity* (London: Routledge, 1990).
Kaiser, S.B. *The Social Psychology of Clothing and Personal Adornment* (London: Macmillan, 1985).
Kellner, D. 'Popular Culture and the Construction of Postmodern Identities', in Lash, S. and Friedman, J. (eds) *Modernity and Identity* (Oxford: Blackwell, 1996).
King, A. *Memories of The Great War in Britain: The Symbolism and Politics of Remembrance* (Oxford: Berg, 1998).
King, S. *Pink Ribbons Inc.: Breast Cancer and the Politics of Philanthropy* (Minneapolis: University of Minneapolis Press, 2006).
Kubler-Ross, E. *On Death and Dying* (London: Tavistock, 1970).
Laing, R.D. *The Divided Self* (London: Penguin, 1960).
Laing, R.D. *The Politics of Experience and The Bird of Paradise* (UK: Penguin, 1967).
Larsen, L. 'The Yellow Ribboning of America: A Gulf War Pheonomenon', *Journal of American Culture*, 17 (1) (1994) 11–22.
Lasch, C. *The Culture of Narcissism: American Life in an Age of Diminishing Expectations* (USA, Warner Books, 1979).
Lash, S., Szerszynski, B. and Wynne, B. *Risk, Environment and Modernity: Towards A New Ecology* (London: Sage, 1996).
Lauver, D., Coyle, M. and Panchmatia, B. 'Women's Reasons for and Barriers to Seeking Care for Breast Cancer Symptoms', *Women's Health Issues*, 5 (1) (1995) 64–72.
Lee, R.M. *Unobtrusive Methods in Social Research* (Buckingham: Open University Press, 2000).
Leech, K. *Youthquake* (London: Sheldon Press, 1973).

Lemert, C. and Branaman, A. (eds) *The Goffman Reader* (Oxford: Blackwell, 1997).

Leopold, E. *A Darker Ribbon: Breast Cancer, Women, and Their Doctors in the Twentieth Century* (Boston: Beacon Press, 1999).

Lewis, J. 'The State and the Third Sector' in Evers, Adalbert and Lavillen, Jean-Louis (eds) *The Third Sector in Europe* (Cheltenham: Edward Elgar, 2001).

Lofland, L.H. *A World of Strangers: Order and Action in Urban Public Space* (New York: Basic Books, 1973).

Lowe, R. *The Welfare State in Britain since 1945* (London: Macmillan Press, 1993).

Lupton, D. *The Emotional Self: A Sociocultural Exploration* (London: Sage, 1998).

Lupton, D. *Risk* (London: Routledge, 1999).

Mailer, N. 'The White Negro' in Mailer, N. *Advertisements for Myself* (USA: Harvard University Press, 2005) 337–59.

Mannheim, K. *Essays on the Sociology of Culture* (London: Routledge, 1956).

Marcuse, H. *One-Dimensional Man: Studies in the Ideology of Advanced Industrial Society* (Boston: Beacon Press, 1964).

Marcuse, H. *An Essay on Liberation* (Middlesex: Penguin, 1972).

Marks, L. U. 'Tie a Yellow Ribbon Around Me: Masochism, Militarism and the Gulf War on TV', *Camera Obscura*, 27 (Summer) (1991) 55–75.

Marwick, A. *The Sixties* (UK: Oxford University Press, 1998).

Marx, K. 'The Fetishism of Commodities', in McLellan, D. (ed.) *Karl Marx: Selected Writings* (Oxford: Oxford University Press, 2004).

Maslow, A. *Toward a Psychology of Being* (New York: Van Nostrand Reinhold, 1964).

Maslow, A. *Motivation and Personality* (London: Harper and Row, 1970).

Mauss, M. *The Gift: The Form and Reason for Exchange in Archaic Societies* (London: Routledge, 2004).

May, R. *Psychology and the Human Dilemma* (New York: Norton and Co., 1967).

Mays, J.B. *The Young Pretenders: A Study of Teenage Culture in Contemporary Society* (London: Michael Joseph, 1961).

McLeod, D.M., Eveland, W.P., and Signorielli, N. 'Conflict and Public Opinion: Rallying Effects of the Persian Gulf War', *Journalism Quarterly*, 71 (1) (1994) 20–34.

Mead, G.H. 'The Self', in Calhoun, C., Gerteis, J., Moody, J., Pfaff, S., Schmidt, K. et al. (eds) *Classical Sociological Theory* (Oxford: Blackwell, 2002).

Melluci, A. *Nomads of the Present: Social Movements and Individual Needs in Contemporary Society* (Philadelphia: Temple University Press, 1989).

Mestrovic, S.G. *The Postemotional Society* (London: Sage, 1997).

Michael, M. *The Miracle Flower: The Story of the Flanders Field Memorial Poppy* (Philadelphia: Dorrance and Company, 1941).

Miedema, B. and Tatemichi, S. 'Breast and Cervical Cancer Screening for Women between 50 and 69 Years of Age: What Prompts Women to Screen?', *Women's Health Issues*, 13 (5) (2003) 180–4.

Miles, A. *Women, Health and Medicine* (Milton Keynes: Open University Press, 1991).

Miller, S. 'The Politics of the "True Self"', *Dissent*, 20 (Winter) (1973) 93–8.

Milles, C.W. *The Sociological Imagination* (New York: Oxford University Press, 1959).

Moeller, S.D. *Compassion Fatigue: How the Media Sell Disease, Famine, War and Death* (London: Routledge, 1999).

Musgrove, F. *Ecstasy and Holiness: Counter-Culture and the Open Society* (London: Methuen, 1974).

Myhre, L. 'The Breast Cancer Movement: Seeing Beyond Consumer Activism', *Journal for the American Medical Women's Association*, 54 (1) (1999) 29–31.

Najar, S. 'Comportement vestimentaire et identification au pluriel', *Société*, 50 (4) (1995) 399–406.

Nelson, E. *The British Counter-Culture: 1966–1973 A Study of the Underground Press* (London: Macmillan Press, 1989).

Nettleton, S. and Bunton, R. 'Sociological Critiques of Health Promotion' in Bunton, R., Nettleton, S., and Burrows, R. (eds) *The Sociology of Health Promotion: Critical Analyses of Consumption, Lifestyle and Risk* (London: Routledge, 1995).

Nolan, J. *Therapeutic State: Justifying Government at Century's End* (New York City: New York University Press, 1998).

Oakley, A. 'Interviewing Women: A Contradiction in Terms' in Roberts, H. (ed.) *Doing Feminist Research* (London: Routledge, 1981).

Oakley, A. 'Tamoxifen – In Whose Best Interests?' in Oakley, A. (ed.) *Essays on Women, Medicine and Health* (Edinburgh: Edinburgh University Press, 1993).

Outhwaite, W. and Ray, L. *Social Theory and Postcommunism* (Oxford: Blackwell, 2005).

Parkin, F. *Middle Class Radicalism: The Social Bases of the British Campaign for British Disarmament* (Manchester: Manchester University Press, 1968).

Parry, G., Moyser, G. and Day, N. *Political Participation and Democracy in Britain* (Cambridge: Cambridge University Press, 1992).

Parsons, G.E. 'Yellow Ribbons: Ties with Tradition', *Folklife Center News*, IV (2) (1981) (www.loc.gov/folklife/ribbons/ribbons_81.html).

Parsons, G.E. 'How the Yellow Ribbon Became a National Folk Symbol', *Folklife Center News*, XIII (3) (1991) 9–11.

Patton, C. *Inventing AIDS* (London: Routledge, 1990).

Patton, C. 'Preface', in Roth, N.L. and Hogan, K. (eds) *Gendered Epidemic: Representations of Women in the Age of AIDS* (London: Routledge, 1998).

Phillips, A. *On Kissing, Tickling and Being Bored* (London: Faber and Faber, 1994).

Phillips, A. and Rakusen, J. (eds) *Our Bodies Ourselves: A Health Book By and For Women* (London: Penguin, 1988).

Pierson, P. (ed.) *The New Politics of the Welfare State* (Oxford: Oxford University Press, 2001).

Pitts, J. 'The Counter-Culture: Tranquilizer or Revolutionary Ideology?' in Harrington, M. and Howe, I. (eds) *The Seventies: Problems and Proposals* (New York: Harper and Rowe, 1972).

Pollack, M. 'Attitudes, Beliefs and Opinions', in Pollock M., Paicheler, G. and Pierret, J. (eds) *AIDS. A problem for sociological research* (London: Sage, 1992).

Pountain, D. and Robins, D. *Cool Rules: Anatomy of an Attitude* (London: Reaktion Books, 2000).

Powell, M. (ed.) *New Labour, New Welfare State?: The 'Third Way' in British Social Policy* (UK: Policy Press, 2002).

Pringle, H. and Tompson, M. *Brand Spirit: How Cause Related Marketing Builds Brands* (Chichester: John Wiley and Sons Ltd, 2001).

Ricoeur, P. 'Personal Identity and Narrative Identity', in Ricoeur, P. (ed.) *Oneself as Another* (Chicago: University of Chicago Press, 1992).

Rieff, P. *The Triumph of the Therapeutic* (London: Chatto and Windus, 1966).

Riesman, D., Glazer, N. and Denney, P. *The Lonely Crowd: A Study of the Changing American Character* (London: Yale University Press, 1957).

Robson, C. *Real World Research: A Resource for Social Scientists and Practitioner-Researchers* (Oxford: Blackwell, 2002).

Rogers, C. *On Becoming a Person: A Therapist's View of Psychotherapy* (London: Constable and Company Ltd, 1967).

Rojas, M. *Beyond the Welfare State: Sweden and the Quest for a Post-Industrial Welfare Model* (Sweden: Timbro, 2001).

Rose, N. 'Authority and Genealogy of Subjectivity', in Heelas, P., Lash, S. and Morris, P. (eds) *Detraditionalization: Critical Reflections on Authority and Identity* (Oxford: Blackwell, 1996).

Roszak, T. *The Making of a Counter-Culture: Reflections of the Technocratic Society and its Youthful Opposition* (London: Faber and Faber, 1970).

Rubinstein, R.P. *Dress Codes: Meanings and Messages in American Culture* (Colorado: Westview Press, 1995).

Rutherford, J. *Identity: Community, Culture, Difference* (London: Lawrence and Wishart, 1990).

Santino, J. 'Yellow Ribbons and Seasonal Flags: The Folk Assemblage of War', *The Journal of American Folklore*, 415 (Winter) (1992) 19–33.

Sartre, J.P. *Being and Nothingness* (London: Routledge, 1957).

Scott, S. and Freeman, R. 'Prevention as a Problem of Modernity: The Example of HIV and AIDS', in Gabe, J. (ed.) *Medicine, Health and Risk: Sociological Approaches* (Oxford: Blackwell, 1995).

Sennett, R. *The Fall of Public Man* (London: Faber and Faber, 1993).

Sennett, R. *The Corrosion of Character: The Personal Consequences of Work in the New Capitalism* (New York: Norton, 1999).

Sennett, R. 'Street and Office: Two Sources of Identity', in Hutton, W. and Giddens, A. (eds) *On the Edge: Living with Global Capitalism* (London: Vintage, 2001).

Sherkat, D.E. 'Counter-Culture or Continuity? Competing Influences on Baby Boomers' Religious Orientations and Participation', *Social Forces*, 76 (3) (1998) 1087–114.

Shilling, C. *The Body and Social Theory* (London: Sage, 1993).

Simmel, G. 'Fashion', in Levine, D. (ed.) *On Individuality and Social Forms* (Chicago: Chicago University Press, 1971).

Simmel, G. 'Prostitution', in Levine, D. (ed.) *On Individuality and Social Forms* (Chicago: Chicago University Press, 1971).

Simmel, G. 'How is Society Possible?', in Levine, D. (ed.) *On Individuality and Social Forms* (Chicago: Chicago University Press, 1971).

Simon, R.W. and Nath, L.E. 'Gender and Emotion in the United States: Do Men and Women Differ in Self-Reports of Feelings and Expressive Behaviour?', *Annual Journal of Sociology*, 109 (5) (2004) 1137–176.

Smith, R. and Gruenfeld, K.E. 'Symbols', *The Encyclopedia of AIDS* (www.thebody.com/encyclo/symbols.html).

Sontag, S. *Against Interpretation* (New York: Dell Publishing, 1966).

Sontag, S. *Illness and Metaphor* (London: Penguin, 1987).

Spates, J.L. 'Counterculture and Dominant Culture Values: A Cross-National Analysis of the Underground Press and Dominant Culture Magazines', *American Sociological Review*, 41 (5) (1976) 868–83.

Stead, S. and Mercer, H. 'Marie Curie Cancer Care', *European Journal of Cancer Care*, 7 (1998) 214–16.

Steadman-Rice, J. *A Disease of One's Own: Psychotherapy, Addiction, and the Emergence of Co-Dependence* (USA: Transaction Publishers, 1998).

Steedman, C. *Landscape for a Good Woman* (London: Virago, 1997).

Stein, A. *Seeds of the Seventies* (London: University Press of New England, 1985).

Strinati, D. *An Introduction to Theories of Popular Culture* (London: Routledge, 1995).

Sturken, M. *Tangled Memories: The Vietnam War, The AIDS Epidemic, and The Politics of Remembering* (University of California Press: London, 1997).

Sznaider, N. *The Compassionate Temperament: Care and Cruelty in Modern Society* (USA: Rowman and Littlefield Publishers, 2001).

Taylor, M. 'The Welfare Mix in the United Kingdom', in Evers, A. and Lavillen, J. (eds) *The Third Sector in Europe* (Cheltenham: Edward Elgar, 2001).

Tester, K. *Compassion, Morality and the Media* (Buckingham: Open University Press, 2001).

Thoits, P.A. 'The Sociology of Emotions', in, *Annual Review of Sociology*, 15 (1989) 317–42.

Thomson, I.T. 'From Conflict to Embedment: The Individual–Society Relationship, 1920–1991', *Sociological Forum*, 12 (4) (1997) 631–58.

Titmuss, R.M. *The Gift Relationship: From Human Blood to Social Policy* (New York: The New Press, 1997).

Trilling, L. 'The Modern Element in Modern Literature', *Partisan Review*, 28 (January) (1961) 9–35.

Trilling, L. *Sincerity and Authenticity*, (London: Oxford University Press, 1972).

Tuleja, T. 'Closing the Circle: Yellow Ribbons and the Redemption of the Past', *Journal of American Culture*, 17 (1) (1994) 23–30.

Turner, R. 'The Real Self: From Institution to Impulse', *The American Journal of Sociology*, 81 (5) (1976) 989–1016.

Vineburgh, N.T. 'The Power of the Pink Ribbon: Raising Awareness of the Mental Health Implications of Terrorism', *Psychiatry*, 67 (2) (2004) 137–46.

Wagner, D. *What's Love Got To Do With It?: A Critical Look at American Charity* (New York: The New Press, 2000).

Walter, T. *The Revival of Death* (London: Routledge, 2002).

Weber, M. *Economy and Society: An Outline of Interpretive Sociology* (New York: Bedminster Press, 1968).

Weeks, J. 'AIDS and the Regulation of Sexuality', in Berridge, V. and Strong, P. (eds) *AIDS and Contemporary History* (Cambridge University Press: Cambridge, 1993).

Weiner, D. and Stillman, D. *Woodstock Census: The Nationwide Survey of the Sixties Generation* (New York: The Viking Press, 1979).

West, P. *Conspicuous Compassion* (UK: Cromwell Press, 2004).

Westhues, K. *Society's Shadow: Studies in the Sociology of Countercultures* (New York: McGraw-Hill Ryerson, 1972).

Whatley, S. *Policing Desire: Pornography, AIDS and The Media* (London: Cassell, 1997).

Whelan, R. *The Corrosion of Charity: From Moral Renewal to Contract Culture* (London: IEA, 1996).

Wilkinson, S. and Kitzinger, C. 'Towards a Feminist Approach to Breast Cancer', in Wilkinson, S. and Kitzinger, C. (eds) *Women and Health: Feminist Perspectives* (UK: Taylor and Francis Ltd, 1994).

Wilkinson, I. *Anxiety in a Risk Society* (London: Routledge, 2001)

Wilkinson, I. *Suffering: A Sociological Introduction* (Cambridge: Polity Press, 2005).

Willis, P. *Profane Culture* (London: Routledge, 1978).

Willis, P. *Common Culture: Symbolic Work at Play in the Everyday Cultures of the Young* (Milton Keynes: Open University Press, 1990).

Wittgenstein, L. *Philosophical Investigations* (Oxford: Blackwell, 2003).

Wouters, C. 'The Quest For New Rituals in Dying', *Body and Society*, 8 (1) (2004) 1–27.

Wrong, D. 'Population Growth and Social Policy', in Harrington, M. and Howe, I. (eds) *The Seventies: Problems and Proposals* (New York: Harper and Rowe, 1972).

Wrong, D. 'Adversarial Identities and Multiculturalism', *Society*, 37 (2) (2000)10–14.

Wuthnow, R. *The Consciousness Reformation* (Berkeley: University of California Press, 1976).

Yankelovich, D. *New Rules: Searching for Self-Fulfillment in a World Turned Upside Down* (New York: Randon House, 1981).

Yinger, J.M. 'Contraculture and Subculture', *American Sociological Review*, 25 (5) (1960) 625–35.

Yocom, M. R. and Pershing, L 'The Yellow Ribboning of the USA: Contested Meanings in the Construction of a Political Symbol', *Western Folklore*, 55 (1) (1996) 41–85.

Zimmerman, M.K. 'The Women's Health Movement: A Critique of Medical Enterprise and the Position of Women', in Hess, B. and Ferree, M. (eds) *Analyzing Gender: A Handbook of Social Science Research* (USA: Sage, 1987).

Art works

James Rosenquist *The President-Elect* (1960–61).

Charity literature

Breakthrough Breast Cancer, 'Be Breast Aware for Life' leaflet (2004), distributed by Marks and Spencer.

Breakthrough Breast Cancer, 'Breast Cancer Risk Factors: The Facts' leaflet, (www. breakthrough.org.uk/upload/documents/328_RiskFactor.pdf 7/11/2004).
Breast Cancer Care, 'Less Bounce Pink Aerobics' poster (October 2004).
Cancer Research UK, Campaign letter for Breast Cancer Awareness Month (September 2004).
Cancer Research UK, 'Walk For Life' Campaign Poster (2004).
Cancer Research UK, 'Definite Risks' web page (www.cancerresearchuk.org).
Cancer Research UK, 'Recent Progress' web page (www.cancerresearchuk.org/ beinghere/recent_research_progress).
Cancer Research UK, 'Stride for Life' leaflet (2003).
Cancer Research UK, 'To the Woman of the House' mail-shot (October 2003).
Jeans for Genes ribbon pin card (2005).
Macmillan Cancer Relief, 'Women still not checking for breast cancer – lack of confidence to blame?' article on web page (25 October 2004) (www.macmillan. org.uk).
The Red Ribbon Foundation web page (www.redribbon.com/).
Socialist Party Lesbian, Gay, Bisexual and Transgender Group, leaflet given out at Manchester Gay Pride (August, 2004).

Discography

Dylan, Bob *The Freewheelin' Bob Dylan*, 1963.
Bob Dylan 'Subterranean Homesick Blues' in Dylan, Bob *Highway '61 Revisited*, 1965.

Fashion designers

'Ossie Clark' exhibition at the Victoria and Albert Museum, London (November 2003 – May 2004).
'Vivienne Westwood' exhibition at the Victoria and Albert Museum, London (April 2004 – July 2004).

Filmography

Alfie (directed by Lewis Gilbert) 1966, Paramount.
Easy Rider (directed by Dennis Hopper) 1969, Pando/Raybert.
Philadelphia (directed by Demme), 1993 Tristar.
Taxi Driver (directed by Martin Scorcese) 1976, Columbia.

Lectures and speeches

Dyson, F.J. 'The World, The Flesh and the Devil. The Third J.D. Bernal lecture', delivered at Birbeck College, London, 1972, in Carey, J. (ed.) *The Faber Book of Utopias* (London: Faber and Faber, 2000).

Kennedy, J.F. *Actual Inaugural Speech of John F. Kennedy: Complete Inaugural Address January 20, 1960* (cassette) New York Miller International Company (1975).
Nixon, R. First Inaugural Address of Richard Nixon, Monday, January 20, 1969 (www.bartleby.com/124/pres58.html).

Literature

Coetzee, J.M. *In the Heart of the Country* (London: Vintage, 1999).
Eliot, G. *Middlemarch* (London: Penguin, 2003).
Ginsberg, A. 'America', in *Howl* (San Fransisco: City Lights Books, 1956).
Huxley, A. *Brave New World* (London: Flamingo, 1994).
Kerouac, J. *On the Road* (London: Penguin, 1991).
Kesey, K. *One Flew Over the Cuckoo's Nest* (London: Picador, 1973).
Orwell, G. *Nineteen Eighty-four* (London: Penguin, 1967).

Magazine articles

The Economist, Vol. 3128, 2 March 1991, p. 43.
Engle, L. *Body Positive* 'Where Have All the Ribbons Gone? AIDS Symbols – Compassion or Fashion?' January/February 2000 (www.thebody.com/bp/jan_feb00/ribbon.html).
Fleury, A. *Brandweek* 'The Most Powerful Icon of the '90s?' 30 November 1992, pp 14–15.
Gleason, R. *Rolling Stone Magazine*, 'So Revolution is Commercial?', 21 December 1968, in Rolling Stone (eds) The Age of Paranoia: How the Sixties Ended (New York: Pocket Books, 1972) pp. 407–9.
Hinckle, W. *Ramparts*, 'A Social History of the Hippies', May 1967, in Howard, G. (ed.) The Sixties: Art, Politics and Media of Our Most Explosive Decade (New York: Paragon House, 1991) pp. 207–32.
InthePINK, 'Superstar', October 2004, p. 29.
Mailer, N. *Esquire* 'Superman Comes to the Supermarket', November 1960, in Howard, G. (ed.) The Sixties: Art, Politics and Media of Our Most Explosive Decade (New York: Paragon House, 1991) pp. 144–177.
Marketing, 3 June 2004, p. 13.
Newsweek, 10 June 1963, p. 4.
Newsweek, 28 June 1993, p. 61
Oz, no. 32, January 1971, pp. 7–9.
Oz, no. 37, September 1971, pp. 8–9.
Pink Ribbon, 'In My Own Words', October 2002, p. 12.
Pink Ribbon, 'Up Front', October 2002, p. 5.
Quattrocchi, A. *New Statesman*, 'Letter to a Dying Underground', 13 February 1970, pp. 214–215.
Seidner, D., *New Yorker*, 28 March 1993, p. 31.
The Usual Gang of Idiots, *Mad About the Sixties: The Best of the Decade* (New York: EC Publications, 1996).

Newspaper articles

Birmingham Evening Mail, 6 November 2002, pp. 1–2.
Daily Record, 4 November 1997, p. 9.
The Daily Telegraph, 5 April 2001, p. 17.
The Daily Telegraph, 13 March 2004, Front Page.
Essex Chronicle, 27 November 2003, p. 45.
Evening Gazette, 1 April 2004, p. 17.
The Express, 5 November 2001, p.13.
The Glasgow Herald, 26 June 1992, p. 14.
The Guardian, 24 February 1994, p. 14.
The Guardian, 25 November 1994, p. 14.
The Guardian, 15 March 1996, T6.
The Guardian, 17 June 1998, p. 5.
The Guardian, 13 November 2000, p. 6.
The Housten Chronicle, 6 May 2004, p. 5.
The Independent, 20 April 1992, p. 3.
The Independent, 21 May 1992, p. 17.
The Independent, 30 March 1993, p. 20.
The Independent, 1 December 1996, p. 10.
The Independent, 1 December 1997, p. 14.
The Independent, 18 November 2003, p. 10.
The Independent, 30 May 2005, p. 6.
The Independent on Sunday, 11 June 1995, p. 5.
The Independent on Sunday, 1 December 1996, p. 10.
Los Angeles Times, 24 March 1993, F1/F6.
Mail on Sunday, 11 July 1993, pp. 8–9.
New York Times, 27 January 1991, XII.
New York Times, 2 February 1991, F2.
New York Times, 3 February 1991, F3.
New York Times, 26 February 1991, F26.
New York Times, 27 February 1991, F27.
New York Times, 28 November 1997, B10.
New York Times, 30 November 1997, 3C.
New York Times, 6 October 2005 (Fashion and Style Section).
The Observer, 8 August 2004, p. 9.
The Telegraph, 13 March 2004, front page.
Time Magazine, 30 December 1996, p. 16.
The Times, 25 March 1915, p. 12.
The Times, 11 May 1915, p. 5.
The Times, 12 May 1915, p. 5.
The Times, 9 July 1915, p. 4.
The Times, 15 July 1915, p. 9.
The Times, 1 September 1915, p. 11.
The Times, 3 September 1915, p. 9.
The Times, 15 September 1915, p. 9.
The Times, 22 September 1915, p. 9.

The Times, 7 October 1915, p. 11.
The Times, 21 October 1915, p. 11.
The Times, 22 October 1915, p. 6.
The Times, 9 December 1915, p. 4.
The Times, 2 March 1916, p. 5.
The Times, 13 March 1916, p. 11.
The Times, 30 June 1916, p. 11.
The Times, 5 July 1916, p. 5.
The Times, 29 July 1916, p. 5.
The Times, 24 October 1916, p. 5.
The Times, 26 October 1916, p. 9.
The Times, 27 October 1916, p. 5.
The Times, 26 February 1918, p. 3.
The Times, 14 March 1918, p. 9.
The Times, 7 November 1918, p. 3.
The Times, 8 June 1920, p. 18.
The Times, 4 October 1920, p. 7.
The Times, 17 October 1921, p. 12.
The Times, 19 October 1921, p. 7.
The Times, 11 November 1921, p. 11.
The Times, 12 November 1921, p. 5.
The Times, 24 November 1921, p. 7.
The Times, 10 May 1922, p. 13.
The Times, 12 October 1922, p. 10.
The Times, 20 October 1922, p. 9.
The Times, 11 November 1922, p. 11.
The Times, 16 November 1922, p. 9.
The Times, 4 October 1923, p. 14.
The Times, 22 October 1924, p. 14.
The Times, 23 February 1925, p. 9.
The Times, 26 May 1925, p. 10.
The Times, 28 May 1925, p. 20.
The Times, 8 September 1925, p. 9.
The Times, 8 December 2001, Features.
The Times, 12 August 2002, p. 10.
The Times, 9 November 2002, Features, p. 98.
The Times, 14 November 2002, p. 4.
Times Union, 27 April 1995, A10.
Washington Post, 25 May 1975, DC1.

Press releases

PR Newswire 'Three-Time Breast Cancer Survivor Judy Pickett Prepares for 100th 5K Race', 6 May 2004.
PR Newswire 'McDonald's Raises Awareness over Breast Cancer During the Mother's Day Holiday', 11 May 2004.

University of Sussex: Press and Communications Office 'Students Organise Yellow Ribbon Charity Tribute', 16 February 2004 (www.sussex.ac.uk/press_office/ media/media387.shtml) (accessed 20 February 2004).

Statistics

'Breast Cancer: Incidence Rate Rises While Death Rate Falls' published by the Office of National Statistics, 31 October 2003 (www.statistics. gov.uk).
'Breast Cancer Facts and Figures', published by the American Cancer Society (www.cancer.org/downloads/STT/CAFF2005BrF.pdf).

Television

BBC News 24, interview with Paul Scott, 10 June 2005.
The Wright Stuff, Channel Five, 14 June 2005.
The Wright Stuff, Channel Five, 15 June 2005.
This Morning, interview with Evelyn Lauder, ITV, 23 October 2003.

Websites

Artists About AIDS (www.artists-about-aids.com).
The Babyloss Awareness Campaign (www.Babyloss.com).
BBC News Archive, 'Pope John Paul II: Your Tributes' http://news.bbc.co.uk/1/ hi/talking_point/2806153.stm (accessed 20 September 2005).
BBC Business Pages, 'Bono Bets on Red to Battle Aids' (www.news.bbc.co.uk/2/ hi/business/4650024.stm).
Carolyn Gargaro's Homepage, 'Ribbon Campaigns' (www.gargaro.com).
Charities Aid Foundation, 'General Facts and Figures' (www.cafonline.org/ research/factsandfigures.cfm).
Charities Aid Foundation, 'UK Giving 2004/2005: Results of the 2004/2005 survey of individual charitable giving in the UK' (www.cafonline.org/ default.aspx?page=7663).
CharitiesDirect.com 'UK Charity Information' (www.charitiesdirect.com/ CharityDetail.asp?orgid=26457).
Eating Disorders Association (www.edauk.com/sub_press_rellaw).
Make Poverty History (www.makepovertyhistory.org/theyearof/).
National Autistic Society 'Prince Charles presented with Autism Awareness Ribbon' News Archive, 22 July 2002 (www.autismawareness.org.uk/ news220702.htm).
National Center for Charitable Statistics, 'Quick Facts' (www.nccsdataweb. urban.org/NCCS/files/quickFacts.htm).
Pin Mart 'Awareness Ribbons' (www.stock-custom-pins-store.com/awareness-ribbons.html).
Six Degrees of Separation (www.sixdegrees.org/Default.aspx).
Visual AIDS (www.visualAIDS.com).
Wikipedia 'Awareness Ribbons' (www.wikipedia.com).
Yellow Ribbon Suicide Prevention Programme (www.yellowribbon.org/).

Index